THE NEW COLD WAR?

Comparative Studies in Religion and Society
Mark Juergensmeyer, editor

THE NEW COLD WAR?

Religious Nationalism Confronts the Secular State

MARK JUERGENSMEYER

UNIVERSITY OF CALIFORNIA PRESS
BERKELEY   LOS ANGELES   LONDON

University of California Press
Berkeley and Los Angeles, California

University of California Press, Ltd.
London, England

© 1993 by
The Regents of the University of California

First Paperback Printing 1994

Library of Congress Cataloging-in-Publication Data

Juergensmeyer, Mark
    The new Cold War? : religious nationalism confronts the
secular state / Mark Juergensmeyer.
        p.   cm. —(Comparative studies in religion and society)
    Includes bibliographical references and index.
    ISBN 0-520-08651-1
    1. Revolutions—Religious aspects—History—20th century.
2. Nationalism—Religious aspects—History—20th century. 3.
Religion and state—History—20th century. I. Title. II. Series.
BL65.R48J84 1993
320.5'5'09048—dc20   92-5609
                                                             CIP

Printed in the United States of America

9 8 7 6 5 4 3 2 1

for Sucheng,
who is small—very, very small—
and quick and bright

Contents

Acknowledgments

Many of the insights in this book have come from field studies and interviews conducted in the past several years in parts of the world where movements of religious nationalism have come to the fore. For that reason, I am especially grateful for the advice of experts in these countries and of colleagues around the world who are familiar with the case studies on which my observations are based.

In Sri Lanka my research was facilitated by S. W. R. deA. Samarasinghe and Radhika Coomaraswamy of the Kandy and Colombo branches, respectively, of the International Centre for Ethnic Studies; Sarath Amunugama of Worldview International Foundation; Mangala Moonesinghe of the Marga Institute, Colombo; and Padmasiri deSilva of the Philosophy Department, Peradeniya University, Kandy. I also appreciate the comments of Stanley Tambiah of Harvard University on the Sri Lankan case and on the theoretical perspective of the project as a whole. Useful advice on initial contacts in Sri Lanka came from Don Swearer, Ashis Nandy, and Diana Eck. Throughout, Antony Charles provided both help and insight.

In India I was assisted by Harish Puri and Surjit Singh Narang at Guru Nanak Dev University, Amritsar; and I greatly benefited from the comments of Manoranjan Mohanty, T. N. Madan, J. P. S. Oberoi, and members of the Department of Political Science at Delhi University, where an initial version of one section of this book was presented. I have also learned from the comments of Gurinder Singh Mann of Columbia University and Mohinder Singh at the National Institute for Punjab Studies in New Delhi on my case study of the Sikhs.

In Israel, my mentors were Ifrah Zilberman in Jerusalem, and Ehud Sprinzak, Emmanual Sivan, and Gideon Aran at Hebrew University. I thank Robin Wright of the *Los Angeles Times* and *The New Yorker,* as well as other journalists in Jerusalem, the West Bank, and Gaza for their help in securing interviews.

In Egypt, I valued the cooperation of Saad Ibrahim, Kent Weeks, and Leila el-Hamamsy of the American University, Cairo; Muhammad Khalifa and Ibrahim Dasuqi Shitta of Cairo University; Mohamed Elmisilhi Salem of Al-Azhar University, Cairo; and Gehad Auda and other scholars and journalists connected with the *Al-Ahram* newspaper and institute. William Brinner and Alan Godlas helped in arranging contacts in Cairo, for which I am very grateful. Juan Campo provided helpful comments on the revision.

In Mongolia, I appreciated the assistance of D. Batsukh and G. Lubsantseren in Ulan Bator, and the kindness of Glenn Paige in arranging contacts. Majid Tehranian and Ahmad Karimi-Hakkak helped provide information on Tajikistan. Regarding Central Asia in general, I valued the suggestions of Dru Gladney and Barnett Rubin. For Russian and Eastern European materials, I am grateful to Amir Khisamutdinov, Lucja Swiatkowski, and the working group on religion and nationalism at the United States Institute of Peace, organized by David Little. I appreciate also the assistance of David Batstone in locating original materials relating to the Christian support for the Nicaraguan revolution. In addition to these scholars, I also wish to thank the many participant-observers who shared their insights with me and whose names appear in the list of interviews at the end of this book.

The research for this book was begun while I was a Fellow at the Woodrow Wilson International Center for Scholars at the Smithsonian Institution, Washington, D.C., in 1986. Additional grants for research in 1987–88 came from the Harry Frank Guggenheim Foundation and in 1989–91 from the United States Institute of Peace in Washington, D.C. I am grateful for the generosity of these foundations and the support of Dr. Anne Sheffield at the Wilson Center, Dr. Karen Colvard at the Harry Frank Guggenheim Foundation, and Dr. Hrach Gregorian at the United States Institute of Peace. Earlier versions of some of the material included in this book have been published as: "The Logic of Religious Violence" in the *Journal of Strategic Studies* and *Contributions to Indian Sociology;* "What the Bhikkhu Said: Reflections on the Rise of Militant Religious Nationalism" in *Religion;* "Sacrifice and Cosmic War" in *The Journal of Terrorism and Political Violence;* and the sections on "India" and "Sri Lanka" in Stuart Mews, ed., *Religion in Politics: A World Guide.*

My colleagues in Berkeley, Washington, and Honolulu have enriched my thinking about these matters enormously, as has my outspoken but diligent research assistant over the years, Darrin McMahon. At Hawai'i my graduate assistant was David Fouse. I have appreciated the care with which they and members of my graduate seminar at the University of Hawai'i read early drafts of the manuscript.

In the final stages of preparation, the book has benefited from the comments of a number of scholars, including Dru Gladney, Richard Hecht, Ehud Sprinzak, and a stellar group of specialists convened by the Harry Frank Guggenheim Foundation in New York for a one-day seminar to discuss a draft of the manuscript. The participants included Karen McCarthy Brown, Karen Colvard, Ainslie Embree, Charles Hale, Jack Hawley, James Hester, R. W. Kaeuper, David Laitin, Bruce Lawrence, Darrin McMahon, Gananath Obeyesekere, David Rapoport, David Little, Ninian Smart, Arthur Waldron, and Joel Wallman. Although none were shy about suggesting ways that the manuscript could be improved, each affirmed the importance of its topic and the value of undertaking the study. My thanks to them all.

The final version has been groomed by Sucheng Chan, to whom this book is dedicated. She has helped immensely in bringing organization and clarity to the manuscript, and her consistent support for it over the years (aided by sweet Cotufa) has helped to keep this project alive. In one way or another, she and all others named above have helped to improve this book's accuracy and flow of thought, and have demonstrated, once again, the benefits of having such patient and intelligent friends.

Preface to the
Paperback Edition

Religious nationalism continues to expand and evolve in various parts of the world, and much has happened since this book first went to press. The World Trade Center in New York was bombed allegedly by Muslim nationalists; Jewish and Muslim extremists angrily responded to the Israeli–PLO accords; India's Ayodhya mosque was destroyed, giving new momentum to that country's Hindu nationalism; the Sikh revolution in the Punjab and the incipient Muslim government in Tajikistan were quelled; and elsewhere in the world, movements of religious nationalism were adopting new forms in competition with their secular foes.

None of these events has altered the main theses of this book. It has become increasingly clear that religious nationalists are more than just religious fanatics: they are political activists seriously attempting to reformulate the modern language of politics and provide a new basis for the nation-state. In many cases they are waging popularist struggles against Western culture and its political ideology, and they aim at infusing public life with indigenous cultural symbols and moral values. Recent events also reinforce the point that they can be hostile, dogmatic, and violent, and that they threaten a confrontation with secular government that is virtually global in its reach.

Although I have tried to revise the text of this book to bring it up to date, I have not changed my analyses of why religious nationalism has emerged at this point in history, how our own ideology and politics play a role in this development, and what

xiii

problems and solutions are in store for the future. I note that several other authors—including Samuel P. Huntington, writing on "The Clash of Civilizations?" in *Foreign Affairs,* and Lloyd and Susanne Rudolph, discussing "Modern Hate" in *New Republic*— also regard religious nationalism as a significant and potentially destructive force in world politics. The question is whether its values can be made compatible with the virtues of secular Western democracy. I still harbor the hope that the new cold war between secular and religious ideologies can be forestalled.

MARK JUERGENSMEYER
Santa Barbara,
September 21, 1993

Introduction:
The Rise of Religious Nationalism

"There is a desperate need for religion in public life," the dean of Egypt's premier school of Islamic theology told me.[1] He meant, he went on to say, that there should be not only a high standard of morality in public offices but also a fusion of the religious and political identities of the Egyptian people. From his point of view, the Islamic religion is "a culturally liberating force," which Egypt as a nation urgently needs in order to free itself from the last vestiges of its colonial past. "Western colonialism has gone," the dean explained, "but we still have not completed our independence. We will not be free until Egypt becomes a Muslim state."[2]

In interviews I conducted in half a dozen troubled countries during the late 1980s and early 1990s, I found that his point of view is not idiosyncratic. The longing for an indigenous form of religious politics free from the taint of Western culture has been expressed by many in countries that have become independent in this century: not only by Egyptians, but by Central Asians and other Muslims from Algeria to Indonesia, and by Ukrainians, Sri Lankans, Indians, Israelis, Mongolians, and intensely religious persons of a variety of faiths throughout the globe. In fact, what appeared to be an anomaly when the Islamic revolution in Iran challenged the supremacy of Western culture and its secular politics in 1979 has become a major theme in international politics in the 1990s. The new world order that is replacing the bipolar powers of the old Cold War is characterized not only by the rise of new economic forces, a crumbling of old empires, and the discrediting of communism, but also by the resur-

1

gence of parochial identities based on ethnic and religious allegiances. Although Francis Fukuyama, among others, has asserted
that the ending of the old Cold War has led to an "end of history" and
a world-wide ideological consensus in favor of secular liberal democracy, the rise of new religious and ethnic nationalism belies that
assertion.[3] Moreover, proponents of the new nationalisms hold the
potential of making common cause against the secular West, in what
might evolve into a new Cold War.

Like the old Cold War, the confrontation between these new
forms of culture-based politics and the secular state is global in its
scope, binary in its opposition, occasionally violent, and essentially
a difference of ideologies; and, like the old Cold War, each side
tends to stereotype the other. According to the major Islamic political strategist in Sudan, the post-Cold War West needs a new "empire of evil to mobilize against."[4] Similarly, he and other religious
politicians need a stereotype of their own, a satanic secular foe that
will help them mobilize their own forces. Unlike the old Cold War,
however, the West (now aligned with the secular leaders of the
former Soviet Union) confronts an opposition that is nether politically united nor, at present, militarily strong. For that reason, it is
often not taken seriously. This attitude, I believe, is a mistake.

For instance, these new forms of cultural nationalism are sometimes dismissed as historical aberrations or as misguided applica-
tions of religion. In an introduction to an article by Conor Cruise
O'Brien on the Punjab crisis in 1988, an editor of the *Atlantic
Monthly* described as "one of the grimmer and more ironic develop-
ments of the late twentieth century" the manner in which religion
had inflamed the Third World. He claimed that religion is "on the
whole a benign force in Western societies"; but in the non-Western
world it "often combines combustibly with nationalism to fuel political murder."[5] The underlying assumption was that something is
seriously wrong with religion in the non-Western world.

In this book, I have adopted a different approach. I have tried to
see the points of view of the activists that the *Atlantic* editor de-
rided. From their perspectives it is secular nationalism, and not
religion, that has gone wrong. They see the Western models of
nationhood—both democratic and socialist—as having failed, and
they view religion as a hopeful alternative, a base for criticism and
change.

Why has secular nationalism failed to inspire them? Why has religion been raised as an alternative? Why has the religious rejection of secular nationalism been so violent? And what ideology and political organization will come in its place? In searching for answers to these questions, I have sought the opinions of politically active religious leaders in various parts of the world. Some I interviewed in person; others I encountered through their published interviews, transcripts of their speeches, and their writings. I have tried to make sense of their positions, determine what they have in common with their counterparts in other parts of the globe, place them in a wider context of political and cultural change, and see why they are so optimistic about their role in what one Algerian Islamic nationalist described as "the march of history."[6]

My interest in this topic began with the Sikhs. Having lived in northern India from time to time and written on religion and politics in the Punjab, and having known the Sikhs generally to be delightful and sensible people, I was profoundly disturbed to witness the deadly spiral of violence involving militant Sikhs and the Indian government that began there in the early 1980s and in which the Punjab is still terribly mired. In trying to make sense of this situation, I turned to the recorded sermons and transcripts of one of the leaders of the militant movement, Sant Jarnail Singh Bhindranwale.[7] His message seemed to be one of despair about the present state of society: he saw it characterized by an absence of a sense of moral community and led by politicians incapable of being anything but corrupt. The despair, however, was tempered by a radical hope: he felt that a religious crusade could bring about a political revolution, one that would usher in a new politics and a new moral order.

The rhetoric of Bhindranwale—at once critical and hopeful, oriented both to modern needs and to traditional values of the past—was not unique, I found, as I began to compare it with other cases. Turning first to the language of Buddhist monks in the militant Sinhalese movement in nearby Sri Lanka and to the rhetoric of India's Hindu nationalists, I soon expanded my interests from the discourse of politically active religious leaders in those two countries to the ideological language of their counterparts in Egypt, Iran, Israel, Israeli-occupied Palestine, Mongolia, Central Asia, and other parts of the world.[8] The differences among these religious leaders are considerable—their religious values and goals, their political and historical settings—but many of their concerns are surprisingly similar. They are united by a common enemy— Western secular nationalism—and a common hope for the revival of religion in the public sphere.

While urging that they be taken seriously, however, I do not want to exaggerate their importance. Although some religious nationalists have already achieved a great deal of political influence in their countries, others have not and never will. Many will forever remain members of a strident minority. I include them in this study, however, because they fit into a larger, virtually global pattern. In what is admittedly an unsystematic sampling, I have singled out members of religious groups that actively criticize the secular political order and attempt to replace it with one founded on religious principles. Even when the voices of these religious activists are relatively insignificant in their own countries, they are worth considering, for they add to what is a major counterpoint to the dominant secular nationalism of our time.

The religious type of nationalism that they advocate receives more attention in the American and European press—and is probably more difficult for Westerners to comprehend—than any other form of cultural nationalism, including those based on ethnicity, race, and a region's legendary past. In many parts of the world, however, religious and ethnic identities are intertwined. The nationalist aspirations of Muslims in China and Central Asia have been rightly described as "ethnoreligious."[9] But even in these locales, the crucial symbols and ideas of the regions' cultural heritages are most often the religious ones. Perhaps for that reason religious activists there, as elsewhere in the world, have become secular leaders' most formidable foes.

It would be easy to characterize these religious activists as *fundamentalists*, but I hesitate to do so for several reasons. First, the term is pejorative. It refers, as one Muslim scholar observed, to those who hold "an intolerant, self-righteous, and narrowly dogmatic religious literalism."[10] The term is less descriptive than it is accusatory: it reflects our attitude toward other people more than it describes them. By implication such persons should not be taken seriously as thoughtful political actors, and that characterization does not fit most of the people whom I encountered in this study, either directly or through their writings.

Second, *fundamentalism* is an imprecise category for making comparisons across cultures. The term stems from the attempt of a group of conservative Protestants early in this century to define what they held to be the "fundamentals" of Christianity, including the inerrancy of scripture, and it is unclear how they can be compared with those who adhere to other forms of revitalized Christianity, much less to religious activists of other faiths in other parts of the world.[11] The only thing that most religious activists around the world have in common, aside from their fervor, is their rejection of Westerners and those like us who subscribe to modern secularism. For that reason, a better comparative category would be *antimodernism*, the term Bruce Lawrence uses to define fundamentalism as a global concept, for it suggests a religious revolt against the secular ideology that often accompanies modern society.[12] One of the advantages of this term is that it allows one to make a distinction between those who are *modern* and those who are *modernists*—that is, between those who simply accept modern society and those who go further and believe in the secular ideologies that dominate modern cultures.[13]

This distinction is important because in most cases religious activists, while opposing the values of modernism, are themselves very modern persons. The dean of Islamic theology in Cairo, to whom I referred in the opening paragraph of this Introduction, lived in London for a number of years and appreciated its modern efficiency. Rabbi Meir Kahane, a right-wing Jewish nationalist in Israel, ran his movement like a political campaign and loved to discuss American baseball. The most politically active mullah in Tajikistan has a fax machine and a cellular telephone. Such religious nationalists are modern in the sense that they are organization-minded and empirical in their outlook.[14] Yet their modernity is such that it also allows them to embrace traditional religious values and reject secular ones.

My third objection to the use of *fundamentalism* in this study is the most salient: it does not carry any political meaning. To call someone a fundamentalist suggests that he or she is motivated solely by religious beliefs rather than by broad concerns about the

nature of society and the world. The religious activists I met and
studied are politically astute and deeply concerned about the society in which they live. No doubt many of them have friends who
are not: these friends may be fixated exclusively on religious matters, and they may rightly be called conservatives, fundamentalists,
or simply antimodernists. But when such people fuse their religious perspective with a broad prescription for their nation's political and social destiny, one must find an inclusive term. For that
reason, I call them religious nationalists.

By characterizing the activists in this study as religious nationalists, I mean to suggest that they are individuals with both religious
and political interests. To understand their perspective is an exercise in both comparative religion and comparative politics, for they
appear—at least from our point of view—to be responding in a
religious way to a political situation. Many of them, however, agree
with the observation of a Palestinian leader, Sheik Ahmed Yassin,
that there is "no clear distinction between religion and politics" and
that the distinction itself is a mark of Western ways of thinking.[15]
Rather, articulators of religious nationalism see a deficiency in society that is both religious and political in character, one that requires a response that is religious as well as political.

Although they reject secular ideas, religious nationalists do not
necessarily reject secular politics, including the political apparatus
of the modern nation-state. To show how this can be possible, I
must explain how I use certain terms. By the *state,* I mean the
locus of authority and decision making within a geographical region. By the *nation,* I mean a community of people associated with
a particular political culture and territory that possesses autonomous political authority.[16] A *nation-state* is a modern form of nationhood in which a state's authority systematically pervades and regu-
lates an entire nation, whether through democratic or totalitarian
means. The modern nation-state is morally and politically justified
by a concept of *nationalism,* by which I mean not only the xenophobic extremes of patriotism but also the more subdued expressions of identity based on shared assumptions regarding why a
community constitutes a nation and why the state that rules it is
legitimate.[17]

The new religious revolutionaries are concerned not so much
about the political structure of the nation-state as they are about

the political ideology undergirding it. They are concerned about the rationale for having a state, the moral basis for politics, and the reasons why a state should elicit loyalty. They often reject the European and American notion that nationalism can be defined solely as a matter of secular contract.[18] At the same time, however, they see no contradiction in affirming certain forms of political organization that have developed in the West, such as the democratic procedures of the nation-state, as long as they are legitimized not by the secular idea of a social contract but by traditional principles of religion.

As a bhikkhu in Sri Lanka explained to me, what he despised was "not democracy, but your idea of nationalism."[19] He and others like him reject the notion that what draws people together as a nation and what legitimates their political order is a rational compact that unites everyone in a geographical region through common laws and political processes. Such secular nationalism underlies both the parliamentary democracies of Europe and the Americas, and the socialist bureaucracies that once characterized Eastern European countries and the formerly Soviet republics of the Commonwealth of Independent States. This way of thinking about nationalism comes naturally to most Americans and Europeans, but it contains assumptions about the universal and secular nature of a moral social order that many religious people in the rest of the world simply do not take for granted.

I find it striking that the religious-nationalist point of view so strongly dismisses secular nationalism as fundamentally bereft of moral or spiritual values. How shocking this rejection would have been to some of the Western social scientists and other observers of global politics who proclaimed two or three decades ago that the advent of secular nationalism in the Third World was not only a triumph of Western political influence but also one of the West's finest legacies to public life throughout the world.

I begin, in the first part of this book, with this sense of promise that so buoyed the spirits of proponents of Western nationalism earlier in this century. I examine how the promise faded and how secular nationalism began to be disdained in many parts of the world. I then turn to the underlying issue: the competition between religion, in its various forms, and the European and American model of secular nationalism. The second part of this book provides case studies from the Middle East, South Asia, and formerly socialist countries. Although this book is largely about the discourse of religious activists, it is important also to look at the particular movements with which they have been associated and to try to discern patterns that indicate how and why religious revolutions develop. The third part of the book looks at several concerns that have been raised about religious nationalists: their proclivity toward violence and their apparent disregard for democracy and human rights. The Conclusion is devoted to the question of where we go from here: how secular nationalists can live in a world increasingly populated with religious nationalists and whether religious nationalism can be made compatible with secular nationalism's great virtues: tolerance, respect for human rights, and freedom of expression.

Part One

Religion vs. Secular Nationalism

Chapter One

The Loss of Faith
in Secular Nationalism

In the celebrations following the first stages of elections that threatened to bring Islamic nationalists to power in Algeria early in 1992, a jubilant supporter of the Islamic Front spied a foreigner on the streets of Algiers and grabbed her by the arm. "Please give my condolences to President Mitterrand," the Algerian said.[1] Behind this amusing bit of sarcasm is an impression shared by many Muslims in Algeria: that the ruling party, the National Front, which came to power in the 1956 war of independence with France and which controlled the country afterward, is, in a cultural sense, an extension of French colonial rule. The independent Algeria that proudly came into being in 1956 has come to be seen as a vestige of the colonial past that is itself in need of liberation.

In the mid-1950s, soon after Algeria and many other former colonies in the Third World received their political independence, it was popular for Europeans and Americans to write with an almost religious fervor about the spread of nationalism throughout the world. Their zeal, however, was invariably for something secular: the emergence of new nations that elicited loyalties forged entirely from a sense of secular citizenship. These secular-nationalist loyalties were based on the idea that the legitimacy of the state was rooted in the will of the people, divorced from any religious sanction.

The secular nationalism of the day was defined also by what it was not: it was not one of the old ethnic and religious identities that had made nations parochial and quarrelsome in the past. For that reason, scholars viewed the spread of nationalism in a hopeful,

11

almost eschatological, light: it was ushering in a new future. It meant, in essence, the emergence of mini-Americas all over the world.

Hans Kohn, his generation's best-known historian of nationalism, observed in 1955 that the twentieth century was unique: "It is the first period in history in which the whole of mankind has accepted one and the same political attitude, that of nationalism."[2] In his telling, the concept had its origins in antiquity. It was presaged by ancient Hebrews and fully enunciated by ancient Greeks. Inexplicably, however, the concept stagnated for almost 2,000 years, in Kohn's account, until suddenly it took off in earnest in the seventeenth century in England, "the first modern nation."[3] Today, he cheerfully observed, the whole world has responded to "the awakening of nationalism and liberty."[4]

Not only Western academics but a good number of new leaders— especially those in the emerging nations created out of former colonial empires—were swept up by the vision of a world of free and equal secular nations. The concept of secular nationalism gave them an ideological justification for being, and the electorate that subscribed to it provided them power bases from which they could vault into positions of leadership ahead of traditional ethnic and religious leaders. But secularism was more than just a political issue, it was also a matter of personal identity. A new kind of person had come into existence—the "Indian nationalist" or "Ceylonese nationalist" who possessed an abiding faith in a secular nationalism identified with his or her homeland. Perhaps none exemplified this new spirit more than Gamal Abdel Nasser of Egypt and Jawaharlal Nehru of India. According to Nehru, "there is no going back" to a past full of religious identities, for the modern, secular "spirit of the age" will inevitably triumph throughout the world.[5]

Donald Smith has written poignantly of the followers of Nehru after India's independence: "The Indian nationalist felt compelled to assert that India was a nation," even though there were some "embarrassing facts"—such as divisive regional and religious loyalties— that had to be glossed over.[6] The reason for this compulsion, according to Smith, was that such people could not think of themselves as modern persons without a national identity. "In the modern world," writes Smith, "nationality and nationalism were the basic premises of political life, and it seemed absolutely *improper* for India to be without a nationality."[7] A similar attitude predominated in many other new nations, at least at the beginning.

Leaders of minority religious communities—such as Hindu Tamils in Ceylon and Coptic Christians in Egypt—seemed especially eager to embrace secular nationalism because a secular nation state would assure that the public life of the country would not be dominated completely by the majority religious community. In India, where the Congress Party became the standard bearer of Nehru's vision, the party's most reliable supporters were those at the margins of Hindu society—untouchables and Muslims—who had the most to fear from an intolerant religious majority.

The main carriers of the banner of secular nationalism in these newly independent countries, however, were not members of any religious community at all, at least in a traditional sense. Rather, they were members of the urban educated elite. For many of them, embracing a secular form of nationalism was a way of promoting its major premise—the separation of religion and politics—and thereby avoiding the obstacles that religious loyalties create for a country's political goals. By implication, political power based on religious values and traditional communities held no sway.

The problem, however, was that in asserting that the nationalism of their country was secular, the new nationalists had to have faith in a secular culture that was at least as compelling as a sacred one. That meant, on a social level, thinking that secular nationalism could triumph over religion. It could also mean making secular nationalism a suprareligion of its own, which a society could aspire to beyond any single religious allegiance. In India, for example, political identity based on religious affiliation was termed *communalism.* In the view of Nehru and other secular nationalists, religion was the chief competitor of an even higher object of loyalty: secular India. Nehru implored his countrymen to get rid of what he called "that narrowing religious outlook" and to adopt a modern, nationalist viewpoint.[8]

The secular nationalists' attempts to give their ideologies an antireligious or a suprareligious force were encouraged, perhaps unwittingly, by their Western mentors. The words used to define nationalism by Western political leaders and such scholars as Kohn always implied not only that it was secular but that it was competitive with religion and ultimately superior to it. "Nationalism [by

which, of course, he meant secular nationalism] is a state of mind,"
Kohn wrote, "in which the *supreme loyalty* of the individual is felt
to be due the nation-state."[9] And he boldly asserted that secular
nationalism had replaced religion in its influence: "An understanding of nationalism and its implications for modern history and for
our time appears as fundamental today as an understanding of
religion would have been for thirteenth century Christendom."[10]

Rupert Emerson's influential *From Empire to Nation,* written
several years later, shared the same exciting vision of a secular
nationalism that "sweeps out [from Europe] to embrace the whole
wide world."[11] Emerson acknowledged, however, that although in
the European experience "the rise of nationalism [again, secular
nationalism] coincided with a decline in the hold of religion," in
other parts of the world, such as Asia, as secular nationalism
"moved on" and enveloped these regions, "the religious issue
pressed more clearly to the fore again."[12] Nonetheless, he anticipated that the "religious issue" would never again impede the progress of secular nationalism, which he saw as the West's gift to the
world. The fact that in some instances this gift had been forced on
the new nations without their asking was noted by Emerson, who
acknowledged that "the rise of nationalism among non-European
peoples" was a consequence of "the imperial spread of Western
European civilization over the face of the earth." The outcome, in
his view, was nonetheless laudable: "With revolutionary dyna-
mism . . . civilization has thrust elements of essential identity on
peoples everywhere. . . . The global impact of the West has . . .
run common threads through the variegated social fabrics of mankind, . . . [and it] has scored an extraordinary triumph."[13]

When Kohn and Emerson used the term *nationalism* they had in
mind not just a secular political ideology and a religiously neutral
national identity but a particular form of political organization: the
modern European and American nation-state. In such an organization individuals are linked to a centralized, all-embracing democratic political system that is unaffected by any other affiliations, be
they ethnic, cultural, or religious. That linkage is sealed by an emotional sense of identification with a geographical area and a loyalty to
a particular people, an identity that is part of the feeling of nationalism. This affective dimension of nationalism is important to keep in
mind, especially in comparing secular nationalism with religion. In

the 1980s, the social theorist Anthony Giddens described nationalism in just this way—as conveying not only the ideas and "beliefs"
about political order but also the "psychological" and "symbolic"
element in political and economic relationships.[14] Scholars such as
Kohn and Emerson recognized this affective dimension of nationalism early on; they felt it appropriate that the secular nation adopt
what we might call the spirit of secular nationalism.

Faith in Secular Nationalism

Despite their admission that secular nationalism is emotional and
that in many cases it superseded traditional forms of faith, scholars
such as Kohn and Emerson and nationalist leaders such as Nasser
and Nehru insisted that secular nationalism was superior in large
measure because it was categorically different from religion. Yet it
seems clear in hindsight that to believe in the notion of secular
nationalism required a great deal of faith, even though the idea was
not couched in the rhetoric of religion. The terms in which it was
presented were the grandly visionary ones associated with spiritual
values. Secular nationalism, like religion, embraces what one
scholar calls "a doctrine of destiny."[15] One can take this way of looking at secular nationalism a step further and state flatly, as did one
author writing in 1960, that secular nationalism *is* "a religion."[16]

More recently, Ninian Smart has enlarged on this way of thinking about secular nationalism and specified the characteristics that
make it akin to a certain kind of religion—"a tribal religion."[17]
Employing six criteria to define the term, he concludes that secular
nationalism measures up on all counts: it includes doctrine, myth,
ethics, ritual, experience, and social organization. This structural
similarity between secular nationalism and religion is comple-
mented by what I regard as an even more basic, functional similarity: they both serve the ethical function of providing an overarching
framework of moral order, a framework that commands ultimate
loyalty from those who subscribe to it. A further point, one that will
be explored later in this book, bears mentioning here: nowhere is
this common form of loyalty more evident than in the ability of
nationalism and religion, alone among all forms of allegiance, to
give moral sanction to martyrdom and violence.[18]

For that reason, I believe the line between secular nationalism and religion has always been quite thin. Both are expressions of faith, both involve an identity with and a loyalty to a large community, and both insist on the ultimate moral legitimacy of the authority invested in the leadership of that community. The rise of secular nationalism in world history, as Benedict Anderson observes, has been an extension of "the large cultural systems that preceded it, out of which—as well as against which—it came into being."[19] For that reason secular nationalism can be said to be a kind of "cultural nationalism" in the way that Howard Wriggins describes Sinhalese national sentiments.[20] It not only encompasses the shared cultural values of people within existing, or potentially existing, national boundaries but also evokes a cultural response of its own.

The implication of this position—that secular nationalism has a cultural dimension—is that there is no such thing as a concept of nationalism that stands above culture. The Western notion of secular nationalism is precisely that, a Western construct. It may be true that in time, as Kohn and Emerson prophesied, the concept may spread throughout the globe, not because it is inherently universal but because it has been consciously adapted to particular situations and clearly accepted within certain regions as a legitimate expression of indigenous sentiments. In contrast, in the 1950s in many regions there was superficial acceptance of a concept that was promoted by leaders of new nations who may have genuinely believed in the idea of secular nationalism but who also found it useful in buttressing their own legitimacy at home and fostering economic support and political liaisons abroad.

The proposition that the Western notion of secular nationalism is a European artifact has been bandied about from time to time in Western intellectual circles. At least one scholar, a Christian theologian, has suggested that the idea of a secular basis for politics is not only culturally European but specifically Christian. In an arresting book, *Christianity in World History*, Arend Theodor van Leeuwen argued that the idea of separating out the things of God from the things of people in such a way as to deny the divine nature of kingship was first formulated in ancient Israel and then became a major motif of Christianity.[21] As Christianity spread across Europe, it brought the message of secularization with it: "Christianization and secularization are involved together in a dialectical relation," van Leeuwen claimed.[22] By secularization van Leeuwen did not mean secularism—the worship of worldly things—but rather the separation of religious and temporal spheres.[23] The great liaison between the medieval church and state was something of a mistake, from this point of view, and the Enlightenment brought Christianity's secularizing mission back on track. In general, van Leeuwen proclaimed, "the revolutionary history of the West up to the present time is rightly held to have been a continuous, ongoing process of secularization"; and, he added, it is a process that "nothing has been able to halt, let alone reverse."[24]

Van Leeuwen noted that the encounter between Western (implicitly Christian) secular culture and the traditional religious cultures of the Middle East and Asia "begins a new chapter in the history of secularization."[25] Secular culture was, in his mind, Christianity's gift to the world, and he fully expected that as a result of the encounter Hindus would shed their "myth of *sanatana dharma*" (traditional duties) and Muslims their "myth of the all-embracing authority of the *shari'a*" (religious law), just as Christians had fled from pagan gods and the ancient Israelites had abandoned the Tower of Babel.[26] This result was inevitable, van Leeuwen thought, for "once the ontocratic pattern of the pagan religions has been disrupted fundamentally, there can be no returning to a pre-Christian situation."[27] Still, in the short run, van Leeuwen anticipated trouble: "Never in the past," he wrote, "has there been such an encounter" as the present one between Christianity "in such a thoroughly secularized phase" and "the great pre-Christian societies and the post-Christian Muslim world." Van Leeuwen concluded, somewhat darkly, "We do not know what may happen."[28]

As it turned out, the encounter between Islamic and other traditional religious societies and the secular West was as unpleasant as van Leeuwen feared. Van Leeuwen's thesis about the Christian origins of modern Western secularism is increasingly regarded as true, especially in Third World countries, by people who have never heard of van Leeuwen and who once were uncritically accepting of Western nationalism as the wave of the future. The finer points of van Leeuwen's argument are still problematic however. The idea that secularism was uniquely Christian can be challenged by the observation that most other religious traditions have as complicated a pattern of church/state relations as Christianity has. In ancient India and in many Buddhist countries, for instance, a distinction similar to that made by the ancient Hebrews and early Christians was drawn between priestly and secular authority. Moreover, the instances of religious complicity with the state are at least as frequent in Christian history as they are in the history of other traditions. Yet van Leeuwen is correct in saying that the particular form of secular society that has evolved in the modern West is a direct extension of its past, including its religious past, and is not some supracultural entity that came into being only after a radical juncture in history.

Van Leeuwen thus stated some years ago what today is taken to be a fact in many parts of the world: the secular nationalism of the West is a mask for a certain form of European Christian culture. This point of view is adopted increasingly by many who have never read van Leeuwen but who agree with his premise: the rise of specific political ideologies is part of a much larger unfolding of ideas in world history, ideas that in most cases are colored in particular religious hues. This position is frequently heard today among the religious and political leaders of previously colonized countries.

The Religious Rejection of Secular Nationalism

Secular nationalism is "a kind of religion," one of the leaders of the Iranian revolution wrote in a matter-of-fact manner that indicated that what he said was taken as an obvious truth by most of his readers.[29] He went on to explain that it was not only a religion but one peculiar to the West, a point echoed by one of the leaders of the Muslim Brotherhood in Egypt.[30] Behind his statement was the assumption that secular nationalism responds to the same needs for collective identity, ultimate loyalty, and moral authority that religion has traditionally responded to and that this similar response makes secular nationalism de facto a religion. One of his colleagues went further and stated that the Western form of secular nationalism is Christian. He claimed that the West is "not as secular as it pretends," for it has "Christian governments."[31] For evidence, he offered the fact that the word *Christian* is used in the title of socialist parties in Europe.[32]

Others have given a more sophisticated version of this argument, saying that although secular nationalism in the West may not be overtly Christian, it occupies the same place in human experience as does Islam in Muslim societies, Buddhism in Theravada Buddhist societies, and Hinduism and Sikhism in Indian society. Thus it is a religion in the same sense that Islam, Theravada Buddhism, Hinduism, and Sikhism are. One might as well call it Christian nationalism or European cultural nationalism, they declare, and make clear what seems to many Muslims, Buddhists, Hindus, and Sikhs to be perfectly obvious: that it competes in every way with religion as they know it.

Behind this charge is a certain vision of social reality, one that involves a series of concentric circles. The smallest circles are families and clans; then come ethnic groups and nations; the largest, and implicitly most important, are global civilizations. Among the global civilizations are Islam, Buddhism, and what some who hold this view call "Christendom" or simply "Western civilization."[33] Particular nations such as Germany, France, and the United States, in this conceptualization, stand as subsets of Christendom/Western civilization; similarly, Egypt, Iran, Pakistan, and other nations are subsets of Islamic civilization.

From this vantage point, it is a serious error to suggest that Egypt or Iran should be thrust into a Western frame of reference. In this view of the world they are intrinsically part of Islamic, not Western, civilization, and it is an act of imperialism to think of them in any other way. One of the things that most exercised the Ayatollah Khomeini in prerevolutionary Iran was what he and others referred to as "West-toxification" or "Westomania."[34] According to Khomeini, Islamic peoples have been stricken with Westomania since the eighth century, and partly for that reason they easily accepted the cultural and political postures of the shah. More recent attempts to capitalize on Westomania, he maintained, have come from the insidious efforts of Western imperialists.[35] The goal of the Islamic revolution in Iran, then, was not only to free Iranians politically from the shah but also to liberate them conceptually from Western ways of thinking.

When the leaders of some formerly colonized countries continue to impose on their people Western ideas—including especially the idea of secular nationalism—they are accused by other indigenous

leaders of perpetuating colonialism. "We have yet to be truly free,"
a Buddhist leader in Sri Lanka remarked in reference to the
Western-style government in his country.[36] In some Middle Eastern Islamic countries, the injury of the colonial experience was
compounded with the insult of having lost their connection with a
great Islamic power, the Ottoman Empire.

Islamic revolutionaries in Iran have also voiced anticolonial sentiments, even though Iran was never a colony in the same sense that
many Middle Eastern and South Asian countries were. The heavy-
handed role of the U.S. Central Intelligence Agency in Iranian
politics and the force-feeding of Western ideas by the shah were
regarded as forms of colonialism all the same. According to one
Iranian leader, Abolhassan Bani-Sadr, the religious character of
Western nationalism makes it a competitor with Islam. He claimed
that Western nationalism suffers from a pretension of universality
so grand it has religious proportions and this claim to universality
makes its cultural and economic colonialism possible by allowing a
"national entity" from the West to assume that it has "prior rights to
the rest of the world."[37]

These leaders regard as especially pernicious the fact that the
cultural colonialism of Western ideas erodes confidence in traditional values. For that matter, it also undermines traditional religious constructs of society and the state. Concerns over both these
matters and over the erosion of religion's influence in public life
unite religious activists from Egypt to Sri Lanka, even those who
are bitterly opposed to one another. A leader of the religious right
in Israel and a spokesperson for the Islamic movement in Palestine,
for instance, used exactly the same words to describe their sentiments: "Secular government is the enemy."[38]

Some Western scholars also use bellicose terms to describe the
relation of religious and secular political authorities in many traditional societies. In Islam, according to Bernard Lewis, "the very
notion of a secular jurisdiction and authority . . . is seen as an impi-
ety, indeed as the ultimate betrayal of Islam."[39] He goes on to say
that "the righting of this wrong is the principal aim of Islamic revolutionaries."[40] For this reason, Lewis asserts, Islamic activists throughout the world have attempted to rid their societies of what they
regard as the corrosive influence of Western secular institutions.

Some religious revolutionaries—although certainly not all of them—deny the possibility that secular institutions can exist in a religious society. According to a leader of the religious right in Israel, "Secular government is illegitimate."[41] A similar sentiment was echoed by one of his rivals, a Muslim leader in Palestine, who declared that "a secular state is anti-Islamic" and that "no such thing exists in Islam."[42] Some would go so far as to denounce any form of secular thinking as illegitimate. When secular ideas are described in articles published by the Islamic wing of the Palestinian liberation movement, they are dubbed *al muniya,* which means "knowledge that does not come from Islam";[43] by implication, it is no knowledge at all.

One of the reasons secular ideas and institutions are so firmly rejected by some religious leaders is that they hold these ideas and institutions accountable for the moral decline within their own countries. The moral impact of Western secularism in Sri Lanka was devastating, according to the calculations of some leaders of Buddhist monastic organizations. One of them, in discussing this matter, carefully identified the evils of the society around him and then laid them fully at the feet of the secular government. "We live in an immoral world," the bhikkhu (monk) stated, giving as his examples of immorality gambling, slaughtering animals for meat, and drinking *arrack* (a locally produced alcohol that is popular in the countryside).[44] In each case the government was implicated: the state lottery promotes gambling, the state encourages animal husbandry, and it licenses liquor shops. The institutions of government were all suspect, the bhikkhu implied: "People in public office are not to be trusted."[45]

Interestingly, one of the concepts that disturbed the bhikkhu the most was an activity that most Westerners regard as a cardinal strength of the secular political system: the ability to respond impartially to the demands of a variety of groups. The political expediency of giving in to the demands of particular interests, such as those of the Tamils, was cited by the bhikkhu as evidence of the government's immorality. He felt that such politicians were incapable of standing up for truth in the face of competing, selfish interests, and their impartiality indicated that they ultimately cared only about themselves. The bhikkhu scoffed at secular politicians who attempted to cloak themselves in Buddhist rhetoric. "They are the enemy of Buddhism," he said.[46]

Secular nationalists within Third World countries are thought to be enemies in part because they are in league with a more global enemy, the secular West. To some religious nationalists' way of thinking, there is a global conspiracy against religion, orchestrated by the United States. For this reason virtually anything the United States does that involves non-Western societies, even when its stated intentions are positive, is viewed as part of a plot to destroy or control them. An example occurred in 1991 during the Gulf War; Islamic political groups in Egypt reversed their initial condemnation of Iraq's invasion of Kuwait when the United States sent thousands of troops to defend the Kuwaitis. These groups then felt it necessary to defend Saddam Hussein against the sinister plotting of the United States, which they regarded as the major obstacle to "the liberation of the Third World" and the establishment of a pan-Islamic consciousness that would unify Arab Muslim people.[47]

The most extreme form of this way of thinking is satanization. During the early days of the Gulf War, the Palestinian Islamic movement, Hamas, issued a communiqué stating that the United States "commands all the forces hostile to Islam and the Muslims." It singled out George Bush, who, it claimed, was not only "the leader of the forces of evil" but also "the chief of the false gods."[48] As the communiqué indicates, this line of reasoning often leads down a slippery slope, for once secular institutions and authorities begin to loom larger than life and take on a satanic luster, the conclusion rushes on, inevitably and irretrievably, that secular enemies are more than mortal foes: they are mythic entities and satanic forces.

Perhaps nowhere was this process of satanization more prevalent than in Iran during the early stages of the revolution when both the shah and President Jimmy Carter were referred to as *Yazid* (in this context, an agent of satan). "All the problems of Iran," Khomeini elaborated, are "the work of America."[49] He meant not only political and economic problems but also cultural and intellectual ones, fostered by "the preachers they planted in the religious teaching institutions, the agents they employed in the universities, government educational institutions, and publishing houses, and the Orientalists who work in the service of the imperialist states."[50] The vastness and power of such a conspiratorial network could be explained only by its supernatural force.

The process of satanization indicates that secular nationalism is seen as a religious entity, albeit a sinister one, and this view can be explained, in part, by the "fallen-angel" syndrome: the more vaunted the expectations, the more severe the recrimination. Many members of formerly colonized countries had had such high expectations of—such great faith in—secular nationalism that their disappointment in its failure was also extreme. Where anticipation of secularism's performance had assumed messianic proportions, the disappointment in the lack of performance reached satanic depths.

For that reason the loss of faith in secular nationalism is linked to another phenomenon: the perception that secular institutions have failed to perform. In many parts of the world the secular state has not lived up to its own promises of political freedom, economic prosperity, and social justice. Some of the most poignant cases of disenchantment with secularism are to be found among educated members of the middle class who were raised with the high expectations propagated by secular-nationalist political leaders. Some of them have now been propelled toward religious nationalism after trying to live as secular nationalists and feeling betrayed, or at least unfulfilled. Many of them also feel that Western societies have betrayed themselves: the government scandals, persistent social inequities, and devastating economic difficulties of the United States and the former Soviet Union in the 1980s and early 1990s made both democracy and socialism less appealing as role models than they had been in those more innocent decades, the 1940s and 1950s. The global mass media in their exaggerated way have brought to religious leaders in non-Western nations the message that there is a deep malaise in the United States caused by the social failures of unwed mothers, divorce, racism, and drug addiction; the political failures of Watergate, Irangate, and the Vietnam War; and the economic failures associated with recession and the mounting deficit.

But mass media or no, religious leaders in the new nations need not look any further than their own national backyards for evidence that the high expectations raised by secular nationalists in their own countries have not been met. "It is an economic, social, and moral failure," a Muslim leader in Egypt said, speaking of the policies of his nation's secular state.[51] Other new religious revolutionaries are disturbed not so much that an experiment in secular nationalism has failed as that a religious nationalism, except in Iran, has never been fully implemented.

The hopes for such a religious nationalism can be utopian. Christian revolutionaries in Latin America have spoken of instituting the "kingdom of God" promised in the New Testament. The "dhammic society" that the bhikkhu in Sri Lanka desired as the alternative to secular nationalism resembled a paradise: "The government would be supported by the people and trusted by them; it would uphold *dhamma* [moral teachings of the Buddha], and it would consult monks regarding proper policies."[52] In a Halakhic society, Jewish leaders in Jerusalem promised, Israel would become more harmonious than it is, all its aspects integrated under religious law. "Man can't live by bread alone," one of the leaders reminded his supporters; "religion is more than just belief and ritual, it is all of life."[53] Another contrasted secular rule with the rule of God: "Secularism lacks God and idealism," he said, pointing out that the state "only has laws, and that's not enough. There is a need to be in touch with the God behind the justice and the truth that secular society espouses."[54] The vision of religious nationalists is appealing in part because it promises a future that cannot easily fail: its moral and spiritual goals are transcendent and not as easy to gauge as are the more materialistic promises of secular nationalists.

Ultimately secular nationalism is perceived by many as having failed not only because its institutions and leaders have disappointed them but also because they have ceased to believe in it. In their own way, they are experiencing what Jürgen Habermas has dubbed a modern "crisis of legitimation," in which the public's respect for political and social institutions has been deflated throughout the world.[55] Perhaps many religious leaders never did believe in the validity of secular nationalism; but they are now able to convince the masses of people within their societies of its invalidity, in part because great numbers of them no longer see secular nationalism as an expression of their own identities or as related to their social and economic situations. More important, they have failed to see how the Western versions of nationalism can provide a vision of what they would like themselves and their nation to become. Secular nationalism is seen as alien, at best the expression of only a small, educated, and privileged few within non-Western societies. As both capitalist and formerly socialist governments wrestle with their own constituencies over the moral purpose of their nations and the directions they are to take, their old, tired forms of nationalism seem less appealing elsewhere.

Chapter Two

Competing Ideologies of Order

It is easy for the new religious activists—the militant ayatollahs, bhikkhus, rabbis, priests, and sheiks—to tag the modern notion of secular nationalism as Western, for the concept frequently travels as the excess baggage of a European or American presence. What they often do not realize is how new the notion is, even in the West. Although Arend van Leeuwen and others are right in saying that the division between church and state in the West has ancient roots, religion in most Christian countries has never been as far removed from politics as it has in the last two or three hundred years.

Secular Nationalism in the West

Secular nationalism as we know it today—as the ideological ally of the nation-state—did not appear in England and America until the eighteenth century. Only by then had the nation-state taken root deeply enough to nurture an ideological loyalty of its own, unassisted by religious or ethnic identifications, and only by then had the political and military apparatus of the nation-state expanded sufficiently to encompass a large geographic region. Prior to that time, as Giddens explains, "the administrative reach" of the political center was so limited that rulers did not govern in "the modern sense."[1] Although there were embryonic forms of secular nationalism before then, the power of the state had been limited.[2] Until the advent of the nation-state, the authority of a political center did not systematically and equally cover an entire population, so that what appeared to be a single homogeneous polity was in fact a congeries of

26

fiefdoms. The further one got from the center of power, the weaker the grip of centralized political influence, until at the periphery whole sections of a country might exist as a political no man's land. For that reason, one should speak of countries prior to the modern nation-state as having frontiers rather than boundaries.[3]

The changes of the late eighteenth and nineteenth centuries included the development of the technical ability to knit a country together through roads, rivers, and other means of transportation and communication; the construction of the economic ability to do so, through an increasingly integrated market structure; the emergence of a world economic system based on the building blocks of nation-states;[4] the formation of mass education, which socialized each generation of youth into a homogeneous society; and the rise of parliamentary democracy as a system of representation and an expression of the will of the people. The glue that held all these changes together was a new form of nationalism: the notion that individuals naturally associate with the people and place of their ancestral birth (or an adopted homeland such as the United States) in an economic and political system identified with a secular nation-state. Secular nationalism was thought to be not only natural but also universally applicable and morally right. Although it was regarded almost as a natural law, secular nationalism was ultimately viewed as an expression of neither God nor nature but of the will of citizens.[5] It was the political manifestation of the Enlightenment view of humankind.

The ideas of John Locke about the origins of a civil community[6] and the social-contract theories of Jean Jacques Rousseau required little commitment to religious belief.[7] Although they allowed for a divine order that made the rights of humans possible, their ideas did not directly buttress the power of the Church and its priestly administrators, and they had the effect of taking religion—at least Church religion—out of public life.

The medieval Church once possessed "many aspects of a state," as one historian put it, and it commanded more political power "than most of its secular rivals."[8] By the mid-nineteenth century, however, Christian churches had ceased to have much influence on European or American politics. The Church—the great medieval monument of Christendom with all its social and political panoply—had been replaced by churches: various denominations of Protestantism and a largely depoliticized version of Roman Catholicism. These churches functioned like religious clubs, voluntary associations for the spiritual edification of individuals in their leisure time, rarely cognizant of the social and political world around them.[9]

At the same time that religion in the West was becoming less political, its secular nationalism was becoming more religious. It became clothed in romantic and xenophobic images that would have startled its Enlightenment forebears. The French Revolution, the model for much of the nationalist fervor that developed in the nineteenth century, infused a religious zeal into revolutionary democracy; the revolution took on the trappings of church religion in the priestly power meted out to its demagogic leaders and in the slavish devotion to what it called the temple of reason. According to Alexis de Tocqueville, the French Revolution "assumed many of the aspects of a religious revolution."[10] The American Revolution also had a religious side: many of its leaders had been influenced by eighteenth-century deism, a religion of science and natural law that was "devoted to exposing [Church] religion to the light of knowledge."[11] As in France, American nationalism developed its own religious characteristics, blending the ideals of secular nationalism and the symbols of Christianity into what has been called "civil religion."

The nineteenth century saw the fulfillment of de Tocqueville's prophecy that the "strange religion" of secular nationalism would, "like Islam, overrun the whole world with its apostles, militants, and martyrs."[12] It was spread throughout the world with an almost missionary zeal and was shipped to the newly colonized areas of Asia, Africa, and Latin America as part of the ideological freight of colonialism. It became the ideological partner of what came to be known as nation building. As the colonizing governments provided their colonies with the political and economic infrastructures to turn territories into nation-states, the ideology of secular nationalism emerged as a by-product. As it had in the West in previous centuries, secular nationalism in the colonized countries in the nineteenth and twentieth centuries came to represent one side of a great encounter between two vastly different ways of perceiving the sociopolitical order and the relationship of the individual to the state: one informed by religion, the other by a notion of a secular compact.

In the West this encounter, and the ideological, economic, and political transitions that accompanied it, took place over many years. Though fundamental, these changes were not complicated by the intrusion of foreign control of a colonial or neocolonial sort. The new nations of this century have had to confront the same challenges in a short period of time and simultaneously contend with new forms of politics forced on them as by-products of colonial rule. As in the West, however, the challenge they have faced is fundamental: it involves the encounter between a religious world-view and one shaped by secular nationalism.

When Europeans colonized the rest of the world, they were often sustained by a desire to make the rest of the world like themselves.[13] Even when empires became economically burdensome, the cultural mission seemed to justify the effort. The commitment of colonial administrators to a secular-nationalist vision explains why they were often so hostile to the Christian missionaries who tagged along behind them: the missionaries were the liberal colonizers' competitors. The Church's old religious ideology was a threat to the new secular ideology that most colonial rulers wished to present as characteristic of the West.[14]

In the mid-twentieth century, when the colonial powers retreated, they left behind the geographical boundaries they had drawn and the political institutions they had fashioned. Created as administrative units of the Ottoman, Hapsburg, French, and British empires, the borders of most Third World nations continued after independence, even if they failed to follow the natural divisions between ethnic and linguistic communities. By the middle of the twentieth century, it seemed as if the cultural goals of the colonial era had been reached: although the political ties were severed, the new nations retained all the accoutrements of Westernized countries.

The only substantial empire that remained virtually intact until 1990 was the Soviet Union. It was based on a different vision of political order, of course, one in which international socialism was supposed to replace a network of capitalist nations. Yet the perception of many members of the Soviet states was that their nations were not so much integral units in a new internationalism as they were colonies in a secular Russian version of imperialism. This reality became dramatically clear after the breakup of the Soviet Union and its sphere of influence in the early 1990s, when old ethnic and national loyalties sprang to the fore.

The current situation is one in which the nation-state continues to be critical to world politics, not only for ideological reasons but also for economic ones: nation-states are the essential units of a global economic system. In the past, religion had little role to play in this scheme, and when it did become involved, it often threatened it.[15] Contemporary religious politics, then, is the result of an almost Hegelian dialectic between two competing frameworks of social order: secular nationalism (allied with the nation-state) and religion (allied with large ethnic communities). The clashes between them have often been destructive, but, as we shall see, they have also offered possibilities for accommodation. These encounters have given birth to a synthesis in which religion has become the ally of a new kind of nation-state.

The Competition between Two Ideologies

How should we describe this conflict between religion and secular nationalism, which occurred in the West several centuries ago and is now reappearing elsewhere in the world? Our choice of terms is important because they color how we think about Western history and how we think about contemporary world affairs. Because the social functions of traditional religion and secular nationalism are so similar, it is useful to designate a general category that includes them both: a "genus" of which religion and secular nationalism are the two competing "species." Benedict Anderson has suggested "imagined communities," and Ninian Smart has suggested "worldviews" as the common term.[16] Their choices have the benefit of including a wide range of concepts, from attitudes toward sexuality and natural science to views about the cosmos, and explicitly include both what we call religion and what we call secular nationalism. Because our discussion is focused on conceptual frameworks that legitimize authority, however, I prefer a term with a political connotation, *ideologies of order.*

I use the word *ideology* with a certain amount of trepidation, knowing that it comes freighted with meanings attached to it by Karl Marx and Karl Mannheim, and a great deal of controversy still lingers over its interpretation today.[17] The term is useful for our purposes, however, because it originated in the late eighteenth century in the context of the rise of secular nationalism.[18] A group of French *idéologues*, as they called themselves, were attempting to build a science of ideas based on the theories of Francis Bacon, Thomas Hobbes, John Locke, and René Descartes that would be sufficiently comprehensive to replace religion. According to one of the *idéologues*, Destutt de Tracy, whose book *Elements of Ideology* introduced the term to the world, "logic" was to be the sole basis of "the moral and political sciences."[19]

The French originators of the term would be surprised at the way it has come to be redefined, especially in contemporary conversations where it is often designated as an explanatory system that is specifically "nonscientific."[20] But in proposing their own "science of ideas" as a replacement for religion, the *idéologues* were in fact putting what they called ideology and what we call religion on an equal plane. Perhaps Clifford Geertz, among modern users of the term, has come closest to its original meaning by speaking of ideology as a "cultural system."[21] Geertz includes both religious and political cultural systems within this framework, as well as the many cultural systems that do not distinguish between religion and politics. Religion and secular nationalism could both be considered cultural systems in Geertz's sense of the word, and, hence, as he uses it, they are ideologies.

I would prefer, then, to call both religion and secular nationalism ideologies and have done with it. But to make clear that I am referring to the original meaning of the term and not to political ideology in a narrow sense, or to a Marxian or Mannheimian notion of ideology, I will refer to what I have in mind as *ideologies of order*. Both religious and secular-nationalistic frameworks of thought conceive of the world in coherent, manageable ways; they both suggest that there are levels of meaning beneath the day-to-day world that give coherence to things unseen; and they both provide the authority that gives the social and political order its reason for being. In doing so they define for the individual the right way of being in the world and relate persons to the social whole.

Secular nationalism, as an ideology of order, locates an individual within the universe. It ties him or her to a larger collectivity associated with a particular place and a particular history. A number of social scientists have recently explored this phenomenon, and in general they link nationalism with the innate need of individuals for a sense of community. Karl Deutsch has pointed out the importance of systems of communication in fostering a sense of nationalism.[22] Ernest Gellner argues that the political and economic network of a nation-state can function only in a spirit of nationalism based on a homogeneous culture, a unified pattern of communication, and a common system of education.[23] Other social scientists have stressed the psychological aspect of national identity: the sense of historical location that is engendered when individuals feel they have a larger, national history.[24] But behind these notions of community is a more stern image of order, for nationalism also involves loyalty to an authority who, as Max Weber observed, holds a monopoly over the "legitimate use of physical force" in a given society.[25] Giddens describes nationalism as the "cultural sensibility of sovereignty," implying that, in part, the awareness of being subject to an authority—an authority invested with the power of life and death—gives nationalism its potency.[26] Secular nationalism, therefore, involves not only an attachment to a spirit of social order but also an act of submission to an ordering agent.

Recent scholarly attempts to define religion also stress the importance of order, albeit in a conceptual as well as in a political and social sense.[27] In providing its adherents with a sense of conceptual order, religion often deals with the fundamental problem of disorder. The disorderliness of ordinary life is contrasted with a substantial, unchanging divine order.[28] Geertz sees religion as the effort to integrate messy everyday reality into a pattern of coherence at a deeper level.[29] Robert Bellah also thinks of religion as an attempt to reach beyond ordinary phenomena in a "risk of faith" that allows people to act "in the face of uncertainty and unpredictability" on the basis of a higher order of reality.[30] Peter Berger specifies that such faith is an affirmation of the sacred, which acts as a doorway to a truth more certain than that of this world.[31] Louis Dupré prefers to avoid the term *sacred* but integrates elements of both Berger's and Bellah's definitions in his description of religion as "a commitment to the transcendent as to *another* reality."[32] In all these cases there is a tension between this imperfect, disorderly world, and a perfected, orderly one to be found in a higher, transcendent state or in a cumulative moment in time. As Emile Durkheim, whose thought is fundamental to each of these thinkers, was adamant in observing, religion has a more encompassing force than can be suggested by any dichotomization of the sacred and the profane. To

Durkheim, the religious point of view includes both the notion that there is such a dichotomy and the belief that the sacred side will always, ultimately, reign supreme.[33]

From this perspective, religion, like secular nationalism, is the glue that holds together broad communities.[34] Members of these communities— secular or religious—share a tradition, a particular world-view, in which the essential conflict between appearance and deeper reality is described in specific and characteristically cultural terms. This deeper reality has a degree of permanence and order quite unobtainable by ordinary means. The conflict between the two levels of reality is what both religion and secular nationalism are about: the language of both contains images of grave disorder as well as tranquil order, holding out the hope that, despite appearances to the contrary, order will eventually triumph and disorder will be contained.

Because both religion and secular nationalism are ideologies of order, they are potential rivals. Either can claim to be the guarantor of orderliness within a society; either can claim to be the ultimate authority for social order. Such claims carry with them an extraordinary degree of power, for contained within them is the right to give moral sanction for life and death decisions, including the right to kill. When either secular nationalism or religion assumes that role by itself, it reduces the other to a peripheral social role.

Earlier in history it was often religion that denied moral authority to secular politicians, but in recent centuries it has been the other way around. Political authorities now attempt to monopolize the authority to sanction violence. They made this attempt long before the advent of the nation-state but usually in collusion with religious authority, not in defiance of it. Seldom in history has the state denied so vehemently the right of religious authorities to be ultimate moral arbiters as in the modern period, and seldom before has it so emphatically taken on that role itself. The state, and the state alone, is given the power to kill legitimately, albeit for limited purposes: military defense, police protection, and capital punishment. Yet all the rest of the state's power to persuade and to shape the social order is derived from this fundamental power. In Weber's view, the monopoly over legitimate violence in a society is the very definition of a state.[35] In challenging the state's authority today's religious activists, wherever they assert themselves around the world, reclaim the traditional right of religious authorities to say when violence is moral and when it is not.

Religious conflict is one indication of the power of religion to sanction killing. The parties in such an encounter may command a greater degree of loyalty than do contestants in a purely political war. Their interests can subsume national interests. In some cases such a religious battle may preface the attempt to establish a new religious state. It is interesting to note, in this regard, that the best-known incidents of religious violence throughout the contemporary world have occurred in places where it is difficult to define or accept the idea of a nation-state. Palestine, the Punjab, and Sri Lanka are the most obvious examples, but the revolutions in Iran, Nicaragua, and the countries of Central Asia and Eastern Europe also concern themselves with what the state should be like and what elements of society should lead it. In these instances, religion provides the basis for a new national consensus and a new kind of leadership.

It may be easy to think of Islam and Christianity as rivals to secular nationalism and less easy to think of Buddhism in this way. Many Western observers perceive Buddhism as an interior, ascetic spiritual discipline that is far from nationalism. Yet, even that definition reveals that the desire for order is the common thread that runs between the two. When the bhikkhus in Sri Lanka speak of the need for discipline in political life and the necessity of having a religious impulse to undergird it, they are speaking about the same essential quality of religious and national identity: the link between personal and social order. Sri Lanka has a long and glorious pre-colonial history of Buddhist rulers and Buddhist warriors, as have other Theravada Buddhist societies. In Thailand, for example, the king must be a monk before assuming political power—he must be a "world renouncer" before he can become a "world conqueror," as Stanley Tambiah has put it.[36] Burmese leaders established a Buddhist socialism, guided by a curious syncretic mix of Marxist and Buddhist ideas, and even the revolution against that order in Burma—renamed Myanmar—had a religious character: many of the demonstrations in the streets were led by Buddhist monks.[37]

Thus, in most traditional religious societies, including Buddhist ones, "religion," as Donald Smith puts it, "answers the question of political legitimacy."[38] In the modern West that legitimacy is provided by nationalism, a secular nationalism. But even there, religion continues to wait in the wings, a potential challenge to the nationalism based on secular assumptions. Perhaps nothing indicates this potential more than the persistence of religious politics in American society, including most recently the rise of politically active right-wing preachers in the 1980s.[30] Religion is ready to demonstrate that, like secular nationalism, it can provide a faith in the unitary nature of a society that will authenticate both political rebellion and political rule.

How Secular Nationalism Failed
to Accommodate Religion

In places like the United States and Europe, where secular nationalism, rather than religion, has become the dominant paradigm in society, religion is shunted to the periphery. This transposition is most dramatically illustrated by the clublike church religion that is common in the United States. Yet, even here, attempts have been made to assimilate some aspects of religion into the national consensus. The reasons for doing so are varied: coopting elements of religion into nationalism keeps religion from building its own antinational power base; it provides religious legitimacy for the state; and it helps to give nationalism a religious aura. To accomplish these goals, national leaders borrow various elements of a society's religious culture. The secular nationalism of the United States is to some extent colored by a religiosity such as this, as Bellah has pointed out in his analysis of the "civil religion" sprinkled throughout the inaugural addresses of American presidents and the rhetoric of other public speakers.[40]

Despite these attempts to coopt it, and despite its relegation to the periphery of society, church religion occasionally intrudes into the political sphere. In what Jaroslav Krejci calls "the American pattern" of society—the attempt to blend "ethnopolitical relationships" into a homogeneous whole—some religious groups resist the blending.[41] This resistance was seen dramatically during the civil-rights movement, when the black church and the black clergy became central political actors, and religious movements such as the Black Muslims arose as vehicles of protest. In a different way the ascendance of Protestant politicians is a new assault on the presumptions of secular nationalism in the United States. Secular nationalism in Europe is also not completely immune from religion. In what Krejci calls "the European pattern," where strong ethnic and religious communities are supposedly insulated from political life, the insulation sometimes wears thin.[42] The events in Eastern Europe in the early 1990s are cases in point.

So the West has found that religion does not always stay tightly leashed. But if accommodating religion has been difficult for the West, efforts to bridle religion in the new nations have been a thousand times more problematic. There the need to deal with religion is much more obvious. Given religious histories that are part of national heritages, religious institutions that are sometimes the nations' most effective systems of communication, and religious leaders who are often more devoted, efficient, and intelligent than government officials, religion cannot be ignored. The attempts to accommodate it, however, have not always been successful, as the following examples indicate.

In Egypt, following the revolution of 1952, Nasser was caught in a double bind. Because his support came from both the Muslim Brotherhood and the modern elite, he was expected to create a Muslim state and a modern secular state at the same time. His approach was to paint a picture of an Egypt that was culturally Muslim and politically secular, and he cheerfully went about "Egyptizing along with modernizing," as a professor in Cairo put it.[43] The compromise did not work, and especially after Nasser attempted to institute "scientific socialism," which the Muslim Brotherhood regarded as anti-Islamic, the Brotherhood became Nasser's foe. It attempted to overthrow his government, and Nasser jailed its members and executed its leader, Sayyid Qutb.

Nasser's successor, Anwar al-Sadat, repeated the pattern, which turned out to be a tragic and fatal mistake. Like Nasser, Sadat raised Muslim expectations by currying favor with the Muslim Brotherhood. In 1971, he released many of them from jail. But by 1974 he and the Brotherhood were at loggerheads, and again the organization was outlawed. Sadat attempted to wear the mantle of Islam by calling himself "Upholder of the Faith," announcing that his first name was really Muhammad rather than Anwar, and promoting religious schools. None of these attempts worked. His wife was thought to be an improper role model for Muslim women, and

Sadat himself was accused of being a Muslim turncoat. With this image in mind, members of the al-Jihad, a radical fringe group of the Muslim Brotherhood, assassinated Sadat in 1981. His successor, Hosni Mubarak, tried to steer more of a middle course, making no promises to the Muslim activists, but making no new secular or socialist departures either.[44]

In India, three generations of Prime Ministers in the Nehru dynasty—Jawaharlal, his daughter Indira Gandhi, and her son Rajiv—all tried to accommodate religion as little as possible. Yet at times they were forced to make concessions to religious groups almost against their wills. Nehru seemed virtually allergic to religion, putting secularism alongside socialism as his great political goal. Nonetheless the Indian constitution and subsequent parliamentary actions have given a great deal of public support to religious entities.[45] Special seats have been reserved in the legislature for Muslims and members of other minority religious communities; religious schools have been affiliated with the state; and temples and mosques have received direct public support. In general the Indian government has not been indifferent to religion but has attempted to treat—and foster—each religion in the country equally. As Ainslie Embree puts it, "Advocates of secularism in India always insisted . . . that far from being hostile to religion, they valued it."[46]

Even so, these concessions have not been sufficient to stem the tide of religious politics in India. The 1980s was a decade of tragedy in that regard. Hindu nationalists wanted more and more access to power, prompting defensiveness on the part of Muslim and Christian minorities and a bloody rebellion on the part of the Sikhs. The assassinations of Prime Minister Gandhi and her son Rajiv did not put an end to their sense of dissatisfaction, and the election of 1991, in which religious parties gained power in several states, demonstrated the potency of the Hindu right.

In Sri Lanka following independence, the urbane and Western-educated leaders of the new nation realized that they would have to give a Sinhalese Buddhist aura to their secular political stance in order for it to be widely accepted. Perhaps no Sri Lankan leader attempted to give in to Buddhist demands as much as did S. W. R. D. Bandaranaike, but even he lost his life at the hands of an irate Buddhist monk who felt that he had not gone far enough. The present

rulers in Sri Lanka face the same dilemma their predecessors did:
they need Sinhalese support, but they feel they cannot go so far as to
alienate the Tamils and other minority groups. They would like to
achieve what might be an impossibility: a national entity that is both
Buddhist and secular. The use of Buddhist symbols is meant to
appeal to the Sinhalese, and the adoption of a secular political ideology is supposed to mollify everyone else.

This dual policy of Sri Lankan leaders has led to flagrant displays
of support for Buddhist culture, such as the rebuilding of grounds
around the Dalada Maligawa, the Temple of the Tooth. This temple
houses one of the most important relics in Buddhism, a tooth that is
said to have been taken from the Buddha's funeral pyre in the fifth
century B.C.E., and is the only thing that remains of the Enlightened One's physical being. How it got to Sri Lanka and eventually
to Kandy is a long story, but there it is, and the temple that houses
it is the central shrine of Sinhalese Buddhism. For that reason no
politician can afford to ignore it. In 1987, when the United Nations
proclaimed "the international year of housing" to encourage
the building of shelter for the world's poor, the first thing that one
of Bandaranaike's successors, J.R. Jayawardene, housed with the
money he collected from international sources was the tooth: he
built a roof over the temple and layered it with a gold sheath that
can be seen throughout the city. It shimmers in the sunlight by day
and gleams in floodlights by night.

In housing the tooth, Jayawardene was responding to a dilemma
faced by many sensitive citizens of Sri Lanka. They want to affirm
that their national identity is distinctively Buddhist, while at the
same time affirming that ultimately a secular Sri Lankan nationalism transcends any particular religious expression of it. This dilemma is acute for those who come from minority communities—
Christians, Muslims, even Hindu Tamils; they would like very
much to identify with the national culture, even if it is Buddhist,
and yet not lose the distinctive aspects of their own religious traditions. An Anglican pastor and scholar in Colombo spoke movingly
about how he had come to embrace the "Christ of Buddhism" and
how his own research in Buddhist theology had brought him more
closely in touch than he was before with his Christian sensibilities.[47] Stanley Tambiah, a Sri Lankan Tamil who is professor of
anthropology at Harvard University, writes in a personal epilogue

to an essay on "ethnic fratricide" in his homeland that his interest in studying Buddhist culture—which has become the center of his professional career—began with a feeling of being excluded from Sinhalese nationalism during the ethnic riots of 1958. By studying Buddhist society in Thailand, Tambiah writes, he was able to "study with the double posture of rapport and distance in someone else's country" many of the things that he "could not aspire to [study], or [study] well, in Sri Lanka."[48] His ambivalent relationship to Buddhism and his ambiguous feelings toward Sri Lankan national identity remain.

The problem with these attempts to accommodate religion in secular nationalism is that they lead to a double frustration: those who make these compromises are sometimes considered traitors from both a spiritual and a secular point of view. Moreover, these compromises suggest that spiritual and political matters are separate, which most religious activists see as a capitulation to the secularist point of view. They sense that behind the compromises is a basic allegiance to secular nationalism rather than to religion.

Can Religion Accommodate the Nation-State?

As secular nationalism's unhappy attempts at accommodating religion have shown, religion is not easily placated. Religious activists are well aware that if a nation is based from the start on the premise of secular nationalism, religion is often made marginal to the political order. This outcome is especially unfortunate from many revolutionary religious perspectives, including the Iranian, the Sikh, and the Sinhalese, because they regard the two ideologies as unequal: the religious one is far superior. Rather than starting with secular nationalism, they prefer to begin with religion.

According to one Sinhalese writer, whose booklet, *The Revolt in the Temple*, was published shortly after Sri Lankan independence and was influential in spurring on the Buddhist national cause, "it is clear that the unifying, healing, progressive principle" that held together the entity known as Ceylon throughout the years has always been "the Buddhist faith."[49] The writer goes on to say that religion in Sri Lanka continues to provide the basis for a "liberating nationalism" and that Sinhalese Buddhism is "the only patriotism worthy of the name, worth fighting for or dying for."[50] In India, Hindu nationalists are equally emphatic that Hindutva, as they call Hindu national culture, is the defining characteristic of Indian nationalism. Similar sentiments are echoed in movements of religious nationalism elsewhere in the world.

The implication of this way of speaking is not that religion is antithetical to nationalism, but that religious rather than secular nationalism is the appropriate premise on which to build a nation— even a modern nation-state. In fact, virtually every reference to nationhood used by religious nationalists assumes that the modern nation-state is the only way in which a nation can be construed. The term *religious nationalism* in today's parlance, therefore, means the attempt to link religion and the nation-state. This is a new development in the history of nationalism, and it immediately raises the question of whether it is possible: whether what we in the West think of as a modern nation—a unified, democratically controlled system of economic and political administration—can in fact be accommodated within religion.

It is an interesting question and one to which many Western observers would automatically answer no. Even as acute an interpreter of modern society as Giddens regards most religious cultures as, at best, a syncretism of "tribal cultures, on the one hand, and modern societies, on the other."[51] Yet by Giddens's own definition of a modern nation-state, postrevolutionary Iran would qualify: the Islamic revolution in Iran solidified not just a central power but a systemic control over the population that is more conducive to nationhood than the monarchical political order of the shah. This issue will be explored further in the last chapter of this book; suffice it to say here that at least in the case of the Iranian revolution, a new national entity came into being that was quite different from both the polity under the old Muslim rulers and the nation-state the shah ineptly attempted to build. The shah dreamed of creating Kemal Atatürk's Turkey in Iran and bringing to his country the instant modernity that he perceived Atatürk brought to Turkey. Ironically, Khomeini— along with his integrative religious ideology and his grass-roots network of mullahs—brought his nation closer to that goal.

Does religion lose some essential aspects in accommodating modern politics? Some religious leaders think that it does. In favoring the nation-state over a particular religious congregation as its major community of reference, religion loses the exclusivity held by smaller, subnational religious communities, and the leaders of those communities lose some of their autonomy. For that reason, many religious leaders are suspicious of religious nationalism. Among them are religious utopians who would rather build their own isolated political societies than deal with the problems of a whole nation, religious liberals who are satisfied with the secular nation-state the way it is, and religious conservatives who would rather ignore politics altogether. Some Muslims accused Khomeini of making Islam into a political ideology and reducing it to a modern political force.[52] Moreover, as Lewis claims, most Islamic rebellions are aimed in the opposite direction: to shed Islam of the alien idea of the nation-state.[53] Yet, even if that is their aim, one of the curious consequences of their way of thinking is the appropriation of many of the most salient elements of modern nationhood into an Islamic frame of reference. Rather than ridding Islam of the nation-state, as we shall see, they too are creating a new synthesis.

Modern movements of religious nationalism, therefore, are subjects of controversy within both religious and secular circles. The marriage between religious faith and the nation-state is an interesting turn in modern history, and one fraught with dangers, for even if it is possible, the radical accommodation of religion to nationalism may not necessarily be a good thing. A merger of the absolutism of nationalism with the absolutism of religion might create a rule so vaunted and potent that it could destroy itself and its neighbors as well. The actions of religious terrorists in the 1980s and early 1990s in South Asia and the Middle East warrant some of those fears. When a society's secular state and its religious community are both strong and respected, the power of life and death that is commanded by any single absolute authority—be it secular or religious—may be held tenuously in check. Without that balance, an absolute power of the worst sort could claim its most evil deeds to be legitimate moral duties. The revolutionary religious movements that emerged in many parts of the world in the 1980s and 1990s exhibit some of the dangers—as well as many of the hopeful aspects—of the religious nationalists' appropriation of the idea of the modern nation-state.

Part Two

The Global Confrontations

Chapter Three

Models of Religious Revolution:
The Middle East

Although the rise of revolutionary movements that embrace a religious nation-state is new, the movements inherit a long tradition of religious protest and social change. Religion and politics have been intertwined throughout history and around the globe, and a number of rebellions against authority, from the Maccabean revolt in ancient Israel to the Taiping Rebellion in China, the Wahhabiya movement in Arabia, and Puritanism in England, have been religious in character. Some of them, like the movements to be discussed here, were rebellions against secular authorities. The Puritans, with their theocratic revolt against the increasing secularism of seventeenth-century English politics, may be regarded as precursors of modern antisecular radicals.[1]

The new movements are different from their historical predecessors in that they are reactions to, and are attempts to forge a synthesis with, a specific political form that originated in the modern West: the nation-state. In responding to it, religious nationalists evoke ethnic loyalties and religious commitments that are by definition specific. These movements are identified with particular geographic and linguistic regions. To understand the phenomenon, then, we have to see it in its diversity.

The Ingredients of a Religious Revolt

In this part of the book, we will look at confrontations involving movements of religious nationalism that have come to the fore in the Middle East, South Asia, and the formerly socialist areas of

45

Central Asia and Europe. I have chosen these cases because they are well known and they show profound similarities. Taken together, they are not just a congeries of particular cases but a worldwide phenomenon.

In general, I have chosen movements that share these characteristics: they reject secular nationalism; they regard secular nationalism as Western and neocolonial; their rejection is fundamental—often hostile and violent; they wage their struggle with religious rhetoric, ideology, and leadership; and they offer a religious alternative to the secular nation-state.

All the movements discussed in the following chapters share these characteristics, although some fit the criteria better than do others. They are all revolutionary, in the sense that they challenge the legitimacy of the old order and call for changes that have far-reaching consequences. Calling them revolutionary, however, does not indicate the kind of politics the revolutionaries desire. In the descriptions that follow we will find great diversity: the religious nation-state they have in mind may be democratic, socialist, theocratic, or autocratic; and in many instances the leaders simply have not thought that far ahead.

Some social scientists have seen past revolutions as the eruption of change along fault lines in a social system where pressure has been building for years, and this model can be applied to the current cases as well.[2] Gary Sick has done so in describing the Iranian revolution as almost a "textbook case" of Crane Brinton's theory that revolutions occur when rising expectations are thwarted.[3] The model is not essential for understanding the cases that follow, however, and I prefer to burden the term *revolution* with a minimal amount of conceptual baggage: in my use of the term, a revolutionary movement is one that attempts to alter the social and political order at a basic level.

Saying that revolutionary movements attempt to change the system does not, of course, mean that they will succeed. Most of the movements described here have not resulted in new regimes. The major exceptions are Iran, Sudan, Afghanistan, and Tajikistan, and in each of these cases it is still not clear whether in the long run the most strident leaders of the regimes will remain in charge. Yet the revolutionary intent of the religious activists in these countries, and in many countries like them around the world, is serious indeed.

Four heads of state have been assassinated by religious radicals—
Anwar Sadat in Egypt, S.W.R.D. Bandaranaike in Sri Lanka, Indira Gandhi in India, and Mohammed Boudiaf in Algeria—and
thousands of others, on both sides of the struggles, have lost their
lives.

One could question whether the sights of these revolutionary
movements are aimed solely at the national level. Like the ideological rhetoric of the old Cold War, the political rhetoric of many of the
movements seems directed toward a supranational ideal. This is especially true of the Muslim movements. The longing for a global state
of religious harmony is an old Islamic dream, and for years the great
Islamic empires appeared to be on the verge of making that dream a
reality. For this reason, many Muslim activists hesitate to speak of
solely national interests and instead express pan-Islamic ideals.
Many espouse Muslim nationalism in general; pictured on the wall of
one of the Palestinian leaders in Gaza is a map of the world on which
is superimposed the Qur'an drawn as if it had hands extending from
Morocco to Indonesia.[4] Some Muslim writers go so far as to regard
the very idea of nationalism as anti-Islamic. One has described nationalism as "the greatest evil that stalks the modern world," and
although he acknowledges that many Muslim movements are indeed nationalist, he sees their nationalism as a short-term goal and
looks forward to a Muslim unity "beyond the Muslim nation-states."[5]

Even though this yearning for a single Islamic nation runs deep
in Muslim consciousness, most Muslim activists seem happy to
settle for an Islamic nationalism that is limited to the particular
countries in which they reside. In the modern period, as Ira
Lapidus explains, "the capacity of Islam to symbolize social identity
has been merged into national feeling."[6] The most obvious example
is Iran; the Shi'ite form of Islam that predominates there is rarely
found elsewhere. But even in Sunni areas, such as Egypt and
Palestine—as the case studies in this chapter show—religious sentiments are fused with national concerns. The religious revolutionaries there fight for an Egyptian or a Palestinian identity as well as a
Muslim one. Even the proponents of a worldwide Islamic nation
concede the necessity for "a succession of Islamic Revolutions in all
Muslim areas of the world."[7] They expect that these will eventually
be united through " 'open' or 'soft' frontiers" to replace the boundaries between Islamic states.[8] My guess, however, is that the bor-

ders will stay immutable and solid, for the pan-Islamic sentiments of Arabs and other Muslims have always been vexed by intra-Islamic rivalries, many of which were exacerbated in 1991 by the Gulf War.[9]

Even so, Islamic nationalism in one country can encourage the growth of Islamic nationalism in other countries. In the 1980s, the Islamic revolution in Iran served as a model for the emergence of modern Islamic nation-states elsewhere in the world. In the early 1990s, Islamic leaders in Sudan promoted Muslim activism throughout the region. After 1989, when Lieutenant General Omar Hassan Ahmed Bashir established an Islamic regime in Sudan, thousands of young Muslim revolutionaries came to study in Sudanese universities and to train in its military camps.[10] Hassan Abdullah Turabi, the Islamic leader described by an American reporter as the "behind-the-scenes power" in Khartoum, is also mentioned as "one of the key architects" of Islamic movements in Algeria, Tunisia, Egypt, Ethiopia, Nigeria, Chad, and Afghanistan.[11]

In each of these countries, however, the impetus toward an Islamic nationalism was distinctively tied to each country's history and culture, and it is doubtful that Sudanese or any other external agents made a decisive difference. In Algiers, for instance, when the Islamic Salvation Front in 1991 soundly defeated the party that had ruled Algeria since its independence from the French in 1956, the Islamic leaders were consciously attempting to emulate the earlier independence movement and promised to fulfill it by giving Algeria "a firm beginning for building an Islamic state."[12] It was a short-lived promise, however, for in January 1992, the army annulled the elections and established a secular military junta, accomplishing, as the leader of a local mosque put it, "a *coup d'état* against the [Algerian] Islamic state before it was created."[13] Leaders of the Islamic Salvation Front were jailed, and a ban was imposed on meetings at mosques, which had become venues of protest and organization for the Islamic opposition. On March 5 the party was officially outlawed. Later in 1992, the standoff between the army and Muslim activists erupted into violence, and the Casbah in Algiers's Old City became an arena of guerrilla warfare reminiscent of Algeria's war of independence from the French.[14] Hundreds of supporters of the Islamic Salvation Front were killed, and on June 29 Boudiaf, the civilian head of the military-supported

Council of State, was assassinated, allegedly by militant supporters of the Salvation Front.[15]

In other nations, Islamic political movements have also been directed toward local and national concerns. In neighboring Tunisia, the outlawed Islamic Renaissance Party and the Nahda movement have mounted a serious opposition to the government, and in Jordan, where Muslim activists' accession to power has been less violent than in Algeria, it has, in many ways, been as effective. In elections held after the Gulf War in 1991, members of the Muslim Brotherhood became the largest single bloc in the Jordanian parliament. Since then, even more extreme Muslim groups have threatened to destabilize the Jordanian government.[16] In Lebanon, Shi-'ite and Christian allegiances have defined the major factions, both of them claiming to represent a true Lebanese nationalism. In Syria, Islamic activists opposed to the Ba'ath Party's socialist ideology and its attempts to pander to Christians and other minority groups have attempted to unseat the party.[17] They disdain the secular style of Hafez al-Asad, whom they accused of "gross corruption, brutal repression of dissent, collusion with Zionism and imperialism, and sectarianism."[18]

In Saudi Arabia, Kuwait, and the other Gulf Emirates, where a kind of state Islamic culture prevails and Islamic law is honored, strident and democratic-minded Muslim activists threaten the status quo. These kingdoms, the last of the old-style Muslim states, have been protected against both the Western secularism of the left and the radical Muslim popularism of the right. In Saudi Arabia, Muslim activists have railed against the royal family and its alliance with the United States by means of fiery speeches recorded on illicit cassette tapes that have been distributed by the thousands.[19]

Outside the Arab sphere, Muslim activists have also taken up local political causes and in some cases have scored spectacular successes. The triumph of Islamic revolutionaries in Afghanistan and Tajikistan will be discussed later in this book. Islam is also linked with the rise of new ethnic politics in such disparate places as Croatia and Bosnia-Herzegovina in Yugoslavia; Kosovo province in Albania; the Aceh region of Indonesia; southern Philippines; Xinjiang, Ningxia, Gansu, and Yunnan in China; Azerbaijan, Uzbekistan, Turkmenistan, Kazakhstan, and Kyrgyzstan; and the Islamic regions of Russia.

Muslim political activism is on the rise throughout the world, but it is not orchestrated by a central command, nor are its goals antithetical to national interests. Many Muslim activists are indeed nationalists; some support subnational, local, and ethnic entities; and a few favor a pan-Islamic federation of states. Most, however, are united in their stand against the adoption of Western secular nationalism. Like religious activists everywhere, they criticize secular rule from a religious perspective; they employ religious language, leadership, and organization in their attempts to change it; and they hold up the promise of a new religious order as a shining ideal.

Iran: The Paradigmatic
Religious Revolution

The event that set the standard for religious revolution throughout the Muslim world was the Islamic revolution in Iran. "An entire population has risen up against the Shah," the Ayatollah Khomeini proclaimed to a professor from the University of California who visited him in France during the last, declining days of the Pahlavi regime.[20] This "revolutionary movement," as the Ayatollah described it, was an "explosion" that occurred as a direct result of "American intervention" and the repression of Islam over the preceding fifty years. At the time of the interview, in 1978, the ayatollah felt that the situation had "intensified to an extraordinary degree."[21] A few days later the Ayatollah was bound for Iran and his headquarters in Qom, where he presided over the new revolutionary Islamic regime until his death on June 4, 1989.

Even though the revolution was marked by the unique personality of the ayatollah, the particular circumstances of Iranian politics, and the distinctive character of Shi'ite Islam, this regime and the remarkable transfer of power that inaugurated it are seen as the paradigmatic form of religious revolution. The demon of the revolution was a nationalism and a secular rule patterned on the West and ineptly promoted by the shah. The critique of the shah's Westernized regime was couched in religious terms, the rebellion was led by religious figures, and the new order was fashioned as a utopian religious state. It was not simply a revival of an earlier form of Muslim rule, but a new form of Islamic politics. In a curious way, it was the shah's vision of an Iranian nationalism come true.

The new politics of the Iranian revolution was fundamentally Muslim—and particularly Shi'ite. Politics of various kinds have always been part and parcel of Islam. The Prophet himself was a military as well as a spiritual leader, and there have been strong Muslim rulers virtually from the tradition's inception. "In classical Islam there was no distinction between Church and state," writes Bernard Lewis, who goes on to say that the concept of secularism did not exist in the Islamic mind until quite recently.[22] There was not even a word in Arabic to express it.[23] All aspects of social and personal behavior were subject to divine guidance, and all political authority ultimately derived from sacred authority. This continues to be a general principle in Islamic societies; what is novel about the new Islamic movements is their struggle to install—in a distinctively modern way—this religious authority in secular states.

Perhaps nowhere in Islam is struggle more a part of its tradition than in Shi'ite societies. The world of Islam is largely Sunni, and only a small minority are Shi'a (partisans). They are found in southern Lebanon, Iraq, Pakistan, and especially in Iran, where 90 percent are Shi'a of a particular form. This dominant, Ithna Ashari (Twelver) brand of Shi'ism is based on the belief that there will be twelve great leaders, or imams, in world history. Shi'ite Islam began with a political struggle, and over time the tradition developed its own separate theological emphases. In his interpretation of the tradition, Khomeini capitalized on traditional Shi'ite themes, sharpening them to fit the situation of revolutionary Iran. The most important of these themes are the Shi'a tradition of struggle against oppression, the investment of political power in the clergy, and a pattern of messianic and utopian expectations.

Struggle against oppression. Shi'ism was born in conflict, in the struggle for power immediately after the death of the Prophet Muhammad. The dispute was between those who felt that the spiritual and temporal authority of Islam resided in the caliphs who followed him and who believed that it dwelled in the members of the Prophet's own family—specifically in the descendants of Ali, who was both the prophet's cousin and his son-in-law. The critical moment in this conflict came in 680 C.E., with the assassination of Ali's son, Husain, who led the Shi'ite community in Karbala (in present-day Iraq). The assassin, Yazid, was a caliph of the Sunni's Umayyad dynasty. To this day that event is recognized

as the somber turning point in Shi'ite history—rather as the crucifixion is regarded in Christian history.

Once a year, the assassination of Husain is remembered in massive and mournful parades throughout the Shi'ite world. Men
stripped to the waist march down the city streets, flagellating themselves with whips and barbed wire until their backs become raw
and bloody. On these occasions—the Ashura celebrations held
every year during the first ten days of the Islamic month of
Muharram—the faithful remember the suffering of Husain and
experience both sorrow for his wrongful death and their own vicari-
ous guilt for not having stood by him in his time of trial. In Iran,
from the early 1960s on, this occasion took a special turn. The
Ayatollah Khomeini and his colleagues began to alter the emphasis
from personal mourning to collective outrage against oppression.
They had in mind especially the shah's oppression of Islam, and
they likened the shah to Yazid, the man who had killed Husain. In
his messages the ayatollah urged his followers to avenge the martyrdom of Husain by attacking the Yazids of the present age. "With the
approach of Muharram," he told his flock, "we are about to begin
the month of epic heroism and self sacrifice—the month in which
blood triumphed over the sword, . . . the month in which the
leader of the Muslims taught us how to struggle against all the
tyrants of history."[24] In case the listener still did not get the point,
Khomeini would soon mention by name the particular tyrant he
had in mind.

Political power of the clergy. Islam is primarily a layperson's
religion, and although political leaders are expected to be religious
and to use the state's apparatus to administer Muslim law, the
clergy in most parts of the Muslim world have little political influence. In such Sunni societies as Egypt and Syria, for instance, they
have been relatively uninvolved in radical Islamic politics.[25] The
Shi'a tradition is different, in part for theological reasons. The idea
of an imam, a great leader who shapes world history, has condi-
tioned Shi'ites to expect strong leadership in what we would regard
as both worldly and religious spheres. During a period of history
when an imam is not physically present—such as the contemporary
period, when the imam is supposedly "hidden"—the power of the
imam is to be found in the mullahs, the Shi'a clergy. Another
source for the power of certain religious leaders is their ancestral

ties to the family of Ali and hence to the Prophet himself. The Ayatollah Khomeini could claim such ties, and even the modern Iraqi leader, Saddam Hussein, has let it be known that he has such connections as well. The shah's Pahlavi family, however, lacked such spiritual links, and from the point of view of the Shi'a clergy, that made them unfit for leadership. The mullahs, however, have been quite ready to speak out on social and political matters when they felt the situation called for it.

Rebellions of one sort or another have been led by the Shi'a clergy in Iran for at least a century. In 1892 a revolt against the use of tobacco was led by the mullahs, and their influence on the Constitutional Revolution of 1905–9 ensured that laws would not be passed that the mullahs deemed injurious to Islam. During the 1950s, after the campaign of the shah to blunt the influence of the mullahs, some of them became involved in conspiratorial plots against secular Iranian leaders, several of whom were assassinated. The groups they organized included the Fedayeen-i-Islam (Supporters of Islam) and the Mujahadin-i-Islam (Fighters for Islam), led by Mullah Nawab Safavi and the Ayatollah Abul Qasim Kashani, respectively. By 1963, the radical opposition to the shah had crystalized around the leadership of the Ayatollah Khomeini, and the Iranian revolution began in earnest.

Messianic and utopian expectations. In the Shi'a view of history, the hidden imam will return again at the end of history in the form of the Mahdi, the Messiah who will overthrow all the evil forces and institute a realm of justice and freedom. It would have been heretical to suggest that the Ayatollah Khomeini was the Mahdi and the Iranian revolution was that realm, and no Shi'ite dared to do so. It is true that the title that most of Khomeini's followers in Iran preferred to give him was *imam* (rather than *ayatollah*, the label by which he is best known in the West), but the title is often applied to Shi'ite religious leaders with no implication that they are in the pantheon of the twelve great imams.[26] Even so, some of Khomeini's followers claimed that he was actually a "mystical emanation issuing directly from the Mahdi," serving as a harbinger of the Mahdi's return.[27] Even if this attitude was not widespread, the very notion of a Mahdi helps to create the cultural conditions in which the figure of a savior/leader is expected and widely accepted.

These three aspects of Shi'ite Islam—its history of struggle against oppression, the political power it has traditionally vested in the clergy, and its tradition of messianic and utopian expectations—made the Islamic movement in Iran a revolution waiting to happen. That it happened so easily was due in part to the vulnerability of its adversaries. Few characters in the Shi'ite drama of the forces of good struggling against the forces of evil have so effectively played the role of evil as the members of the Pahlavi dynasty—Riza Shah, who established a military dictatorship in 1921, and his son Muhammad Riza Shah, who succeeded him in 1941. The Pahlavi reign was interrupted from 1951 to 1953 by a democratically elected prime minister, Mohammed Mossadegh (Musaddiq), who attempted to nationalize the oil industry and, with the help of the American Central Intelligence Agency, was promptly overthrown.

When the shah returned he attempted to mollify the mullahs by giving them a free reign in developing their organizations and publications, and helping them to finance Islamic schools. To some extent this policy was successful, and even Khomeini's predecessor, Ayatollah Hosain Burujirdi, supported the shah in the 1950s; at this time the clergy was accused of being a "pillar of the Pahlavi state."[28] This accommodation of the mullahs changed in the 1960s, however, when the shah attempted land reforms that threatened religious institutions and extended the right to vote to women. Impressed by Atatürk's experiment at secularization in Turkey, the shah attempted similar sweeping reforms, replacing most of Islamic law with a secular code adopted from the French. Although they tried publicly to appear to be good Muslims, the Pahlavis were seen as destroying traditional Muslim schools and seminaries, Westernizing the universities, and creating a modern bureaucracy to administer the state. Women were forbidden to wear the veil. In Teheran and other cities Western culture began to thrive, bringing in its wake not only Coca-Cola and Western movies but also discos, girlie magazines, and gay bars. It was not the Islamic utopia the mullahs had in mind. The mullahs described it, in fact, as "a satanic rule."[29]

The government's control of the media and the presence of the sinister SAVAK, the secret police, made opposition difficult. It was "impossible to breathe freely in Iran."[30] The group that was most difficult to contain and most able to organize was the clergy, who found a natural leader in Ruhullah al-Musavi al-Khomeini, who began his career as the protégé of one of Iran's leading theologians,

Sheik 'Abd al-Karim Ha'iri of the pilgrimage city of Qom. Following the death of Ha'iri in 1937, the leadership fell to the Ayatollah Burujirdi; when he died in 1961, there was no immediate consensus over who the new leader at Qom should be. It is probably not a coincidence that Khomeini's increasingly outspoken public pronouncements against the shah at that time and the rise of his public popularity occurred simultaneously with the solidification of his power within his own religious community. In any event, the protest, and Khomeini's leadership of it, surfaced in a massive demonstration in Qom in the spring of 1963. This demonstration led to Khomeini's imprisonment, his release in 1964, and imprisonment again in that year followed by expulsion from the country Khomeini was to remain abroad—first in Turkey, then in Iraq, and finally in France—until after the revolution was completed in 1979. Although he was out of the country during those critical years, he was certainly not silent, and perhaps he was able more effectively to articulate the grievances and lead the revolution from Neauphle-le-Chateau than from Qom.

To the surprise of everyone, the end came quite suddenly. Perhaps most caught off guard were the Americans, who had great difficulty even conceiving the possibility that a band of bearded, black-robed rural mullahs could seriously confront the poised and urbane shah with all his worldly connections and military might.[31] Even more inconceivable was that the power of the shah should crumble so effortlessly. Only a few months before, Jimmy Carter had praised the shah for creating an "island of stability" in the region.

Although the new revolutionary regime has not lived up to its utopian promises, the changes it has wrought have made a dramatic difference. Islamic law is now the law of the land, and most marks of "Westoxification" have been systematically erased. These reforms have not always been brought about with subtlety—some 7,000 people were executed for crimes as varied as homosexuality and believing in the Baha'i faith—and the revolutionary spirit has not easily been bridled. For a time bands of young people in the Hizbollah (Party of God) roamed the streets, attacking anyone or anything that appeared anti-Islamic, and a group of rowdy youth, without government authorization (at least at the beginning), precipitated a foreign-policy crisis by taking hostages at the American

Embassy in Teheran.[32] The course of the revolution and the attention needed for domestic problems were also deflected by a bloody, protracted war with Iraq.

In the thirteen years between 1979 and 1992 the revolutionary regime went through three stages. It began as a moderate, secular regime led first by Mehdi Bazargan and then by Abolhassan Bani-Sadr, until Khomeini used the hostage crisis as a way of continuing the revolution and forcing the moderates out.[33] After Bani-Sadr fled the country in 1981, a period of repression set in, during which thousands of persons were killed, moderate and leftist political forces were destroyed, and the power of the clergy was consolidated.[34] In 1985, the revolutionary regime began something of a Thermidorian return to a more pragmatic and moderate rule.

After the death of the Ayatollah Khomeini on June 4, 1989, his son, Ahmad Khomeini, remained as virtually the only radical clergy in the inner circles; the new president of Iran, Ali-Akbar Heshemi-Rafsanjani, continued to steer a pragmatic course. During the Gulf War, Rafsanjani refused to side with Iraq or to criticize the United States seriously, to the disappointment of the conservative clergy.[35] At the end of 1991, Iranian leaders arranged for the American hostages held in Lebanon for years to be released. In the first months of 1992, apparently to impress the conservative clergy that he had not fully capitulated to the Americans, Rafsanjani denounced the American-sponsored Arab-Israeli peace talks and referred to the United States as "an arrogant power."[36] Although the April 1992 election was a triumph for the moderates, it resulted largely in economic reforms. In 1993 Iran greatly increased its financial aid to Islamic political movements in Algeria, Bosnia, Lebanon, Pakistan, Tajikistan, and elsewhere in the world.[37]

Iran has become the grandfather of the current generation of revolutionary Islamic nationals. Perhaps the most enduring contributions of its revolution are the creation of the sense of Iranian nationalism that the shah tried but failed to achieve and the constitutional privilege granted to religion in Iran's public life.[38] There is now a fusion of Iranian nationalist goals with Shi'ite political ideology, access to power for the Muslim clergy, and provision for religious guidance at the top of the country's administration. This provision is particularly interesting, for the leaders of the revolution have taken the concept of the just ruler (*al-sultan al-'adil*) in

Shi'ite Islam and made it into a political position—an elder states-
man who guides and advises the president and other governmental
officials.[39] During Khomeini's lifetime he played that role, and after
his death he was succeeded by the former president, Ayatollah Ali
Khamenei. The position is intriguing, for, as Khomeini explained,
"the religious leaders do not wish to be the government, but neither are they separate from the government."[40] Separate or not,
the ayatollah warned that they would be prepared to "intervene" if
the secular leaders of the government make "a false step."[41] Religious revolutionaries in other parts of the world would give almost
anything to acquire this remarkable leverage of power.

Egypt's Incipient Religious Revolt

Can the religious revolution that Khomeini created in Iran be ex-
ported to other places in the Islamic world? Many observers think
that it can, and the country that is often mentioned as a candidate
for a Khomeini-style revolution is Egypt.[42] In fact, Iran is said to
have given financial support to some of Egypt's most radical Muslim movements, including the group accused of bombing the World
Trade Center in New York City and plotting to blow up the UN
in 1993.

The al-Jamaa al-Islamiyya ("the Islamic group") began as a student
movement in Egypt in the 1970s and became linked with the militant
al-Jihad in the 1980s. Its spiritual authority, Sheik Omar Abdul-
Rahman, a former professor of Islamic law, fled to America in
1990, soon becoming the leader of the storefront mosque in New
Jersey with which many of the accused conspirators in the World
Trade Center bombing were affiliated. He and his followers were
committed to a vision of Islamic rule in Egypt that would rival
Khomeini's Iran.

This concept of an Egyptian religious nationalism has been
around long before Khomeini, but the demand for it increasingly
has been expressed in violent acts. In 1981, President Sadat was
assassinated by members of al-Jihad. In 1990, the speaker of the
Egyptian Assembly, Rifaat al-Mahgoub, who at the time of his
death was second in power only to President Hosni Mubarak,
was brutally killed. Members of the al-Jamaa al-Islamiyya were
charged with the crime, but were acquitted in 1993 through lack of

evidence. At the time, Mahgoub's death was linked to Egypt's stand in the Gulf War, but another factor may have been his efforts to block the use of Islamic law in Egypt's courts.[43] In Egypt, as in many other Arab countries, trifling with the spread of Islam is a serious business.

However, Egypt is not necessarily going the way of Iran. The radical Islamic movements in Egypt are different in basic ways from their Iranian counterparts. Sunni Muslims have neither the theological nor the organizational connection to politics that Shi-'ites do, nor has Egypt had the same pattern of suppression of Islam that Iran has had. The Egyptian movements are much less centralized. Despite the fear of many Westerners that the virus of Khomeinism would spread (and perhaps Khomeini's wish that it had), Muslim activists throughout the Sunni world seem surprisingly ignorant of and uninterested in the Iranian experiment.[44] "They have their political problems," a member of the Muslim Brotherhood in Cairo told me, referring to the Iranians, "and we have ours."[45] Although there is sometimes a tremor of admiration in their voices when they speak of the power of the Iranian revolution, the Egyptians seldom offer that upheaval as a model for their own.[46]

Although some scholars see more of an Iranian influence in Egypt than meets the eye,[47] the more obvious interaction is the other way around: the influence of radical Egyptian Muslim movements on the Iranians. In the late 1940s and early 1950s, the Iranians' Fedayeen-i-Islam was created in imitation of the guerrilla Muslim Brotherhood (Jam'iyat al-Ikhwan al-Muslimin), which was spreading terror at the time throughout Egypt. Egypt's Muslim Brotherhood had been founded in 1928 by Hasan al-Banna, and another radical Muslim movement, the Young Egypt Society (which advocated a kind of Islamic socialism), was founded soon after, in 1933.[48]

The leaders of these early Egyptian movements of Islamic politics were reacting against the transnational modernism that remained as the legacy of the British Empire (and before it, the Ottoman). Western culture, political influence, and economic control were the elements of a modernity that some of the early nationalists wished to reject. For that reason, Egyptian nationalism from the outset grew in both religious and secular directions. The Mus-

lim Brotherhood represented the Islamic form of Egyptian nationalism, and the Wafd Party represented its secular side. When King
Faruk (Farooq) and the whole tradition of Egyptian monarchy were
overthrown in 1952, it was largely the Wafd vision of a secular
Egypt that emerged triumphant.

Yet even after Faruk, Islamic nationalism continued to be a potent force in Egyptian politics. The great leader of the revolution,
Jamal 'Abd al-Nasir (whom the Western world knows as Gamal
Nasser), had at one time been allied with the Muslim Brotherhood, as had his successor, Sadat. Despite their willingness to
defend the Islamic aspects of Egyptian nationalism, neither Nasser
nor Sadat was sufficiently strident in his ideology nor obsequious
enough in his response to the Muslim leadership to remain in the
favor of Islamic extremists. By the 1960s, the leaders of the Muslim
Brotherhood and Nasser were locked in bitter opposition; some of
the leaders attempted to overthrow Nasser's regime, and he
promptly threw them in prison.

The love-hate relationship between Muslim leaders and secular
politicians continued in the 1970s during Sadat's regime. On the
one hand, Sadat released the leaders of the Muslim Brotherhood
from prison, lifted a ban on the writings of Muslim radicals, and
was instrumental in the drafting of the 1971 version of the Egyptian
Constitution, which proclaimed, in Article Two, that the goal of the
judicial system was eventually to make shari'a (Islamic law) the law
of the land. On the other hand, he did little to carry out this goal or
the other Islamic reforms he had earlier touted. Sadat's concessions
to Coptic Christians were widely denounced, and his wife was
portrayed as being promiscuous. Pictures of her dancing with Gerald Ford at a formal occasion at the White House were circulated as
evidence of her infidelity. The accords with Israel arranged by
Carter were considered further signs of Sadat's moral decay, and he
eventually succeeded in "having everyone turn against him," as
one Egyptian scholar explained, in part because "he tried too hard
to please everyone."[49] His killers were members of al-Jihad.

Although al-Jihad has been at the fringes of the Muslim Brotherhood, and its various splinter organizations have made a deep political impact, its ideology is the antithesis of Sadat's moderate Muslim
stand. But despite its violence, its leaders have not been lunatics.
One of them, Abd Al-Salam Faraj, was the author of a remarkably

cogent argument for waging war against the political enemies of Islam. His pamphlet, "Al-Faridah al-Gha'ibah" ("The Neglected Duty"), states more clearly than any other contemporary writing the religious justifications for radical Muslim acts. It was published and first circulated in Cairo in the early 1980s.[50] This document grounds the current activities of Islamic terrorists firmly in Islamic tradition, specifically in the sacred text of the Qur'an and the biographical accounts of the Prophet in the hadith.

Faraj argues that the Qur'an and the hadith are fundamentally about warfare. The concept of jihad, holy war, is meant to be taken literally, not allegorically. According to Faraj, the "duty" that has been profoundly "neglected" is jihad, and it calls for "fighting, which means confrontation and blood."[51] Moreover, Faraj regards anyone who deviates from the moral and social requirements of Islamic law to be fit targets for jihad; these targets include apostates within the Muslim community as well as the more expected enemies from without.[52] Perhaps the most chilling aspect of his thought is his conclusion that peaceful and legal means for fighting apostasy are inadequate. The true soldier for Islam is allowed to use virtually any means available to achieve a just goal.[53] Deceit, trickery, and violence are specifically mentioned as options available to the desperate soldier.[54] Faraj sets some moral limits to the tactics that may be used—for example, innocent bystanders and women are to be avoided, whenever possible, in assassination attempts—but emphasizes that the duty to engage in such actions when necessary is incumbent on all true Muslims. The reward for doing so is nothing less than an honored place in paradise. Such a place was presumably earned by Faraj himself in 1982 after he was tried and executed for his part in the assassination of Sadat.

This way of thinking, although extreme, is not idiosyncratic to Faraj. He stands in a tradition of radical Islamic political writers that reaches back to the beginning of this century and earlier. Among Sunni Muslims worldwide, the most important radical thinker has been Maulana Abu al-Ala Mawdudi, the founder and ideological spokesman for Pakistan's Jamaat-i-Islami (Islamic Association).[55] His ideas were echoed by Egypt's most influential writer in the radical Muslim political tradition, Sayyid Qutb. Qutb was born in 1906 and, like Faraj, was executed for his political activities.[56] Although he was not as explicit as Faraj in indicating the techniques of terror that were acceptable for the Islamic warrior, Qutb laid the groundwork for Faraj's understanding of jihad as an appropriate response to the advocates of those elements of modernity that seemed to be hostile to Islam. Specifically, Qutb railed against those who encouraged the cultural, political, and economic domination of the Egyptian government by the West. Qutb had spent several years in the United States studying educational administration, but this experience only confirmed his impression that American society was essentially racist and that American policy in the Middle East was dictated by Israel and what he regarded as the Jewish lobby in Washington, D.C.[57] Alarmed at the degree to which the new government in Egypt was modeled after Western political institutions and influenced by Western values, Qutb, in the early 1950s, advocated a radical return to Islamic values and Muslim law. In *This Religion of Islam*, Qutb argued that the most basic divisions within humanity are grounded in religion rather than race or nationality, and that religious war is the only form of killing that is morally sanctioned.[58] To Qutb's way of thinking, the ultimate war is between truth and falsehood, and satanic agents of falsehood were to be found well entrenched in the Egyptian government. It is no wonder that the government found such ideas dangerous. Qutb was put in prison for most of the rest of the 1950s and was silenced forever in 1966.

The radical ideas of Mawdudi, Qutb, and Faraj have circulated widely in Egypt through two significant networks: universities and the Muslim clergy. The two networks intersect in the Muslim educational system, especially in the schools and colleges directly supervised by the clergy. The most important of these are the ones connected with Cairo's Al-Azhar University. They enroll only a small percentage of Egyptian students—perhaps 5 percent or so— at all levels of the educational system.[59] It is a significant number, nonetheless, because of the impact of the Muslim teachers in relating the traditional truths of Islam to modern ideas. As the dean of the Faculty of Education at Al-Azhar University explained to me, the school's mission is to show how modern academic subjects and fields of professional training—including business, medicine, law, and education—can be taught from an Islamic perspective.[60] Not surprisingly, the university is often viewed as a fountainhead of radical Islamic ideas, and a great number of militant Muslim activists receive their training there.

Despite its dreams, the radical Muslim movement has yet to be sufficiently united to threaten President Mubarak with anything like the revolution in Iran. Even though it showed its destructive power in the 1990 assassination of the speaker of the Assembly, it remains a small splinter organization. The larger parent movement, the Muslim Brotherhood, has become somewhat more moderate. Though not accepted as a legal party, it has been well represented in the legislature. Members of the Brotherhood, running as independent candidates in the 1987 elections, won 38 seats out of the 448 in the People's Assembly. The platform of the Brotherhood was clearly articulated by its leader, Abu al-Nasr, in an open letter to President Mubarak in February 1987. According to Nasr, the movement has four main positions: pride in its Egyptian identity and tradition, the conviction that the current problems of Egypt are largely spiritual and moral in nature, the expectation that Islamic values will be made the basis for all aspects of Egyptian society, and the desire for Islamic organizations to have the freedom to operate as they wish.[61]

These relatively reasonable positions make the Muslim Brotherhood look quite respectable—especially compared with the strident rhetoric of the extremists. In 1991, during the Persian Gulf War, divisions between moderate and radical factions widened.[62] In 1992 and 1993 the terrorist acts of al-Jamaa al-Islamiyya further alienated it from the Muslim mainstream. In addition to the World Trade Center explosion in New York, tourists were attacked near Luxor and in a cafe in Cairo, a luxury ship was fired on as it cruised down the Nile, and a bomb was placed in one of the pyramids. In contrast, the Muslim Brotherhood presented a more viable, if gradual, Islamic revolution. What worries its secular opponents is that the shifts of ideology and power in a gradual revolution are equally unsettling.

Religious Revolt in a Jewish State

Religious revolutionaries in Israel face a situation more like that in Egypt than in prerevolutionary Iran: rather than confronting a thoroughly secular shah, they oppose moderate leaders who are more than nominally committed to their nation's dominant religion. In fact, one might think of Israel as an example of religious nationalism achieved, and many Arab opponents of Israel regard it exactly that

way. Muslim nationalism in the Middle East has been fueled in part
by the fact that Jews have their own religious state, and some
Egyptians feel the religious zeal in the Jewish nation—in contrast
to the secular indifference in their own—contributed to Israel's
victory and Egypt's defeat in the 1967 war.[63]

However, within Israel itself a sizable contingent of politically
active Jews regard their homeland, at best, as the expression of an
incomplete form of religious nationalism. Although Israel is hospita-
ble to Jewish refugees, it is essentially a secular state, one that
follows the rules and mores of European and American society, and
that leaves many Jewish religious nationalists deeply dissatisfied.

One of the most vocal of these Jewish nationalists was the late
Rabbi Meir Kahane, the strident spokesman for the radical Kach
('Thus!') Party. Not surprisingly, perhaps, he had a certain admiration for the Ayatollah Khomeini.[64] He told me that he felt closer to
Khomeini and other militant Muslims than he did to such framers
of secular political thought as John Locke or even to secular Jews.[65]
The reason, he explained, was that Khomeini believed in the rele-
vance of religion to everyday life and especially in the importance
of religion in shaping the morality and communal identity of a
nation. From Kahane's point of view, that belief was far more important than any politically expedient secular arrangement, even if, as
in the case of Israel, it was one made primarily to favor Jews.

Kahane's views on Jewish nationalism are not entirely idiosyncratic in Israel. Tensions between the religious and secular dimensions of modern Israel have existed throughout the almost 100-year
history of the movement for nationhood. When the first meeting of
the World Zionist Organization (WZO) was held in 1897, the goal
was to form a modern national community based on the common
cultural and historical heritage of the Jewish people and explicitly
not to re-create the biblical Israel. The founder of the WZO, Theodor Herzl, had dreamed of Jewish assimilation into European society and hoped to achieve that dream by providing the Jews with "a
new, modern symbol system—a state, a social order of their own,
above all a flag."[66]

For other Jews, however, a flag—especially the secular flag that
Herzl designed, which featured symbols for the seven hours he
proposed for the modern working day—was not enough. They
formed another nationalist group, the Merkaz Ruhani, or Mizrahi,

which called for the formation of a religious state, one that would follow the rules of the Torah. At the same time, another group of orthodox Jews, Agudat Israel, adopted a somewhat different attitude: its members were in favor of Jews settling in Palestine but were largely indifferent to whether it should become a Jewish state. From the Agudat Israel's point of view, until the Temple was rebuilt and a new David installed as king, there could be no true Israel.

These and other groups continued their assaults on secular Israel after the establishment of an independent state in 1948, even though significant compromises had been made. For one thing, Jewish religious courts created during the British Mandate from 1923 to 1947 became integrated into the new legal system. For another, the "status quo agreement" made between the religious parties and the prestate administration, the Jewish Agency, called for certain religious concessions. Among these were the government's observance of dietary laws and the state's maintenance of religious schools.

Yet many nationalist Jews in Israel regarded these concessions as insufficient. The most influential advocate of further religious reforms, the Mafdal party, was a direct descendant of the old Mizrahi party and its various offshoots. The Mafdal has consistently held a dozen or so seats in the Knesset and has been a coalition partner in virtually every government formed since Israel's independence. The Agudat Israel party, despite its ambivalence toward a Jewish state, maintains representation in the Knesset as well. The ties of these two parties to the Likud party during its long rule helped to pass laws against public obscenity, working on the sabbath, and the sale of pork.

A new force has been growing in Israel based on the idea that the present secular Jewish state is the precursor of an ideal religious Israel.[67] It is the revival of an old idea, one advocated by Rabbi Avraham Yitzhak ha-Kohen Kuk (Kook), the chief rabbi of pre-Israeli Palestine. According to Kuk (and, following him, his son and successor, Z. Y. Kuk) the secular state of Israel is the forerunner of the religious Israel to come; it contains a "hidden spark" of the sacred.[68] The implications of this way of thinking are that the coming of the Messiah is imminent and that the religious purification of the state of Israel could help make that arrival come about.

Kuk's ideas began to take on an electric charge after Israel's six-day war in 1967. The war had two results that were significant for the movements for Jewish nationalism. The very success of the military engagement led to a great sense of national euphoria, a feeling that Israel was suddenly moving in an expansive and triumphant direction. At the same time, the spoils of that success created huge problems, the most critical of which were the question of what to do with the conquered territory, and, even more important, the question of what to do with the conquered people, especially Palestinian Arabs on the West Bank and in the Gaza Strip.

Jewish nationalists who were impressed with the theology of Rabbi Kuk felt strongly that history was quickly leading to the moment of divine redemption and the re-creation of the biblical state of Israel. This meant that the Palestinians living in the West Bank were in the way: at best they were an annoyance to be controlled, at worst an enemy to be destroyed. The *intifada,* or 'rebellion,' that has been waged in the Arab areas of Gaza, Jerusalem, and the West Bank since December 1987, has not done anything to dampen the sentiments of the Kukists. If anything, it has sharpened their attacks. The influx of Soviet and Ethiopian Jews has increased the pressure on living space and visibly supported the claim that Jews throughout the world are looking toward Israel as a redemptive nation.

Perhaps the most vocal of the Jewish nationalists to diverge from the Kuk lineage was Rabbi Kahane. Kahane, an American who had a long history of Jewish political activism in Brooklyn, formed the Jewish Defense League (JDL) in the 1960s to counter acts of anti-semitism.[69] In 1971 he came to Israel and turned to a more messianic vision of Jewish politics; in 1974 he created the Kach party. The main position of the party was that Israel should be ruled strictly according to Jewish law; non-Jews—for that matter, even secular Jews—had no place in this sacred order. Unlike Kuk, Kahane saw nothing of religious significance in the establishment of a secular Jewish state: the true religious creation of Israel was yet to come. Unlike other Jewish conservatives with this point of view, however, he felt that it was going to happen fairly soon and that he and his partisans could help bring about that messianic act. Kahane was elected to the Knesset in 1984, but after he served a term, his party was banned in 1988 because of its "racist" and "undemocratic positions."[70]

Kahane adopted a "get-tough" stance toward Judaism's detractors that had worked well in the liberal political atmosphere of the United States. There the Jews were in the minority, and Kahane's JDL was portrayed in the mass media as a Jewish version of the Black Panthers, defending the rights of the oppressed. In Israel, however, where the Jews controlled the status quo, the same belligerence struck secular nationalists as a perverted form of racist bigotry—some called it a kind of Jewish Nazism. His statements about Arabs were compared word for word with those of Hitler's about Jews and were found to be surprisingly similar.[71] In the same vein, a biography of the rabbi appearing in the mid-1980s was sardonically titled *Heil Kahane.*[72]

The main inspiration for Kahane was not Hitler's thought, however, but the messianic ideas of Judaism. In Kahane's view, the coming of the Messiah was imminent, and the Arabs were simply in the wrong place at the wrong time. Kahane told me that he did not hate the Arabs; he "respected them" and felt that they "should not live in disgrace in an occupied land."[73] For that reason they should leave. The problem, for Kahane, was not that they were Arabs but that they were non-Jews living in a place designated by God for Jewish people since biblical times.[74] From a biblical point of view, Kahane argued, the true Israel is the West Bank of the Jordan River and the hilly area around Jerusalem—not the plains where modern Tel Aviv is located.[75] The desire to reclaim the West Bank was therefore not just a matter of irredentism: it was a part of a sacred plan of redemption. Kahane felt that modern Jews could hasten the coming of the Messiah by beginning to reclaim the sacred land. "Miracles don't just happen," Kahane said, referring to the messianic return, "they are made." And, he added, his own efforts and those of his followers would help to "change the course of history."[76]

Although most Jewish settlers do not agree with Kahane's catastrophic messianism and subscribe, instead, to Kuk's incremental theory of messianic history, they view their occupation of the West Bank not only as a social experiment but as a religious act. Rabbi Moshe Levinger, a leader of the Gush Emunim—an organization that encourages the new settlements and claims Rabbi Kuk as its founder—told me that the settlers' "return to the land is the first aspect of the return of the Messiah."[77] The religious settlers are by no means the majority of those who have established residential colonies on the West Bank—they are only a small percentage—but their presence colors the whole movement. Many of them regard the Palestinian Arabs around them with a certain contempt. Hostility from the Arabs—and, for that matter, from many secular Jews— has hardened many of the members of the Gush Emunim and turned what began as a romantic venture into a militant cult.[78]

Much the same can be said about those who long for the rebuilding of the Temple in Jerusalem. According to Kuk's theology, the final event that will trigger the return of the Messiah and the start of the messianic age is the reconstruction of the Temple on Temple Mount.[79] Again, like the Jewish conquest of biblical lands, it is an act of God that invites human participation: Jewish activists can join this act of redemption by helping to rebuild the Temple. The main constraint against doing so is the fact that the most holy place in Judaism is simultaneously one of Islam's most sacred sites. The Dome of the Rock (Qubbat al-Sakhra) occupies precisely the Temple site, which is known by Arabs as Haram al-Sharif, the location from which the Prophet Muhammad is said to have ascended into heaven. No other location is acceptable for rebuilding the Temple, however, and for that reason many messianic Jews are convinced that sooner or later the Dome has to go.

This conviction has led to several attempts to destroy the existing Muslim shrine, some of them involving elaborate tunnels bored from a site near the Western Wall, the only portion of the original Temple still standing. According to a former colleague of Kahane who was once imprisoned for his involvement in a plot to blow up the Dome of the Rock, the three conditions necessary for messianic redemption are the restoration of the biblical lands, the revival of traditional Jewish law, and the rebuilding of the Temple on Temple Mount.[80] He told me that Israel is well on its way to fulfilling the first two conditions; only the absence of the Temple persists as an obstacle to the realization of this messianic vision.

Another Jewish nationalist who laments the absence of the temple is Gershon Salomon; he heads a small group known as the Faithful of Temple Mount—one of several groups committed to rebuilding the Temple. Salomon explained to me that the construction of the Temple will precipitate an "awakening" of the Jewish people and the advent of the messianic age.[81] Each year, on the seventh day of the festival of Sukkot, Salomon and his small band of followers have marched on Temple Mount and attempted to pray, and, according to some, also lay the cornerstone for rebuilding the Temple.[82] Each year, the Waqf organization of Muslim clergy, which polices the area, has nervously turned Salomon away.

During the celebration of Sukkot in October 1990, the charged atmosphere of the *intifada* and the presence of American troops in nearby Saudi Arabia made the situation more tense than usual. As Salomon and his group slowly moved toward Temple Mount, the Waqf leaders were joined by a large number of young people associated with the Islamic Palestinian resistance movement, Hamas, and by a contingent of Israeli police who were, as it turned out, insufficient in number to control what became the ugliest incident between Muslims and Israelis in recent years. Salomon and his group were barred from the Temple Mount area, but the damage had been done: in the confusion rocks were thrown, bullets were fired, and ultimately seventeen Palestinians were killed by the Israeli police in the melee.[83] The Security Council of the United Nations censured Israel for its heavy-handedness and called for an outside investigation, which Israel refused to allow.

Less than a month after the Temple Mount incident, the messianic wing of Jewish nationalism received another shock with the killing of Kahane in New York City, where he had come to give a speech. The suspected assassin, El Sayyid A. Nosair, was a recent immigrant from Egypt associated with the al-Salam Mosque in Jersey City. Other members of the mosque had been arrested for attempting to send ammunition to the Palestine Liberation Organization (PLO), and leaders of the mosque echoed the theology of Muslim nationalists such as Qutb and Faraj. They explained that the killing of Kahane did not violate the Qur'an because Kahane was an enemy of Islam.[84] Within a day of Kahane's death, two elderly Palestinian farmers were shot dead along the roadside near the West Bank city of Nablus, apparently in retaliation for Kahane's killing. Thus the spiral of violence that Kahane encouraged continued even after his death. An editorial writer for the *New York Times*, who described Kahane's life as "a passionate tangle of anger and unreason," referred to his death as the product of a "legacy of hate."[85]

In September, 1993, when many Israelis were celebrating the

mutual recognition of Israel and the PLO, leaders of Kahane's Kach party denounced the historic accord, claiming it a fraud. They joined members of opposition parties, the Gush Emunim, and West Bank settlers in launching a campaign of civil disobedience against it, and vowed to fight by "any means." The passion of their protest—reminiscent of the style of Rabbi Kahane, whom they consider a martyr—comes from the conviction that an Israeli retreat from the biblical lands of the West Bank is not only bad politics but bad religion. In their view, a religious state ruled by Jewish law and located on the site of biblical Israel is essential for the redemption of the entire cosmos. For this reason the followers of Salomon, Kuk, Kahane, and other messianic religious nationalists will continue to wage their political fights with sacred passion. Though few in number, they will be a potent force in the political life of Israel for some years to come.

The Islamic *Intifada:* A Revolt within the Palestinian Revolution

The day that Israel's Yitzhak Rabin and PLO's Yasser Arafat boarded airplanes to fly to Washington D.C. to witness the historic signing of an Israeli–PLO accord in September 1993, protests erupted in Israel, the West Bank, Gaza, and much of the adjacent Arab world, and eight were killed in Gaza alone. The demonstrations were waged not only by Jewish nationalists but also by their Muslim counterparts. Both Israeli Jewish and Palestinian Muslim activists have been conducting a double struggle: one against each other and the other against their own secular leaders. The anti-secular attacks are often more vicious. Some say that the secular leaders, Rabin and Arafat, were propelled into the September 1993 alliance in part because they feared the rising strength of the religious nationalists in their camps. In Israel, the most ardent opposition to the secular government was Kahane's Kach party and the Gush Emunim; in Palestine, it was Hamas.

Hamas is an underground movement—actually a coalition of several movements with no single leader. Prominent among those identified with the movement are several religious figures: Sheik 'Abd al-Aziz 'Odeh (Uda); Sheik As'ad Bayud al-Tamimi, a resident of Hebron who was a preacher at the al-Aksa Mosque in Jerusalem; and Sheik Ahmed Yassin from Gaza.[86] Yassin, who is described as "a charismatic and influential leader," commands the Islamic Assembly, which has ties to virtually all the mosques in Gaza and is able to gain 65 to 75 percent of the votes of both students and faculty in Gaza's Islamic University.[87] Yassin claims that he and his Muslim colleagues initiated the *intifada*, the popular uprising against the Israeli occupation of Gaza and the West Bank.[88]

Although Yassin is virtually incapacitated by a degenerative nerve condition and has to be carried from place to place, when I visited him in 1989 his small house at the outskirts of Gaza City was crowded with admirers and associates who came for his advice. They sat on the carpeted floor of a plain meeting room adjacent to his bedroom and listened patiently to the sheik's rambling discourse. His monologue on the evils of Israeli occupation and the virtues of Muslim society was interrupted only by an occasional question and by daily prayers. These Yassin managed with great difficulty, tottering back and forth as he uttered the words of the Qur'an. His mind was sharp, however, and his opinions on current political matters were crystal clear.

Yassin described his Islamic resistance movement as the heart of the Palestinian opposition. He said that the idea of a secular liberation movement for Palestine is profoundly misguided because there "is no such thing as a secular state in Islam."[89] At that time, prior to the September 1993 accords, he nominally supported the PLO. He referred to Arafat as "President Arafat" and claimed that after the liberation of Palestine, "the people will decide" whether there should be an Islamic state.[90] Clearly, Yassin was confident that the people would decide in favor of Islam.

Leaders of the PLO, however, are not as convinced as Yassin about the outcome of the vote, if it should ever come to that.[91] They are clearly nervous about the Hamas challenge to their legitimacy, and before I was allowed to interview Yassin, representatives of the PLO in Gaza stopped my car and insisted that the driver take me to a pro-PLO refugee camp where I could hear the other Palestinian point of view. On another occasion, Yasir Arafat's brother, Fathi, assured me that only "a small percentage of Palestinians are in favor of an Islamic state."[92] He felt that religion should be a personal matter. He would not want his daughter to wear the Islamic veil, he said, but he would respect the right of others to do so if they wished. Yet he affirmed that his movement is democratic: should the Palestinian people vote in favor of an Islamic state, he would support it.[93]

Most Palestinians are caught between these two competing visions of an independent Palestine. Some observers feel that it would be a tight race if Islamic nationalism became the issue. In Gaza, supporters of Hamas are said to be in the majority, and there is considerable support for Islamic nationalism on the West Bank as well.[94] Yet this sort of support is difficult to gauge because many Palestinians are as impressed with Arafat as they are with Yassin. "The distinction between the PLO and Hamas is artificial," said a Palestinian student leader who is now studying Islamic theology in Cairo. "We should now be united against a common enemy; tomorrow, when we are free, we can discuss our differences."[95]

Still, the differences are considerable. Arafat expects Palestine to be a modern nation-state, one that is patterned largely on the Western secular model, while Yassin thinks that "shari'a should be the sole basis for Islamic politics."[96] Although Yassin admires Khomeini's revolution in Iran and appreciates the conservative Islamic rule in Saudi Arabia, he has been critical of both the Iranians and the Saudis. Yassin has been influenced most by Islamic nationalist leaders in nearby Egypt; he is said to have read the writings of both Qutb and Faraj.

Even though militant Islamic organizations such as Hamas are fairly new in the PLO, the idea of an Islamic Palestine has been around for some years. In the 1970s, when the PLO was consolidating its power among the various movements of the Palestinian resistance, an Islamic alternative to the PLO was proposed: a united movement that based its ideological and political strategy on traditional Islamic values.[97] One of the constituent groups of the short-lived movement was a Palestinian version of the Muslim Brotherhood. This group, in which Sheik Yassin has been active, was kin to its namesake in Egypt. For many years, however, it did not play a significant role in Palestinian politics.

In the 1980s, many Palestinian Islamic activists associated with the Muslim Brotherhood became impatient with its quiescent stance and split off to form several new associations. Sheik Yassin became president of the al-Mujamma' al-Islami (the Muslim Gathering). It had ties to another confederation of groups known as the Islamic Jihad, over which Sheik 'Odeh presided.[98] In 1983 the Jihad was implicated in the killing of a young Israeli settler in the occupied territories. In October 1984 Sheik Yassin and his colleagues were arrested and put in jail for stockpiling weapons to be used for "the destruction of Israel and the creation of an Islamic state."[99] In 1986, after Yassin and other prisoners were freed through a prisoner exchange, the Islamic Jihad launched a cluster of new military actions aimed at Israeli military officers; in Gaza, especially, a number of Israeli soldiers were killed, as were members of the Jihad. Sheik 'Odeh was arrested and expelled from the country.[100] At the same time the Islamic resistance began to organize Palestinians outside the Israeli-occupied areas. Communiqués were circulated in Paris and London, and a magazine, *al-Islam wa Filastin* (*Islam and Palestine*), began publication in Cyprus, with circulation throughout Europe and the United States. The magazine lists a mailing address in Tampa, Florida, in addition to the main Cyprus office.[101]

The last month of 1987 saw the beginning of the *intifada*—a popular uprising that relied not on sophisticated weapons used by a few well-trained cadres, but on rocks, barricades, and any other materials that ordinary Palestinians could marshal in their resistance to Israeli occupation. It was a dramatic turn in the liberation struggle, not only because the simplicity of the weaponry enabled virtually any Palestinian to be involved but also because its populist style gave the cause an image of a moral crusade rather than a terrorist plot. It also changed the nature of the Islamic resistance. As a popular and moral crusade, the *intifada* was easily identified with the religion—and the religious leaders—of the people. The Islamic resistance movement Hamas emerged at roughly the same time that the *intifada* did, and although there is no question that there is a connection between the two, there is some debate over Yassin's boast that he and other Muslim activists created the *intifada*. It is equally possible that the *intifada*, in a sense, created Hamas. Without the *intifada*, a broad-based Muslim activist movement outside the PLO would have been unrealizable.

The word *hamas* means zeal or enthusiasm, but it is also an acronym for the formal name of the movement: Harakat al-Muqawama al-Islamiyya (Islamic Resistance Movement). The name

Hamas first appeared publicly in a communiqué circulated in mid-February 1988. The communiqué was one in a series that appeared about the time that the *intifada* began in December 1987, but it was not clear whether the Muslim Brotherhood, the Jihad organizations, or some other group was behind these early communiqués. Jean-François Legrain suggests that Yassin and the Muslim Brotherhood were not involved in sending the early communiqués or with the *intifada* but joined the *intifada* bandwagon only in February 1988.[102] The February communiqué that mentions the name *Hamas* describes the movement as "the powerful arm of the Association of Muslim Brothers."[103] It is possible, therefore, that Hamas marked a new phase in the Islamic resistance movement, one in which militant Palestinian Muslim activists were united under an old Muslim Brotherhood leadership based in Gaza for the purpose of capturing the leadership of the *intifada*.

Hamas places the ideology of Islam and the organization of the mosque at the service of *intifada*. The struggle between the Palestinians and the Israelis is described in eschatological terms as "the combat between Good and Evil."[104] Committees are set up in mosques to provide alternative education when schools are closed because of the *intifada,* and other mosque committees collect *zakat* (donations) to give to victims of the uprising. Most of the leaders of Hamas have religious titles. The movement's communiqués justify its positions on the basis of Islamic beliefs and tradition, and cast even the most specific issues of policy in a theological light. The communiqués include criticisms of the Arab states' compromises with Israeli and U.S. positions and call for general strikes to protest the sponsorship of peace envoys by the Americans. In August 1988 Hamas published a forty-page covenant, which presented its vision of an Islamic Palestine, and implied that the only true course was to reject the secular ideology and compromising strategy of the PLO and wage a direct jihad against Israel.[105]

The PLO did not take kindly to the Hamas declaration of independence from it, and for a month or so the PLO and Hamas seemed to be competing for public support. They announced general strikes at different times, and although the Hamas strikes were usually smaller, the movement was especially successful in garnering support in Gaza and increasingly in such West Bank cities as Nablus, Ramallah, Bethlehem, and Hebron. By late September

1988 Hamas and the PLO had at least temporarily patched up their differences; for some months after that, most of the general strikes were called by both groups at the same time.

The mutual suspicion that mars relations between Hamas and the PLO may be goaded, in part, by the Israeli government. In the last months of 1988, while members of the PLO were being put in prison, Sheik Yassin was interviewed on Israeli television. There were rumors that he and Hamas were being tolerated by the Israeli government because they were putting an Islamic obstacle in the path of the PLO.[106] By the middle of 1989, however, the leaders of Hamas were regarded as too troublesome to be ignored. The Israeli government rounded up many of them, including Sheik Yassin, who was put under house arrest.

Despite the suppression of its leaders, Hamas did not disappear. Its message was spread through underground circulars and journals, such as *Al-Sabil* (*The Way*), which is printed in Oslo, Norway, and smuggled into Israel. For several reasons, the Islamic resistance movement in Palestine continued to grow. For one thing, the longer the *intifada* continued, the more restless the Palestinian populace became with the official PLO leadership. Moreover, the educated PLO elite was often aloof from the masses—and, in the case of those who were in exile, physically distant—whereas the Islamic leaders were a part of the local communities and close at hand. In addition, the masses of American troops assigned to Saudi Arabia in 1990 following Husein's invasion of Kuwait were seen by many Palestinians as a direct threat to them. The *intifada* became rejuvenated and, with it, the growing feeling that the conciliatory attitude of the PLO was not working and that further direct action was necessary.

This feeling was heightened by a second event in 1990, the October confrontation on Temple Mount. Temple Mount had become an increasingly important symbol in the Hamas resistance struggle. Unlike the PLO, which had only the utopian vision of a Palestinian capital to defend, Hamas had a real one: the Dome of the Rock and the al-Aksa Mosque. Defending the sacred shrine and cleansing it of "foreign" (Israeli) influence became a major theme in Hamas publications. The sacred hill also became an important site for the recruitment of young Palestinian men from Jerusalem—

many of them former members of street gangs—to the cause. Many of them were initiated into the Hamas movement in a dramatic nighttime ritual at the Dome of the Rock.[107] When the Israeli activist Gershon Salomon and his followers in the Faithful of Temple Mount let it be known that they were going to march on the site and lay the cornerstone for a new temple, Hamas leaders excitedly spread the word among their youthful followers that the time had come to defend the faith against the Israeli intruders. What happened then, as I recounted in the previous section of this chapter, was one of the bloodiest incidents of the *intifada*.

Hamas made the most of the incident. The Temple Mount confrontation had the immediate effect of consolidating Hamas power in Arab Jerusalem and the West Bank. It also dramatically illustrated that the Palestinian struggle was not only about land and political rights but also about religion. "The massacre at al-Aksa," leaders explained in one of their communiqués, "showed that our fight with Zionism is a fight between Islam and Judaism."[108] Moreover, it demonstrated that members of the religious resistance would lay down their lives in defense of the faith at a time when their more secular compatriots were quiescent.

Several violent incidents involving Hamas in November and December 1990 indicated either that the movement was now becoming bolder and more aggressive or that bolder and more aggressive persons were now joining the movement and championing its cause as their own. In either event it was a significant change from the earlier position of Hamas. During those two months at least eight Israelis were killed by attackers associated with Hamas. Following the knife slaying of three Israeli workers in Jaffa in mid-December, nearly a thousand Palestinians associated with Hamas were said to have been arrested.[109] The number included 600 in Gaza and another 200 on the West Bank. Included among them was Abdul Aziz al-Rantisi, a colleague of Sheik Yassin, who was described by the *New York Times* as "the co-founder of Hamas."[110]

By 1991 the Islamic resistance movement had become a significant contender for Palestinian leadership, in large part because of the weakening of Arafat's power following the defeat of the PLO's ally, Iraq, in the Gulf War. Unlike Arafat, whose disastrous support of Hussein had decimated the PLO's coffers and undermined its political support, the leaders of Hamas took a restrained approach—perhaps stimulated by the fact that the government of Kuwait had been by far a greater financial supporter of Hamas than of the PLO.[111] After the Gulf War, Hamas began to demand greater representation on Palestinian councils, and for the first time in recent years Arafat's authority began to be challenged by local leaders. By the middle of 1991 internal feuds between religious and secular Palestinian leaders had turned violent.[112] Supporters of Hamas were beginning to win elections on the West Bank as well as in Gaza.[113] In October 1991, Sheik Yassin was imprisoned.

In 1992, the peace talks between Israeli and Palestinian leaders commanded the attention of most Palestinians, and the *intifada* degenerated from a popular uprising of largely peaceful protestors into armed struggle conducted by small groups of youthful cadres. Among these were groups associated with the Fateh and Marxist branches of the PLO as well as groups associated with Hamas.[114] Many of the older leaders of Hamas adopted a wait-and-see attitude toward the peace talks, while the younger members fought, at times violently, against the members of the PLO who favored them.[115] Supporters of Hamas questioned the degree to which Islamic law and leadership would be factors in the settlement eventually negotiated with the Israelis.

As it turned out, Islamic principles were not even mentioned in the September 1993 accord sponsored by Israel's Rabin and the PLO's Arafat. From the Hamas point of view, the circumstances surrounding the accord could not have been worse: It was a thoroughly secular document, negotiated in secret with Israeli leaders, and signed in Washington with the blessings of what is often seen as Islam's global enemy, the government of the United States.

The day the document was signed, Hamas supporters in Gaza City used wooden clubs to disperse a rally sponsored by a new pro-agreement political party. Arafat supporters opened fire with submachine guns over the heads of those attending a rally organized by Hamas in the Gaza town of Rafah. And in Damascus, a coalition of ten anti-PLO groups—including Hamas and another radical Islamic group, the Islamic Jihad—pledged to demolish the accord, identifying Arafat as a traitor. The continuing tensions and attempts on his life prove the seriousness of these accusations. Many outside the Middle East wondered why Palestinians could be so adamantly opposed to what seems to be a major Israeli concession and a giant step towards their own independence.

One one level, it is a matter of who leads the movement: the Hamas leadership comes from the poorest areas of the villages and towns. Like the Islamic revolution in Iran, this struggle has the potential for bringing into power an uneducated local leadership. On another level, Hamas asks what sort of Palestinian movement there should be and what sort of new Palestinian state should come into being. Sheik 'Odeh saw the increased Islamicization of the *intifada* as "a sign from God to the people that they need Islam as a center."[116] This attitude seriously challenges the PLO's monopoly of power. For although Sheik Yassin admits that a secular Palestinian government could go far in helping to protect Islamic values in Palestine, it could never go far enough. It ultimately would be an illegitimate form of government because, according to Yassin and many of his followers in Hamas, "the only true Palestinian state is an Islamic state," and that means strict adherence to shari'a and its moral rules.[117]

The establishment of a secular Palestinian government transformed the Palestinian Islamic movement. Rather than being a revolt within the Palestinian revolution, it became the vanguard of a new revolutionary movement: the enemy of the secular Palestinian state. In this sense, then, it became like its counterparts in Iran, Egypt, Israel, and elsewhere in the Middle East.

Each of these movements oppose not only secular nationalism but also the efforts of secular leaders to offer halfhearted compromises with religion. Each offers its own model of religious protest: the Shi'ite movement in Iran achieved a total revolution; the Sunni Muslim movement in Egypt combines violent extremism with nonviolent measures; the Israeli religious right attempts to move its nominally religious nation further in the direction of religious commitment; and the Muslim wing of the Palestinian liberation movement attempts to change the course of what had been a solely secular movement. Although the particular course that each movement has taken is distinctly its own, the pattern of religious reform that each illustrates has been replicated in movements for religious nationalism elsewhere in the world.

Chapter Four

Political Targets of Religion: South Asia

Although the Islamic revolution in Iran captured world attention, the pattern of religious revolt found in Egypt—and to some extent in Israel—more truly represents the great majority of religious revolutions. As in Egypt, religious activists in many parts of the world are reacting against leaders who appear to us to be moderate and sympathetic to religion: these are the Western-style secular nationalists who subscribe at least nominally to the dominant religion of their country but stop short of proclaiming their country a religious state. The secular leaders are constrained from doing so in part because strong minority religious communities prohibit them and in part because it would violate their own ideals: they have been led to believe that secular nationalism defines a modern nation. South Asian religious activists, like their Egyptian counterparts, have reacted intensely against these secular visions of modern nationalism, scorned their leaders' secularism, and belittled their professed religious loyalties. The major difference is that most South Asians are not Muslims: they are Hindus, Sikhs, and Buddhists.

Perhaps even more than their Middle Eastern colleagues, the South Asian religious activists have employed a great variety of strategies for change. Their targets have sometimes been traditional political parties, sometimes the political process itself, and sometimes the political culture undergirding the process. This diversity holds not only for the activists in the three case studies in this chapter—Hindu nationalists and Sikh separatists in India, and

Sinhalese nationalists in Sri Lanka—but also for members of other movements in South and Southeast Asia.

In South Asia, Islamic parties in Pakistan such as the Jami'at al' Ulama-i-Islam (Party of the Community of Islam) and Jami'at al' Ulama-i-Pakistan (Party of the Community of Pakistan) have been joined by even more extreme Islamic political groups, including a virulent coalition in Pakistan's Punjab region, the Islami Jamhoori Ittehad (Islamic Democratic Front), which opposed Benazir Bhutto's brief rule and was a critical factor in her electoral defeat in 1990. Since then, the Islamization of politics has become a major theme. The Islamic legal code, the shari'a, has been proclaimed the law of the land; secular civil laws have been repealed. Observers fear that Pakistan provides the most accessible model and base of support for Islamic revolutionaries in the nearby Central Asian states. After the 1992 coup in Kabul, however, Pakistani officials were hesitant to do anything that would encourage Muslim extremists in Afghanistan.[1] In Bangladesh, mounting pressure from Islamic political parties forced the government to emulate Pakistan and publicly endorse the idea that Bangladesh is an Islamic state. In Nepal, Hindu religious activists so influenced the committee assigned in 1990 to draft a new democratic constitution following the political abdication of King Birendra that the committee's chairman made public assurances that Nepal would not be described as secular. "The moment we declare a secular state," he said, "we would have religious riots."[2]

In Southeast Asia, Buddhist monks in Myanmar (formerly Burma) were among the leaders of the 1988 riots against the ruling Burma Socialist Program party and many continue to participate in the underground revolutionary movement based along the Myanmar-Thai border. In Cambodia, the peace accord in 1991 ushered in a wave of Buddhist activism and helped Prime Minister Hun Sen consolidate his relationship with his former rival, Prince Norodom Sihanouk. In Thailand, Buddhist monks also have been involved in political movements, and Chamlong Srimvang, the leader of the 1992 rebellion that toppled a military dictatorship, was a member of an activist Buddhist sect that aims at establishing a new national religion in the country. In the southern tip of Thailand Islamic revolutionaries associated with the Pattani United Liberation Organization and Barisan Nasional Revolusi have fought for the independence of Pattani, Yala, Narathiwat, and Satun provinces. In Malaysia, the Parti Islam Se Malaysia and other Islamic political groups have had considerable influence on Malaysian ethnic policy, usually at the expense of the Chinese minority community. In Indonesia, a movement for Islamic nationalism, Darul Islam, has flourished since the country's independence in 1949, and in the Aceh region Islam is part of an ideology of separatism. In the early 1990s Islamic protests mounted against the Suharto government's attempts to maintain a secular stance, and in the 1992 elections the Muslim-based United Development Party made significant gains at Suharto's expense. In the Philippines, the Moro National Liberation Front has fought for some years for an independent Islamic state, a Bangsa Moro homeland, in the southern island of Mindanao. The involvement of Roman Catholics in Philippine politics, however, has received worldwide attention. The support of Cardinal Jaimi Sin for Corazon Aquino during the revolt against the Marcos regime in 1986 is credited with having made the critical difference in her success and further underscored the Catholic character of Philippine national identity in the northern islands.

What is striking about these South and Southeast Asian cases of religious activism is how consistently they aim at political targets in order to solve religious problems or to bring about a consolidation of religious identities and values. This connection with politics also occurs in the Middle East, where new political parties have been formed in the name of religion, terrorist squads have focused on political figures, and—in the case of Iran—a new constitution was created with religious rules in mind. In India and Sri Lanka, however, the magnitude of the movements is staggering. In sheer numbers, India's Bharatiya Janata Party is probably the largest movement of religious nationalism in the world. The level of violence in the movements is intense: the number of political assassinations in the name of religion in South Asia rivals or exceeds that in the Middle East. The South Asian cases, therefore, are useful for understanding the variety of ways in which religious revolutionaries have been politically involved: from militant guerrilla movements fomenting religious revolution to organized involvement in electoral politics. At the extreme religious revolutionaries have been responsible for spontaneous riots and the breakdown of law and order caused by their total rejection of the legitimacy of the secular state.

Militant Hindu Nationalism

In India, the strategies of Sikh nationalists and Kashmiri Muslim separatists have often been desperate and violent, but because the constituency to which Hindu nationalists appeal is the majority community in the country, they have recourse to a different form of protest: the ballot box. In 1991 the Bharatiya Janata Party (the BJP, or Indian People's Party) made a remarkable showing in their electoral battle against what the BJP leader, Lal Krishna Advani, called the "pseudosecularism" of secular politicians. The BJP gained over 120 seats, making it the largest opposition party in India's parliament, and it gained control of several state governments including that of the largest, Uttar Pradesh. These impressive gains were the crowning achievement of almost a century of Hindu nationalist efforts, including protest movements; militant encounters with Muslims, minority leaders, and secular politicians; and the development of sophisticated mass-based organizations.

One of the reasons India has been vulnerable to the influence of Hindu nationalists is that Hinduism can mean so many things. It is the name for India's traditional culture and the title of a specific religious community. In traditional India there was no clear distinction between religion and the general culture of a region: even the words *India* and *Hindu* are etymologically linked. Both were coined by outsiders to refer to the land and the people along the Indus River.[3] Today, one can speak of Hindu as one among several religious communities in India, and the census takers can confidently state that 83 percent of the population is Hindu, 11 percent Muslim, 2.6 percent Christian, and slightly over 1 percent Sikh, with small communities of Jains, Parsis, and Buddhists. Yet Hindu culture traditionally embraced all people and aspects of life in the Indian subcontinent.

In classical Hindu social thought, religious and political dimensions of life were linked. Each economic or political role in society, including kingship, had its own dharma (moral responsibility), and the prime duty of the king, as enunciated in the *Artha-sastra* by the Hindu political theorist Kautilya in the fourth century B.C.E., was to maintain power and uphold the dharma of the social whole.[4] In the great Hindu epics, the gods are portrayed as playing regal roles. During most of India's history, however, there has not been a single centralized monarchy. Instead there have been hundreds of small princedoms and a pattern of local governance involving representative committees, called panchayat (a council of five).[5] The vacuum of leadership at the center made it possible for Muslim rulers from Central Asia and Persia, including the Mogul dynasties that ruled during the sixteenth to nineteenth centuries, to establish great empires. The Moguls and their British successors formed alliances with local kings and left traditional Hinduism largely untouched. Hinduism remained unscathed in its cultural contacts in part because of its "tolerance"—a stance that is, in fact, an ability to absorb an opposition and ultimately to dominate it. What Ainslie Embree calls the "Brahmanical ideology" of high-caste Hinduism has a way of swallowing up other points of view and making them its own.[6]

Hinduism has not remained unchanged over the years however. One interesting development was the popularity of the bhakti (devotional-love) movements led by North Indian poet-saints of the fifteenth to seventeenth centuries and by South Indian bards who lived centuries before. The saints are portrayed as being uninvolved in politics, but because their poetry belittles the spiritual value of ritual and social status, they are sometimes touted today as prophets of social as well as spiritual reform. The sixteenth-century Guru Nanak, who is regarded by the Sikhs as their founder, was one of these introspective and devotional saints.

Whether or not India's religious groups were socially involved in an earlier period, they certainly became so in the eighteenth and nineteenth centuries, in part because of the stimulus of outsiders. Mogul military might and Muslim religious organization became models for the Sikh community in the Punjab. British civilization and Christian missionaries challenged Hindu movements, including the Brahmo Samaj and the Arya Samaj, in the nineteenth century throughout North India. These movements promoted a socially engaged and intellectually respectable form of Hinduism and championed such social causes as mass education, rights for women, and the improvement of conditions for untouchables. Although not overtly political, they were the first modern efforts to link Hindu religious values to public life and were predecessors of the groups that eventually formed the BJP.

In the twentieth century religion and politics began to interact more directly than they had before. Although officially secular, India's independence movement preached nationalist loyalties in terms that echoed the Hindu notion of dharmic obligation, and its espousal of devotion to "mother India" incorporated some of the characteristics of worship of Hindu goddesses. Mohandas Gandhi attempted to forge a compromise between the religious and secular wings of the independence movement by applying Hindu ethical values to the nationalist movement. He adhered to a form of Hinduism that had wide appeal beyond its sectarian origins, and he successfully applied religious concepts to political tactics in his use of what he called *satyagraha* (the force of truth) and *ahimsa* (nonviolence) in political conflict.

Not all Indian political leaders were enthusiastic about Gandhi's compromise with religion: Nehru and other secular nationalists, for example, felt uncomfortable with it, while Muslim leaders felt betrayed by it. Mohammed Ali Jinnah and his Muslim League, suspicious of what they regarded as Gandhi's Hinduization of the nationalist movement, demanded that the British create a separate nation for Muslims. When the British withdrew from India in 1947, they carved Pakistan out of portions of Bengal in the east and sections of Punjab, Sindh, and other areas in the west. Jinnah was named Pakistan's first governor general. Not all Muslims in the remainder of India moved to the areas designated as Pakistan, but eight million people did shift from one side of the borders to the other, and as many as a million lost their lives in the communal rioting that occurred during the transition. Gandhi strongly protested the partition of the country and the communal hatred it unleashed. Militant Hindus felt that he had capitulated to the Muslims, and a former member of a radical Hindu organization, the Rashtriya Swayamsevak Sangh (RSS), assassinated Gandhi in 1948.

The RSS had been founded in 1925 by middle-class Hindus in Maharashtra and Madhya Pradesh, many of whom had been associated with the Arya Samaj movements. The main mission of the RSS was to train young Hindu men to stand up to the temptations of secular society and to revive the traditional values of Hindu India.[7] For years its main activities consisted of weekly meetings in urban homes and summer camps that were similar to Boy Scout outings except for their nationalist-religious ideology and training sessions in self-defense. Despite their Hindu rhetoric, the leaders of the movements were not priests and holy men and other traditional Hindu leaders, and the RSS did not—until much later—become a part of mainstream Hindu culture.

Nonetheless, the RSS set the standard and defined the terms of Hindu nationalism so effectively that they continue in force today. The ideas were shaped by the writings of Vinayak Damodar Savarkar, who called on "the undying vitality of Hindu manhood" to assert itself "so vigorously as to make the enemies of Hindudom tremble."[8] Savarkar advanced the concept of *hindutva*, the idea that virtually everyone who has ancestral roots in India is a Hindu and that collectively they constitute a nation.[9] On the basis of this idea the RSS, in its constitution, called on all Hindus to "eradicate differences" and realize "the greatness of their past" in the "regeneration of Hindu society."[10] The RSS joined the Indian National Congress in opposition to British rule but became increasingly disenchanted with Nehru and his emphasis on secular nationalism.

When India became independent in 1947, Nehru proclaimed it a secular state and exhorted India to "lessen her religiosity and turn to science."[11] But the tension between secular and religious nationalism remained.[12] The gnawing suspicions about Hindu influence persisted among Sikhs, Muslims, and members of other minority communities, but the government appeared eager to dispel these suspicions and attempted to treat all religions equally. It protected and maintained religious institutions of all faiths; it allowed colleges sponsored by Sikhs and Muslims, as well as by Hindus, to be incorporated into state universities; and it permitted aspects of traditional Islamic law pertaining to marriage, divorce, and inheritance to apply to members of Muslim communities. Christians and other minority religious communities were also given legal sanctions similar to those given the Muslims.

Despite the government's claims of impartiality, it has been accused of leaning one way or the other, and Advani's charge that the government has been only "pseudosecular" is widely perceived to be correct. Many Hindus think that the government bends over backward to support Muslims, Sikhs, and other minorities. Members of minority religious communities, however, see the situation the other way around: they feel that the government is implicitly Hindu. In 1987–89, for instance, the government television network, Doordarshan, sponsored a serialized presentation of one of the great Hindu epics, the *Ramayana*, followed in 1988–89 by the other great Hindu epic, the *Mahabharata*. In both cases the government justified its support with the claim that these were traditional stories and not religious myths. In fact, these televised epics may have worked against secular politicians because their enormous popularity—they were the most widely watched programs in India's history—is credited with fueling the revival of religious politics.[13] Even members of the secular parties have attempted to appease the religious right, and during the 1980s many Sikhs regarded Mrs. Gandhi and her Congress party as pandering to the interests of Hindu religious figures. The rise of militant Sikhism was, in part, a response to what many Sikhs saw as the increasing Hinduization of Indian politics.

Hindu nationalism has always been strongest in North India's "saffron belt" running from Rajasthan to Bihar and encompassing India's largest state, Uttar Pradesh. There, religious parties such as the venerable Jan Sangh labored for thirty years to build a political base on the interests of conservative Hindus, but for most of those years it was not able to make a significant dent in the popular support given the reigning Congress party. The Jan Sangh's latest incarnation in the Hindu political lineage, the BJP, has been enormously successful, not only in the saffron belt but throughout the country.

The BJP achieved its success partly by default: the 1980s were not a good time for the Congress and other secular parties, and at least half the voters who cast their ballots for the BJP in 1991 did so out of unhappiness with the other choices and "to give the new party a chance."[14] But the BJP succeeded for other reasons as well: the popularity of its ideology of Hindu nationalism and its alliances with other, more strident, movements for the creation of a Hindu state. Among these was an old one—the RSS—and a potent new coalition of Hindu activists.

The RSS supplied the dedication, energy, and staff to make the new party work. Its network of several thousand *pracharaks*—full-time, educated, unmarried staff workers—was put at the service of the BJP, giving the party overnight an effective political apparatus. Yet the RSS had a mixed image in the Indian public eye. Many regarded it as a Nazi-like group of nationalist fanatics. It gained respectability and a link with traditional Hinduism through its association with the Vishva Hindu Parishad (World Hindu Council, or VHP).

The VHP did not begin as a political organization, and its ties to the RSS were at first unclear.[15] It was founded in 1964 when 150 Hindu leaders were invited to a religious retreat center near Bombay, Sandeepany Sadhanalaya, by its leader, Swami Chinmayananda.[16] The swami, who had a large following in urban areas of India and abroad, including the United States, was in many respects a modern Hindu, but he and the other leaders who founded the movement—including the Sikh leader Master Tara Singh— were concerned about what they regarded as the relatively slight influence their religious groups had on the social values of Indian society.[17] They were determined to make a difference. Chinmayananda was elected the first president of the VHP, and Shivram Shankar Apte was elected its general secretary. Apte was a long-time leader of the RSS, and some say that the RSS was behind the organization from the very beginning. Others say that the RSS gained control gradually through the involvement of its *pracharaks* in the VHP organization. The VHP offered the RSS—and Hindu political parties such as the Jan Sangh and BJP—not only the legitimacy of connections with large religious groups but the manpower of the celibate sadhus (holy men) and other workers who were connected with it.

The politicization of the VHP occurred largely in the 1980s. It first came into national prominence by organizing protests against mass conversions of lower-caste Hindus to Islam at Meenakshipuram in South India in 1981. Allegedly the Islamic states in the Persian Gulf had sent large sums of money to India to encourage raids on Hindu society. The secular government became a target for the Hindu leaders' wrath because they saw the state's policy of religious neutrality as protecting these Muslim assaults. In 1983, a great Procession for Unity organized by the VHP brought over a million people to New Delhi in one of the largest gatherings of its type in history.

The VHP's momentum increased with another issue: control over the alleged birthplace of the god Ram. In a situation hauntingly reminiscent of the Temple Mount dispute in Jerusalem, this issue involved a contest over certain sacred sites. For some time, conservative Hindus had been incensed over the government's protection of a number of mosques built on the sites of Hindu temples during the Mogul period. In 1984 the VHP called for a reassertion of Hindu control over a dozen of these. Chief among them was the Babri Mosque, built by a lieutenant of the Emperor Baber on the location of a Hindu temple in the city of Ayodhya, which is traditionally identified as the home and capital of the God-king Ram. At some point in history—exactly when is a debated issue—the site of the Babri Mosque was identified as none other than the birthplace of Ram. Soon after India's independence, during a time of Hindu/Muslim tensions, it is said that an image of Ram magically manifested itself in the mosque, so some Hindus insisted on worshiping there. Riots broke out between Muslims and Hindus over the use of the site, and the government barred them both. In 1986, after the VHP demanded that Ram be liberated from what they called his Muslim jail, a judge again opened the site for worship. Violent encounters between Muslims and Hindus soon ensued, with the VHP calling for the mosque to be destroyed or removed and a new temple built in its place.

The VHP was linked in 1985 to a new all-India organization, the Dharma Sansad. Based in Karnataka in South India, it consisted of 900 representatives of a variety of Hindu sects and orders of sadhus who vowed to fight for Hindu purification and the propagation of Hindu nationalism. It also forged ties with another potent movement, the Shiv Sena, which had organized protest rallies in Maharashtra, Gujarat, and Punjab over what it regarded as the government's pro-Muslim and pro-Sikh policies. By 1986 the VHP claimed to have over 3,000 branches throughout India and over a million dedicated workers. It targeted for defeat politicians who it felt were unfaithful to the Hindu cause and lobbied for pro-Hindu legislation.

The VHP also persisted on the Ayodhya issue. Although the Archeological Survey of India published a report in January 1989 concluding that it was unlikely that Ram was born on the site, the public continued to see it as an important matter. According to national polls in 1991, Ayodhya rivaled economic issues as one of the most important concerns of India's voters.[18] Over 300 persons had been killed in incidents related to the struggle, including a communal clash in Meerut on May 18–26, 1987, with over a hundred deaths.[19]

Largely through the Ayodhya issue the BJP became directly

linked with the VHP. There had been a relationship between the two
for years through the RSS, whose workers supplied the organizational energy for both the party and the movement. The old Hindu
political party, the Jan Sangh, had merged with the Janata party in a
united front against the Congress in 1977. When the Janata party
broke up, the leaders of the Jan Sangh regrouped in 1980 to form the
BJP. The president of the party was Atal Behari Vajpayee, a former
leader of the Jan Sangh; the vice-president was Vijaye Raje Scindia,
a rather remarkable and outspoken woman who was a member of the
former ruling family of the princely state of Gwalior; and as general
secretary the BJP named Lal Krishna Advani.

Advani's background indicates much about the character of the
BJP. He was born in 1928 and was raised in Karachi, but was forced
to flee in 1947, when Pakistan was created. He was educated in
Catholic schools, worked as a lawyer and a journalist, and was a
member of the RSS. He seldom worshiped in a temple or performed Hindu religious rites, and at one time he ate meat, contrary
to the usual upper-caste Hindu preference for vegetarianism.
When asked why the BJP had become so phenomenally popular,
he said it had nothing to do with religious sentiment; it was purely a
matter of "nationalism" or, rather, as he put it, "patriotism."[20]

Initially the BJP's appeal was not all that great. In the first
national election in which it participated, in 1984, the BJP won
only 2 seats out of a total of 545 in the lower house of parliament (for
all practical purposes the sole legislative body of the national government). In the 1989 elections the BJP won 86 seats and was a
supporter of the new prime minister, V. P. Singh (although it was
technically not part of his coalition). In the 1991 elections the BJP
won 120 seats—compared with only 220 seats for the leading Congress party.

The BJP's smashing electoral success in 1991 was due partly to the
tragic assassination of the Congress party's main candidate, Rajiv
Gandhi.[21] The BJP leaders could claim that theirs was now the party
of stability—one of the claims that Rajiv Gandhi had made about the
Congress. Yet even before Rajiv Gandhi's death, the bookies in
Bombay who were placing bets on the election had given odds in
favor of the BJP's winning over a hundred seats.[22] The main reason
was Ayodhya and all that it had come to symbolize.

The year before the election, in October 1990, Advani joined the

VHP's call for faithful Hindus throughout the country to make bricks and bring them to Ayodhya to rebuild the temple at the site of the Babri Mosque, at the place where Ram was allegedly born. Advani himself attempted to march to the site, and he called on the government to move the mosque "with dignity and honor" to another location a short distance away.[23] Long before Advani got near Ayodhya, however, the government arrested him and 20,000 other Hindu volunteers (including the vice-president of the BJP, Scindia) who were prepared to march to the mosque. The BJP immediately withdrew its parliamentary support from Prime Minister Singh, whereupon his national-front government collapsed. At the Ayodhya site the protest continued, and over thirty Muslims and Hindus were killed in the clash. "My conscience is clear," Singh said in a television interview broadcast after his government's collapse, claiming that he had "sacrificed the highest office for the cause of the unity of the country and the oppressed."[24]

Ayodhya had become a symbol for both sides. For Singh it was a test of the will of the secular state to stand up for its policy of neutrality on religious issues. Behind this policy, however, was an even more fundamental cause: the nature of India as a modern state. In a speech made during the crisis, Singh recalled Mohandas Gandhi's struggle for Hindu/Muslim unity at the time India became independent and said that he, like Gandhi, was fighting for the survival of "India as a secular nation."[25] Several scholars, in a book rushed into print soon after the event, evoked the image of Nehru when they concurred with Singh that Ayodhya was ultimately about the ability of politics to stay free of religion.[26]

On the other side, the leaders of the VHP and the BJP saw Ayodhya as the symbol of the government's inability to stand up for the Hindu majority and its tendency to pander to the interests of religious minorities. From the BJP's point of view, this stand was tantamount to selling the soul of the country for the sake of Muslim votes. Behind their position was the desire for India to be a Hindu, rather than a secular, state. In a curious way, Advani seemed to agree with Singh and the other secular nationalists about the importance of unifying India. The fundamental difference is that Singh thought that only secularism could be the unifying force, while Advani and his colleagues were equally convinced that only India's Hindu culture could provide the cement to hold the nation together and form the basis for modern progress. For this reason Advani could state that in India "politicians do not command respect," for they are only "opportunists." Instead, he claimed, because his followers were motivated by principle, only his party was truly disciplined; only it held a truly "nationalist viewpoint."[27] Invoking Mohandas Gandhi, the party in its May 1992 meetings claimed that it embraced Gandhi's "holistic" approach to politics and economics, "different from capitalism and communism."[28]

Yet once the Hindu nationalists came to power in several states in 1991, they found how difficult it could be to hold onto both their religious ideals and the reigns of power. In Uttar Pradesh, one of the states in which the BJP was victorious, the symbol for their political dilemma was, once again, Ayodhya. The city, which is located in Uttar Pradesh, became the beneficiary of one of the BJP government's efforts at urban renewal: it bought the land around the site of the disputed mosque in order, it claimed, to construct facilities for tourists and pilgrims—an action that angered Muslims and moderate Hindus who saw it as a ploy to take over the mosque. Meanwhile, some of the BJP's radical Hindu followers—the "boys," as the leaders called them—grew impatient with this slow strategy of encroachment, and they launched their own campaign to seize the mosque immediately. The attack failed, but the incident greatly embarrassed the government and divided the Hindu nationalist movement.[29] In 1992 the government abandoned its pretenses, transferred the land to the VHP, and began building a temple.

On December 6, 1992, the mosque was destroyed. Hundreds were killed in riots throughout India, and BJP leaders were briefly jailed. In part because it was ostracized, however, the party's popularity increased. In 1993, the BJP attempted to widen its support in anticipation of the 1994 elections, but it continued to be plagued by internecine quarrels. Beneath a struggle over leadership lay a deeper tension: whether the BJP was just a political party, or the vanguard of a Hindu revolution.

The Sikh War against Both Secular and Hindu Nationalism

In January 1992 the Hindu nationalist BJP party organized a convoy of buses in a unity march to journey from India's far south to its far north, hoping to demonstrate popular support for its message of cultural unity. When the buses reached the Punjab city of Phagwara, they were set upon by a band of militant Sikhs. Five of the Unity Marchers were killed on the spot; sixteen others lay wounded.[30] From these militant Sikhs' point of view, the BJP form of Hindu unity was precisely what they were against: that, and the Congress party's idea of a unified secular nation. To these Sikhs, both Hindu activists and secular politicians were equally foolish and equally dangerous: both threatened their own nationalist aspirations for a Sikh state.[31]

Often, however, the Sikh rhetoric is strikingly similar to the language of Hindu nationalists. I heard one example of this in a dark and sparsely decorated room behind one of the main centers of Sikhism in New Delhi, where a group of intense young men were explaining to me why their hero—the fiery preacher Jarnail Singh Bhindranwale, who fell as a martyr to the militant Sikh cause in 1984—has come to be their symbol for radical opposition to the Indian government. They told me that not just his politics but his religious commitment attracted them: "He went to his death for what he believed."[32] Other leaders are just politicians, they implied, and ultimately they are looking out only for themselves. This same criticism has often been made by the members of the Hindu movements, the RSS and the BJP: secular politics is a cynical and self-serving business.

Sikh leaders, like their Hindu counterparts, state that religious politics offer a positive alternative. "Politics can be beautiful," I was told by a former head priest of Sikhism's central shrine.[33] "But it must be the right kind of politics." By this he meant a politics fused with religion, where "religion dominated politics," rather than the other way around.[34] He felt that Bhindranwale represented this sort of politics. For this reason, he explained, intense young men throughout the Punjab carried crumpled pictures of the preacher alongside their automatic weapons as they moved from village to village under cover of night.

Their hero Bhindranwale is sometimes portrayed in the press and by secular Indian politicians as a hater of Hindus, his message nothing more than the poison of intercommunal hatred. Yet during his heyday in the 1980s, Bhindranwale was always careful to say that he had nothing against Hinduism as such. "I preach Hindu-

Sikh unity," he proudly proclaimed.[35] What he disdained—indeed loathed—was "the enemies of religion." These included "that lady born in a house of Brahmans"—the phrase he used to describe Indira Gandhi—and heretics who had fallen from the disciplined Sikh fold and sought the easy comforts of modern life.

Bhindranwale's epithet for Indira Gandhi seems to indict both secular and Hindu politicians—secular politicians because of her party, Hindu politicians because of her caste—and, in fact, he often regarded the two as twin enemies. He was reflecting a belief of many Sikhs: that secular politics in India is in fact a form of Hindu cultural domination. So conscious are many Sikhs of what they regard as the oppressiveness of Hindu culture that they are uneasy when scholars locate the origins of their tradition in a medieval Hindu milieu. As mentioned, the founder of Sikhism, Guru Nanak, was one of the introspective and devotional saints of the medieval bhakti movement.[36] Many Sikhs would like to think of him as having no significant theological connections with the Hindu tradition that preceded him.

Whether or not Guru Nanak thought of himself as unique, the movement that survived him became increasingly aware that it was a distinctly separate community, in part because the Mogul military leaders regarded it that way and in part because of the cultural influence of the Jats—the dominant landholding caste of the Punjab, who began joining the Sikh community at the end of the sixteenth century. The Jats were great warriors, and they imposed their martial values and symbols on the whole of the Sikh community.[37] The tenth and final teacher in the historical lineage of Sikh masters, Guru Gobind Singh, presided over an army of considerable size, and martyrdom was the supreme honor bestowed. The symbols that Guru Gobind Singh is said to have imposed on his followers in 1699 and that are still meaningful to the faithful include such emblems of militancy as a sword and a braceletlike shield worn on the wrist. The most frequently displayed symbol of Sikhism today is a double-edged blade, surrounded by a circle and surmounted by a pair of swords.

Thus the Sikh community grew from a small group of devotees of an introspective spiritual teacher into an army, one that eventually had its own kingdom. Early in the nineteenth century the land and the armies of the Sikhs were consolidated by Maharaja Ranjit

Singh, whose kingdom spanned most of the Punjab and lasted until the middle of the century; it was one of the last independent regions in India to fall to the British, conquered only after a series of wars.

The British colonial period initially saw a decline of the Sikh community until a reform movement in 1873 began reviving the tradition and imposing standards of faith and practice. This movement, the Singh Sabha, was especially exercised about what it regarded as the display of Hindu artifacts in the Golden Temple and other Sikh shrines and *gurdwaras* (religious meeting places). In 1920, groups of Sikhs began agitating for reforms in the management of its *gurdwaras*, calling for an ouster of those who had been in control of the shrines, including the Udasis (a sect that traced its origins to the son of Guru Nanak, revered Hindu gods and texts, and venerated Guru Nanak to the exclusion of the other nine founding gurus of Sikhism).

The British government capitulated to these demands in 1925 and established a board of control, the Shiromani Gurdwara Parbandhak Committee (Central Gurdwara Management Committee, the SGPC), consisting of elected representatives. The SGPC became an arena for Sikh politics. One group of partisans in the reform movement, the Akali Dal (the Band of the Immortal One), later became a political party, and after independence they successfully contested elections for legislative seats, sharing with the Congress party the ability to form ruling governments in the state.

Sikh politicians, like other minority religious leaders, supported India's fight for freedom from the British but, like Jinnah and other Muslims, mistrusted the influence of Hindu nationalists in the independence movement.[38] Moreover, the creation of Pakistan had raised the expectations of many Sikhs that they should have an independent state as well.

Independence brought a certain amount of disillusionment to many Sikhs who had supported the struggle against the British. They felt outside the mainstream of national politics, and they did not even have control of their area of India because they constituted less than half the electorate in the state of Punjab. In the 1950s they spawned a new political movement that called for a redrawing of the boundaries of the Punjab to include only speakers of the Punjabi language, a demand that was tantamount to calling for a Sikh-majority state. The charismatic leader of the time, Sant Fateh Singh, went on a well-publicized fast and threatened to immolate himself on the roof of the Golden Temple's Akal Takhat (the Throne of the Immortal One, a building that housed the main Sikh organizations). The Indian government, captained by Prime Minister Indira Gandhi, conceded, and in 1966 the old Punjab state was carved into three to produce Haryana and Himachal Pradesh, states with Hindu majorities, and a new, smaller Punjab with a Sikh majority.

The violent movement that erupted in the 1980s had some ties to these earlier campaigns for Sikh autonomy and political power, but it was in many ways more fanatical, more religious.[39] The movement began during a clash in 1978 between a group of Sikhs and the Nirankaris, a small sect that had splintered from the Sikh tradition and followed its own gurus. The leader of the Sikhs attacking the Nirankaris was Bhindranwale, a young rural preacher who at an early age had joined the Damdami Taksal, a religious school and retreat center founded by the great Sikh martyr Baba Deep Singh. Bhindranwale eventually became its head. Bhindranwale had found the Nirankaris' worship of a living guru to be presumptuous and offensive. In the escalating violence between the two groups, lives were lost on both sides. In 1980 the Nirankari guru was assassinated. Bhindranwale was accused of the crime but was found not guilty.

Soon Bhindranwale became busy with a new organization, the Dal Khalsa (the Group of the Pure), which was supported by the prime minister's younger son, Sanjay Gandhi, and other Congress party leaders, including the president of India, Zail Singh. It was supposed to replace the Akali Dal's control of the SGPC, but it never succeeded. In 1981 the publisher of a chain of Hindu newspapers in Punjab who had been a critic of Bhindranwale was shot dead; again, Bhindranwale was implicated. In response to his arrest and the destruction of his personal papers, Bhindranwale turned against the government. Bands of young Sikhs began indiscriminately killing Hindus, and later that year a group of Sikhs hijacked an Indian Airlines plane in Pakistan. The violence had begun.

The sermons of Bhindranwale offer clues to his religious sensibilities and their political implications.[40] In a rambling, folksy manner, he called on his followers to maintain their faith in a time of trial, and he echoed the common fear that Sikhs would lose their identity in a sea of secularism or, worse, in a flood of resurgent Hinduism.[41] One of his more familiar themes was the survival of the Sikh community; for *community* he used the term *qaum,* which carries overtones of nationhood.[42] As for the idea of Khalistan, a separate Sikh nation, Bhindranwale said he "neither favored it or opposed it."[43] He did, however, support the Sikh concept of *miri-piri,* the notion that spiritual and temporal power are linked.[44] He evoked the image of a great war between good and evil waged in the present day: "a struggle . . . for our faith, for the Sikh nation, for the oppressed."[45] He implored his young followers to rise up and marshal the forces of righteousness. "The Guru will give you strength," he assured them.[46]

By 1983, Bhindranwale's power and the fear of it had grown so enormously that Mrs. Gandhi had suspended the Punjab government and was ruling it directly from Delhi. Bhindranwale had set up an alternative government of his own in the protected quarters of the Sikhs' most sacred shrine, the Golden Temple, in Amritsar. The Akali leader, Sant Harchand Singh Longowal, was also sequestered in the Golden Temple but in separate quarters because he and Bhindranwale had had a falling out that led to a series of killings in both camps. From time to time lists of demands to be presented to the government would be drawn up by one group of Sikhs or another, but the groups could seldom agree among themselves on which items to include. Besides, the larger issue was one of political legitimacy for Sikh identity—religious nationalism—so the specific demands were, in a sense, irrelevant. Government officials who focused on these demands in trying to negotiate a settlement were invariably frustrated. In 1984, shortly before she gave the command to the Indian army to invade the Golden Temple, an exasperated Indira Gandhi itemized everything she had done to meet the Sikh demands and asked, "What more can any government do?"[47]

The situation came to a head on June 5, 1984, when Mrs. Gandhi sent troops into the Golden Temple in a venture code-named Operation Bluestar. In a messy military operation that took two days to complete, 2,000 or more people were killed, including a number of innocent worshipers. Bhindranwale was one of the first to die. Longowal was taken into custody. Even moderate Sikhs throughout the world were horrified at the specter of the Indian army stomping through their holiest precincts with their boots on, shooting holes in the temple's elaborate marble facades. Avenging this act of desecration of the Golden Temple, two of Mrs. Gandhi's Sikh bodyguards assassinated her on October 31, 1984.[48] On the following day, over 2,000 Sikhs were massacred in Delhi and elsewhere by angry mobs.[49] Rajiv Gandhi, who became prime minister after his mother's death, entered into an agreement with Longowal in July 1985 to bring the violence to an end, but Longowal himself was assassinated, presumably by members of Bhindranwale's camp, later that year.

In the years since, the "Rajiv-Longowal accord" has never been completely implemented, nor has the violence in the Punjab completely abated. The followers of Bhindranwale have become more strident, increasingly aiming at wiping out the Longowal faction of Akalis, led by Punjab's chief minister, Surjit Singh Barnala, and other moderate Sikhs. Despite this, the moderate leaders of the Akalis attempted a daring strategy of accommodation by appointing several religious leaders who were sympathetic to the extremists' cause to the council of five, which has traditionally made decisions regarding religious matters in Sikhism. (These are often misleadingly referred to in the press as the "five priests" of Sikhism—largely a misnomer because Sikhism is a lay community and the religious function of *granthi*, the word rendered here as *priest*, is minor, similar to the role of a Jewish cantor.)

The newly appointed council of five declared its support of Khalistan and excommunicated Chief Minister Barnala. The least radical of the five religious leaders took "a leave of absence" from his position, and Jasbir Singh Rode, nephew of the martyred Bhindranwale, became the leader (*jathedar*) of the Akal Takhat. Radical organizations such as the Khalistan Commando Force, the Khalistan Liberation Force, and extremist factions of the All-India Sikh Students Federation had direct control of the official Sikh leadership. Violent assaults in the villages increased, and during 1987 over a hundred people a month were being killed by extremists.

The Golden Temple again became a hideout for militants seeking protection from the police, and again the Indian security forces entered the Golden Temple to rout the militants. This spurred the Indian parliament to enact a law prohibiting religious shrines from being used for political and military purposes. Although the law applied to all religious institutions throughout the country, it had immediate applicability to the Sikh situation. Meanwhile, the moderate Akali leaders broke with the militants and dismissed the five leaders of the Golden Temple. In response, bombs were thrown in the major cities in the Punjab, killing seventy-three people. To ameliorate the situation, the popular musician Darshan Singh Ragi was appointed *jathedar* of the Akal Takhat, and he allowed Chief Minister Barnala to undergo acts of penance, including cleaning the shoes of Sikh worshipers, in order to reverse his excommunication from the faith.

In May, 1987, Rajiv Gandhi, claiming that Barnala was not able to control the situation, ousted him from office, suspended parliamentary government in the state, and again ran the state's affairs from the central government. As chaotic as Barnala's rule had been, the situation that year deteriorated even further. After the national elections in November 1989 removed Rajiv Gandhi and his Congress party from control of the government, the new prime minister, V. P. Singh, inaugurated his rule with a ceremonial visit to the Golden Temple. Unfortunately, neither he nor his successor, Chandra Shekar, was able to handle the communal difficulties of the country any better than their predecessors had done.

In 1991, over 3,000 people were killed in the Punjab's triangular battle among the police, the radicals, and the populace.[50] It was the largest number in recent years. Along with the increase in violence was a general collapse of law and order, especially in rural areas of the state. This collapse was due in part to the erosion of idealism in the Sikh movement and in part to the movement's being used by street gangs and roving bands of thugs. The anarchy in the villages was also caused by the failure of the Sikh movement to achieve its political goals, leaving a cynical and demoralized public in its wake. In that sense the public disorder proved what the Sikh religious nationalists had been saying all along: without a government legitimized by religion, there can be no credible government in the state at all. It was not surprising, therefore, that few Sikhs bothered—or dared—to vote in the 1992 elections.

In the absence of a legitimate government in the Punjab, the rural area became a no man's land in the battle between militants and armed police. The war was exacerbated by caste: the militants were largely poor, young members of the dominant farming caste in the Punjab, the Jats. The leaders of the police and central administration of the Punjab were often urban Hindus and Sikhs from merchant castes—traditional rivals of the Jats. The armed police waging the war in the villages on the urban Hindus' behalf were often members of the lower castes, who in the past often acted as serfs for Jat Sikhs. Thus young Jats had to bear both the injury of being dominated by urban Hindus and the insult of being controlled by young police whom they regard as being of lower status than themselves.[51]

In a poignant attempt to break through this vicious cycle and reestablish a leadership to which the central government could maintain ties, Rajiv Gandhi, in virtually his last act of office, released the Akali leader, Simranjeet Singh Mann, from prison. This was an extraordinary act on the prime minister's part because Mann was in prison awaiting trial for his role—which according to some published accounts was central—in the plot that had led to the murder of Rajiv Ghandi's mother. Rajiv claimed that his pardon was an eleventh-hour effort to "heal wounds."[52] Following his release from prison, Mann served as a member of parliament until October 11, 1990; in January 1991 all the major factions of the Akali party united under his leadership. His was a short-lived success, however, since it was based on the support of militant cadres whose political grip on the Punjab would soon come to an end.

The Punjab state government finally gained an upper hand over the militants in 1992. The Congress Party leaders who came to power in the February elections used their mandate to unleash the police in search and destroy missions that literally eradicated the militant network. Several thousand were killed—dedicated revolutionaries, thugs, and innocent bystanders—in what amounted to a government-led massacre. The result, however, was a state of calm in the Punjab that most residents had not experienced in over ten years.[53] By October the police barricades were dismantled in the streets of Amritsar and other urban areas, and by Spring, 1993, it was possible to move freely though the countryside, even at night. The Sikhs' war was over; the secular state had won.

The tensions between the Sikh community and the secular government were not really resolved, however. The government won the war against the militants not because it persuaded the Sikh masses that it was right, but because the public and the moderate Sikh leadership had grown weary of the militants' posturing. They were ready to accept the restoration of law and order at any cost. A great number of Sikhs continue to hope for a public order that gives greater recognition to the authority of their religious community, and many continue to wage their own small wars against the secularism of society, including what they regard as the insidiousness of Western-style scholarship on Sikh history and texts. Moreover, a few of the militants survived the annihilation: the detonation of a car bomb in New Delhi in September 1993, killing eight, indicates their continuing struggle against the secular state. Their movement could rise again.

If it does, it will be part of India's quarreling camp of anti-secularists, which includes Hindu nationalists in the BJP and Muslim separatists in Kashmir.[54] These religious activists all deem India's political structure as illegitimate because secular politics does not encourage candidates to be based in a religious community or claim credibility through cultural ties. Although the politics of religion are thought by many of India's secular leaders to be a step backwards to the worst of its divisive history, some concession to religion may be necessary to assure that India's future is more peaceful than its terrible recent past.

Sri Lanka's Unfinished Religious Revolt

Sri Lanka, like India, was once part of Britain's vast South Asian empire. Today both countries are ruled by secular parties that are caretakers for the political apparatus the British left behind. In both countries voices protest these vestiges of Western secular nationalism and demand a national identity more in touch with the nation's cultural past. In Sri Lanka, as in India, these demands come from two directions: separatist minority movements and religious nationalists from the majority community. In Sri Lanka, however, the Hindus are in the minority. They regard themselves as oppressed; but then, in a curious sort of way, so does the majority.

The Sri Lankan majority community is Sinhalese Buddhist, and a politically active bhikkhu in the highlands near Kandy explained to me why they were so defensive of their cultural tradition. "Look at the map," he implored, "and see how tiny, how fragile Sinhalese Buddhist society is." Other cultures, the bhikkhu explained, including Muslim, Christian, Hindu, and even other Buddhist ones, are "enormous and secure, but our Sinhala society is only a teardrop, a grain of sand, in an enormous sea." And, he concluded, lowering his voice, "it is in danger of being forever dashed away."[55]

The bhikkhu did not feel that the Tamils in the north and east of Sri Lanka are a threat to Buddhism, nor did he fear Hinduism, which he regarded as part and parcel of Buddhist heritage. Rather, the bhikkhu blamed his country's nominally Buddhist but largely secular politicians for what he regarded as too soft an attitude toward Tamil demands and too negligent a response to the Sinhalese. "They are attempting genocide," he proclaimed, for they are "deliberately" trying to annihilate Sinhalese Buddhist culture.[56]

The bhikkhu symbolizes the second of two rebellions that the government of Sri Lanka has faced: one, a popular uprising in the rural Sinhalese area of the central and southern provinces, and the other, a better known, well-organized movement for Tamil separatism in the northern and eastern sections of the country. The Sinhalese movement is in some ways more threatening to the secular government because it challenges the state's legitimacy on a fundamental level and because it touches a sensitive nerve in all quarters of the 70 percent of the Sri Lankan population that is Buddhist.

The Sinhalese rebellion was fueled by the sentiments of many Buddhists, such as the bhikkhu, who felt that independence from the West has yet to be won on a cultural and ideological level. "Those politicians who use English language and British customs and force the British political system on us," the bhikkhu explained, "continue colonialism in Sri Lanka as surely as if the British never left."[57]

It is easy for some Buddhists in Sri Lanka to feel this way because their form of Buddhism has been associated with Sinhalese culture and kings throughout Sri Lanka's history. (The term *Sinha-*

lese, of which the word *Ceylon* is a variation, derives from an ancient name for Sri Lanka, Sinhala, meaning lion.) Theravada Buddhist dynasties have ruled Sri Lanka—or have struggled with contending Tamil kings to do so—ever since the time of Mahinda, the son of the great Indian king Asoka. He is said to have journeyed to Sri Lanka and established the first Buddhist throne there in the third century B.C.E., bringing with him an offshoot of the Bodhi tree (under which the Buddha was enlightened) and the Buddha's tooth, a sacred relic that is housed in Sri Lanka's most important shrine, the Dalada Maligawa (Temple of the Tooth) in Kandy. From a Sinhalese perspective, the governments established by the Portuguese, Dutch, and British from 1505 to 1948 were all merely interruptions in the overall course of Sinhalese Buddhist history.[58]

Sri Lanka never had much of a nationalist movement, although a small number of Western-educated leaders in the country attempted to introduce to Sri Lanka some of the same civilized, secular nationalism that they saw Nehru and the other leaders of India's Congress party bringing to their large neighbor to the north. So, when the British suddenly offered independence to Sri Lanka in 1948, these people were prepared to rule. They had not had much time to develop an ideology of secular nationalism, however, and even in the nationalist movement, such as it was, a sizable contingent of religious leaders had no use for the rhetoric of secularism. The first person to carry a flag for the country's freedom was a Buddhist monk, and today a statue in front of the Dalada Maligawa celebrates his patriotic act.

After independence there was a great deal of controversy over the role of Buddhism in the country's symbols of nationalism. In 1972 the name of the country was changed from the Anglicized form of Sinhala—Ceylon—to a less specifically Buddhist one, Sri Lanka (the name given to the island nation in the great Hindu epic the *Ramayana*). The symbol chosen for the national flag, however, was the Sinhalese lion. The suggestion that it would be more appropriate to have on the flag an ethnically neutral symbol such as Adam's Peak—the mountaintop in the central part of the island that is revered equally by Hindus, Sinhalese, and Muslims—was rejected.[59] Many Sinhalese felt that the time had come to restore Buddhism as the national religion, and in 1953 a popular tract, *The Revolt in the Temple,* urged the populace to reject the emerging secular nationalism and embrace a Buddhist version instead.[60] Political leaders found it increasingly useful to employ the rhetoric of Buddhism to buttress their own power.[61]

An emphasis on Buddhist culture and Sinhalese language was the vehicle on which Bandaranaike and his Sri Lanka Freedom Party (SLFP) rode to power. In 1956 they even supported legislation that made Sinhala the sole official language of the nation. As soon as the bill was passed, they backed away from its extreme implications in order to protect Tamil minority interests, but in doing so they alienated some of their Buddhist supporters (such as the Rasputin-like monk Mapitigama Buddharakkhita Thero) and left an opening for political rivals—including one of Bandaranaike's successors, J. R. Jayawardene—to gain Sinhalese support by claiming that the SLFP had reneged on its promises. On September 25, 1959, Bandaranaike was killed by a Buddhist monk in a conspiracy allegedly masterminded by Buddharakkhita, who among other things was unhappy with the pace of Bandaranaike's efforts to make Buddhism the state religion.

The idea of Buddhist nationalism, even the tepid form proposed by Bandaranaike, did not sit well with minority communities. The largest of them, the Hindu Tamils, had lived for centuries in the northern and eastern sections of the island, and claimed it as a Tamil homeland. According to one Tamil writer, his community stemmed from the "aboriginal people of Sri Lanka," who had lived in the island long before the Sinhalese arrived.[62] Tamil unrest in the north led to a severe backlash in the south. In 1983 a storm of violence was unleashed against Tamils living in Colombo and elsewhere; hundreds—some say thousands—were killed in the riots.[63] Soon after, a Tamil separatist movement began in earnest.

The Tamil position is not explicitly religious. The nationalism of the movement is directed toward a separate Tamil nation, Thamil Eelam, and is one in which religious identities—specifically Hindu and Christian—are not immediately apparent. As one separatist writer explained, "The original link between Tamil ethnicity and the Hindu religion has come to be severed."[64] Instead, Tamil ethnicity replaces Hinduism as the focal point of nationalist pride among Tamils. As a result, some of the most active participants in the Tamil separatist movement have been Christians, even Christian clergy. The cyanide capsules that dedicated members of the

Black Tigers—the most militant Tamil movement—wear around their necks are suspended from the same black rope necklaces that Christians wear in displaying the crucifix. The fanaticism of the Tigers, especially after their successful assassination of India's former prime minister Rajiv Gandhi in 1991, led one Western writer to describe them as "the Asian guerrilla equivalent of the Rev. Jim Jones and his Guyana suicide cult."[65] Yet Tamil rebels seldom choose religious targets. Although Buddhist monks have sometimes been caught up in the violence—in 1987, twenty-nine monks were dragged out of a bus near the ancient Buddhist capital, Anuradhapura, and systematically gunned down—the Tamil movement's main enemy has been the government. Ironically, the favorite target of Buddhist militants has been the government as well.

The growth in Sinhalese Buddhist militancy in the 1980s was in part a response to the Tamil separatist movement and in part a response to the government's attempt to be secular and neutral in the face of communal conflict. The Sinhalese militants were bitterly opposed to the pact between President Jayawardene and India's Rajiv Gandhi on May 1987 to bring in Indian troops to quell the Tamil uprising in the northern and eastern sections of the island. The pact gave increased political autonomy to the Tamils, which appeared to many Sinhalese to be a sellout to Tamil demands. Moreover, the pact did not quiet the most extreme of the Tamil separatists, the Liberation Tigers of Thamil Eelam, who persisted in fighting to the death. The occupation troops of the Indian Army Peacekeeping Force, for their part, did not quickly leave. Rather, their numbers swelled to over 60,000—more soldiers than the British had in India even at the height of the British Empire.[66] The fear spread throughout Sri Lanka that Rajiv Gandhi's gift of peace was a Trojan horse and that even when the Indian army left, the military and political ties to India would remain.

The antipathy to Sri Lanka's pact with the Indian military greatly boosted support for the Janatha Vimukthi Peramuna (JVP)—the People's Liberation Front.[67] The present JVP is a revival of an earlier movement of the same name that in 1971 attempted an abortive coup against Sirimavo Bandaranaike, the widow of the slain leader, who succeeded him in office. Both the present and previous forms of the movement were said to have been led by Rohana Wijeweera, until he was captured and killed in police custody in 1989.

Wijeweera was a secular radical with Marxist credentials—he once attended college in Moscow—and he was never fully accepted by many of the religious activists who followed the JVP banner, especially those in its most recent incarnation. Yet the movement was not so closely organized as to require strict obedience to any single leader, and Wijeweera himself claimed to have no influence over many aspects of the Sinhalese movement, including its most violent wing, the Deshapremi Janatha Viyaparaya.

Taken as a whole, the new movement could be described as one of cultural nationalism; it was in many ways a Sinhalese Buddhist revolt. Leaders of the movement would recall Sir Lanka's glorious Buddhist past, and they regarded the secular, democratic government of Colombo to be an enemy of Buddhism and an obstacle to social progress. But although the new JVP was more Buddhist in its rhetoric than its previous incarnation had been, it was perhaps even more savage in its actions. Hundreds, some say thousands, of villagers were killed. In many cases, the killings took the form of gang slayings, as old rivalries were brought into the open and old grudges were avenged. In other cases, the violence was an attempt to assert the militants' own control over rural areas and to undercut the legitimacy of the government.

This movement, like the original JVP, was a "youthful revolt."[68] The most active members of the movement were young men aged eighteen to twenty-six.[69] Thus, its constituency was entirely different from that of its 1971 predecessor. Members of the earlier movement had become middle-aged and in some cases they were targets of the wrath of the new JVP youth.[70] Many of the most active supporters of the new movement were unemployed villagers in the southern part of the island; some observers said that a majority of the young people there were sympathetic to or at least did not resist JVP activities.[71] Fieldworkers in the Sarvodaya relief-and-development agency reported difficulties in carrying out their activities owing to JVP interference: they were harassed and their vehicles were stolen.[72] The main targets, however, were government officials.

In 1987, President Jayawardene was targeted for assassination. When shots fired at him during a parliamentary meeting missed, hand grenades were tossed in his direction; they bounced across the table in front of him and exploded. Jayawardene escaped unscathed, but a member of his cabinet was killed and seventeen others were wounded. In 1988, a popular Sinhalese film star and politician, Vijaya Kumaranatunga, who was in the process of creating a new alliance among three socialist parties, was shot dead by gunmen on a motorcycle as they sped past his house in Colombo. Later in the day two bombs that had been planted inside a crowded Hindu temple near the film star's home exploded while priests were chanting their evening prayers; seven people were instantly killed, and thirteen more were seriously injured. Although the Reuters report of the incident said that "police could not say who was responsible," the JVP was "blamed" for the attack and the bombing.[73]

The government was clearly the enemy in what amounted to a Sinhalese holy war. One indication of the JVP's antipathy to the government—and its influence in the countryside—was given on Sri Lanka's Independence Day in 1988, when leaders of the JVP sent out word that no one was to display the Sri Lanka national flag; and in those areas dominated by the JVP virtually no one did. Black flags were flown instead.[74]

One place black flags were prominently in evidence—with no national flags in sight—was the campus of Peradeniya University, near Kandy, where strongly worded antigovernment slogans were scrolled across the walls of classroom buildings. "JR [the President] is a monkey," some of the graffiti proclaimed, "a pest that should be destroyed!" Behind the pro-JVP activities at Peradeniya was a secret Student Action Committee. Its membership was mixed: it included Muslims and even Tamil supporters, and some of the most active members of the committee were student Buddhist monks.[75] Only 400 monks were enrolled at Peradeniya, but a disproportionately large number of them were political activists. The more established leaders of Buddhist monastic orders admonished them to resist the temptation to use violent means, but even elder monks had a great deal of sympathy for the JVP cause.[76]

The young monks in the rural areas were especially vulnerable to the appeal of the JVP and particularly impatient: "They don't listen to us," one of the bhikkhus I interviewed said, referring to the admonition of the older monks to keep quiet and not be involved in movements for radical change.[77] There was a certain pride in his voice as he spoke about these young firebrands. He explained that the concerns behind movements such as the JVP were valid, even if not all their means could be approved. "What is the message of these people?" the bhikkhu asked, and then answered his own question: "They want jobs and fair elections, they want order to be restored, and a peaceful Buddhist rule." The image he presented was of a fair-minded but oppressed generation that had been pushed to its limit. It was reasonable, from this point of view, for emotional and socially concerned monks to join in the revolution: they "struggle for *dhamma*" in their own way. Politicians, according to the bhikkhu, "are not interested in Buddhism" but "only in themselves."[78] By implication this left only the younger, more strident, and more selfless leaders to take the interests of the Sinhalese Buddhist nation truly to heart.

By mid-1989, the JVP was entering its most active—and most brutal—phase. Increasingly, young Buddhist monks who had secretly supported the movement came out in the open. On April 7, over 200 of them demonstrated in front of the Temple of the Tooth, protesting against government policies in general and the government's attempts to crush the JVP in particular. They were assaulted by the police and a good number were injured.[79] One scholar estimates that 100 monks were killed in police encounters during 1989.[80]

The decisive change in the government's war with the JVP came after Ranasinghe Premadasa was elected president on December 19, 1988. Although some observers had hoped that he would be regarded as a greater friend of Buddhism and traditional Sinhalese culture than his predecessor, the JVP boycotted the elections and vowed not to relax their activities until all their demands—including the demand for a Sinhalese Buddhist state—were met. Between January 10 and 26, 1989, eight candidates for parliamentary seats were dragged from their homes and killed by JVP supporters. Further acts of violence occurred after the parliamentary elections on February 15, 1989. The JVP initiated a series of highly effective strikes demanding higher wages for workers and the withdrawal of Indian troops, and on June 12, 1989, several people were killed when police broke up a JVP-sponsored demonstration in western Sri Lanka that called for a boycott of Indian goods and for the departure of all Indians—civilian and military—from Sri Lankan soil.

Eventually Premadasa won the JVP war and the movement was

crushed. By engineering the retreat of Indian forces from Sri
Lankan soil in 1990, Premadasa removed one of the major sources
of irritation that had fueled JVP discontent. Moreover, he dealt
with the Sinhalese movement both directly, through confrontation,
and indirectly, through cooptation of the Buddhist leadership.

The government confronted the militants directly on the militants' own terms. It fought terrorism with terrorism. The army let it
be known that for every one of them killed it would kill twenty
members of the JVP or their sympathizers. In one case an assault on
an entire village near Kandy left over 200 dead.[81] On June 20, 1989,
President Premadasa declared a state of emergency and arrested
3,200 suspected JVP sympathizers and other leftists; scarcely a week
later he survived a bomb attack on his life at a crowded religious
festival. The JVP was implicated in the attempt.

For the rest of 1989 and throughout the first half of 1990, the
army was unleashed to use whatever means it wished. One of its
most terrifying tactics was to kill young JVP activists and leave their
bodies on the main roads, sometimes for days, as public examples.
A taxi driver in Colombo told me that he had counted forty-seven
such bodies while driving the short stretch of road between the
towns of Humbantota and Tangalle in a day in January 1990.[82] The
total number of JVP members and their sympathizers killed is a
subject of some dispute. Some put the numbers in the tens of
thousands.[83] Most estimates are in the thousands, but even if the
accurate number is somewhere between 3,000 and 6,000, as many
claim, that is a significant figure. It was sufficient to destroy the
leadership and break the momentum of the movement.

By the middle of 1990, the JVP had effectively been crushed.
The main outcry against the government's brutal repression of the
movement came from civil libertarians and liberal Buddhists who
feared that the government's reign of terror would not soon be
contained. Yet even students in Peradeniya University, including
those whose friends "disappeared" as a result of the army's action,
seemed relieved that the JVP was no longer around to intimidate
them. They claimed that the "excesses" of the government are
sometimes necessary to maintain law and order.[84]

One of the reasons that there was not more of an outcry against
the government's actions is that several of Premadasa's attempts to
coopt the Buddhist leadership were quite successful. In 1991 and

1992 he spent an enormous amount of time visiting Buddhist shrines, temples, and monasteries, and the newspapers became crowded with pictures of the president giving offerings at such Buddhist shrines as the Temple of the Tooth. Genuinely religious—even superstitious, in a traditional Sri Lankan–village way—the lower-caste, rural Premadasa has traveled with a coterie of dancers and musicians who bless the floor that he steps on at official functions. He has proclaimed that *rajdharma* (the age of religious righteousness) has begun, ordered the construction of a gold-painted replica of the throne used by ancient Sri Lankan kings for his use at official functions, and appeared on television and elsewhere seated on a specially blessed chair with all the aura of a religious master.[85]

Perhaps Premadasa garnered the most Buddhist support from his creation of a new cabinet-level agency, the Ministry of Buddhist Affairs, of which he appointed himself the first minister.[86] The leaders of the four main monastic chapters were appointed as the ministry's council. Premadasa presented the council with some twenty-five million rupees to use in establishing an endowment for Buddhist causes. The council was also given the responsibility of adjudicating matters of Buddhist concern and suggesting appropriate government policies on religion and morality. The council was instrumental in getting the government to rescind its support for the establishment of fish-breeding ponds (because the purpose of the ponds was to kill animate life). The monks felt that their voice was finally being heard. One of the members of the council, a leader of a monastic order that had previously been critical of the government, said in January 1991 that the government was now beginning to "reflect Buddhist values."[87]

Not all monks were impressed with Premadasa's new policies however. One of the most strident of the bhikkhus that I had interviewed in the heyday of the JVP movement seemed despondent over the destruction of the movement and the wanton killing of so many young activists, including a good many idealistic Buddhist monks.[88] When I interviewed him in 1991, he told me that all the efforts of the government to put on a Buddhist front were just that, a show designed to win public support. "Supporting things like temples and stupas does not make one a good Buddhist," he explained; "you have to be Buddhist inside."[89] Moreover, he was not certain that the Sinhalese movement had been entirely crushed. "You can lese nationalists will appear again.

On May 1, 1993, during a May Day parade in Colombo, a bicyclist strapped with explosives rammed into President Premadasa, instantly killing him and a dozen members of his entourage. Although Tamil rebels were implicated in the attack, the political chaos that ensued encouraged the tattered remnants of the government's other political enemy, the Sinhalese nationalists, to regroup. They hoped to capitalize on the absence of Premadasa's charismatic leadership and his uncompromising stance toward his opposition.

If and when the Sinhalese nationalist movement is revived, most likely it will again target the secular government. Like Hindu and Sikh religious nationalists in India and elsewhere in South Asia, Sinhalese nationalists regard the secular parliamentary process— often touted in the West as the hallmark of freedom and democracy— as a purveyor of Western cultural colonialism. At one time Marxism provided an alternative to activists who were looking for an ideological base different from the American or Western European models. Increasingly, however, they look to their own cultural traditions for a distinctive national identity that they can call their own.

Chapter Five

Religious Ambivalence toward Socialist Nationalism: Formerly Marxist States

"The real struggle," a politician in Tajikistan explained, "is the battle between two ideologies: Islam and Communism."[1] In his country, the Communist Party remained strong even as the Soviet Union was falling apart in the early 1990s, in part because it was regarded as the nation's bulwark against the rising tide of Islamic nationalism in the Central Asian region. The demise of the Soviet Union set the stage for a confrontation between religious nationalism and socialist forms of secular nationalism. In the Soviet context, religion and socialism were both ideologies of order, and they are now competitors for the political allegiance of residents of many former Soviet states, including Mongolia and the nations of Central Asia. Yet in places such as Sri Lanka and Nicaragua the two have been allies, and the relation of religious-nationalist movements to Marxist states and socialist struggles is anything but predictable.

Today, especially in the former Soviet Union, socialist governments are seen by religious activists as part of the problem. In the rallies held in Moscow during the failed coup in August 1991, religious icons and bearded Orthodox priests were at the forefront of many of the processions against the Communist Party. The party was viewed as a vestige of an old secular nationalism—in the guise of a communist internationalism—that needed to be overthrown.

According to Marxist theory, such an outcome should never have occurred. Religious identities, and all other parochial forms of social organization, should have been subsumed under a political relationship to the state that was beyond nationalism.[2] Marxist theory calls for large, international political identities that are based on alliances of working-class people rather than on any local religious or ethnic allegiance. As for the practice of religion, Marx regarded it as, at best, the expression of travail, "the sigh of the oppressed." At its worst it was an "opiate"—a narcotic that exploiters used to ease the pain of exploitation.[3] In the Soviet Union the old ethnic and religious identities persisted, however, despite Marxist doctrine and the various attempts of Communist leaders to enforce it. In fact, Lenin's policy of "divide and rule" in the 1920s led to an increased sense of ethnic identity and a rigid demarcation of ethnic boundaries that, in turn, led to the unraveling of the Soviet Union in the 1980s and 1990s.[4]

When, in the late 1980s, Mikhail Gorbachev offered to the Soviet people the possibilities of *perestroika,* restructuring, and *glasnost,* openness, he got more than he bargained for. He opened not only the doors for economic changes and political reform but also the lid on the Pandora's box of resurgent ethnic and religious nationalisms. In the months immediately following the fall of the Soviet Union in January 1992, many Americans and Europeans focused on the economic and political changes in celebrating their victory over communism. Yet in the long run the people who live in the former Soviet states will be far more affected by the dissolution of the union and the rise of new national states. In fact, in Russia and many other states, a new nationalism and an increase in religious freedom are virtually the only differences that the collapse of the Soviet Union and the death of communism as an ideology have wrought. Despite efforts at economic reform and democratization, the economic system and the political apparatus remain much as they were before, although some political leaders have abandoned their Communist Party cards in favor of newfound ethnic and religious identities. A few of the former Communist leaders in Central Asia have even become Muslim mullahs. In places like Turkmenistan, Kazakhstan, and Mongolia, however, political power remains largely in the hands of the old socialist leaders, albeit often under new party labels.

In some ways, the situation in the last decades of the twentieth century is much like that in the first ones, when socialism initially appeared on the Russian scene as an economic alternative to tsarist feudalism and before it became the ideological ally of an international empire. In the first years following the October 1917 revolution, religion was relatively untouched by the new communist leaders. In Lenin's 1918 decree on the separation of religion and state, he took a laissez-faire position toward religious institutions. Neither he nor other Communist leaders were friends of religion, but for the first ten years their attitude toward it was relatively liberal.

All that changed in 1929, when Joseph Stalin—a former seminary student who had once prepared for the priesthood—solidified his power and brought cultural institutions more firmly under control of the state than they had been.[5] Legislation passed in 1929 limited religion to "performance of the cult"—the performance of rites and rituals—and disallowed the church a role in education and social matters. During the same year, legislation granted "freedom of antireligion propaganda," and more than a decade of repression followed.[6] In the 1930s a great number of churches were closed, monastic communities were dissolved, and theological schools were abandoned. Perhaps the most vivid symbol of the antireligious mood of the time was the burning of religious icons on huge bonfires in public squares.

In Central Asia and other Muslim areas of the Soviet Union religion was similarly repressed. As early as 1927, shari'a courts and *madrassah* (Islamic schools) were phased out, *waqf* (Muslim charity) lands were confiscated, and mosques were closed. In the 1930s the situation changed from bad to worse. Muslim institutions were required to change the alphabet in which their sacred writings and teachings were published: first from Arabic to Latin in 1930, then from Latin to Cyrillic in 1940 (in the first wave of Russification).

In Mongolia and other Buddhist areas under Soviet control, religion was also suppressed. In 1930, Mongolia still had over 80,000 active lamas associated with some 800 monasteries. Tied to the monasteries were over 7,700 plots of land. Two years later, the number of lamas had been reduced to 20,000, and the size of the monastic properties was scarcely a fraction of what it had been.[7] With the defeat of the "Left Deviationists" and rise of a "New Turn" policy in 1932, forcible secularization was stopped, and some lamas returned to the monasteries, but the grandeur of the monasteries seemed to be a thing of the past.

During the Second World War, Stalin was too busy with the war to keep up his attacks on religion. Moreover, he needed the support of the Russian Orthodox Church in his attempt to culturally unify the whole of the Soviet Union through Russification. In 1943, Stalin signed a concordat with church officials that led to the state-approved revival of the Moscow patriarch of the Russian Orthodox Church. In some areas of the Soviet Union, including the Ukraine, this policy of support for the Russian Orthodox Church resulted in even greater repression of regional religious communities, as their property was confiscated and given over to Russian Orthodox leaders, and local clergy were forced to give allegiance to Moscow. In non-Christian areas of the Soviet Union, however, any attempt to make Muslim mullahs and Buddhist monks into Orthodox priests must have seemed futile, and during the 1940s they experienced small improvement in their situation.

When N. S. Khrushchev came to power after the death of Stalin in 1953, he led a new campaign against religion, which, in its most virile stage, lasted from 1958 to 1964. During this period two-thirds of the Russian Orthodox churches opened in the 1940s were again closed. Muslim and Buddhist institutions were also affected. In 1961, a bishops' council organized and controlled by the state abolished the power of the clergy and allowed only lay leadership in religious congregations—in effect destroying the parish church. Leonid Brezhnev, who followed Khrushchev from 1964 to 1982, continued this policy, even encouraging the establishment of Scientific Atheist Clubs in abandoned churches. Brezhnev's successors, Yuri Andropov (1982–84) and Konstantin Chernenko (1984–85), did little to ameliorate the situation.

The great revival of religion came as the direct result of the policies of Gorbachev. Soon after he came to power in 1985, he adopted a gentle policy toward religious organizations and in 1987 called for a release of religious prisoners. In the March 1988 consultation between government officials and church leaders, which happened to coincide with the celebration of a millennium of Christianity in Russia, major changes for the churches were charted, and in a historic meeting between Gorbachev and church leaders on April 29, 1988, the walls of government repression began to tumble down. New rules allowed churches to run themselves democratically, through assemblies established on a parish, diocese, and national level. In 1989, for the first time since the revolution in 1917, several Orthodox clergy were elected to parliament.

The complete restoration of religious freedom in the Soviet Union came in 1990 with the passage of the Freedom of Conscience and Religious Organizations Act on October 9. On November 10, 1990, the Russian Federation passed the even more comprehensive Law on Freedom of Worship. Both gave free reign to religious leaders and religious institutions. The election of a new patriarch in 1990 was accomplished without interference from the state for the first time since the Bolshevik revolution, and the choice of sixty-one-year-old Metropolitan Aleksy of Leningrad over the acting patriarch, Metropolitan Filaret of Kiev, a hardliner described as a "KGB puppet," was regarded as a victory for freedom and reform.[8]

The church had little time to enjoy its newfound freedom, however, for it was drawn into the turmoil of new nationalist movements surrounding the breakup of the Soviet Union on New Year's Day 1992. In Russia today, the relation of the church to Russian nationalism is complicated because of its on-again, off-again co-optation by the state over the years. The exploitation of the church by Stalin during his attempts at Russification has kept it from becoming the symbol of nationalism that religion has become in many other parts of the former Soviet Union.[9] And in some parts of the former Soviet empire, such as Ukraine, the Orthodox Church is part of a Soviet past that new religious nationalists are seeking to expunge. Even so, the church's symbols of nationalism—such as its concept of the Russian people as a united religious community— were exploited by the politicians who surfaced in the wake of Russia's independence in 1992. One deputy in the Russian legislature predicted that the church would now play "a great economic and political role."[10]

Russia, then, may eventually find itself affected politically by the spiritual wave breaking over other areas of the former Soviet Union, where religion is enjoying a peculiar sort of revival. On the one hand, the free expression of religion is part of the burst of democracy that is bringing the citizens of former Soviet states closer to their counterparts in the West. On the other hand, however, their religious affiliations link them with nationalist identities of a bygone era. Through religion, they are able to revive the past.

Religious Revival in Mongolia

"Communism tried to conquer religion," the founder of a new Mongolian religious party told me. "But now," he proudly asserted, "religion is replacing communism."[11] This claim of S. Bayant-sagaan, president of the Association of Mongolian Believers, is somewhat exaggerated because many of Mongolia's old socialist leaders are still very much in power, and his own party thus far has only a limited following. But he is correct in stating that the old ideology has lost its force, and a new public consciousness is emerging in Mongolia—one that compounds nationalism and religion, and replaces Marxism as the legitimizing force in public life. In this sense, what is happening in Mongolia is paradigmatic of what is occurring throughout the former Soviet Union and its client states.

As elsewhere in the region, much of the force of new nationalism is fueled by a pent-up hostility against what was regarded by many as a long period of Russian colonialism. In Ulan Bator,[12] a research historian for the government archives who is a member of the ruling socialist party—the Mongolian People's Revolutionary Party—was adamant in claiming that her party was not communist. It was founded before it came under Russian communist influence, she told me, and now the truth could come out about how her party had been "exploited and controlled" by the Russians all these years.[13]

The colonial control of the Russians was a mixed blessing, she explained, offering the architecture of the city as an illustration of how the benefits of Russian economic support were purchased at the expense of Mongolian national identity and pride. In the middle of a barren, wind-swept valley that rises above the chilly emptiness of the Gobi desert is the new center of Ulan Bator, which appears to be almost a movie set of a modern Soviet city. Row after row of sturdy Soviet institutional buildings line the broad streets, punctuated by statues of Lenin and Mongolian revolutionary heroes. Behind these mammoth concrete showcases are bland cinderblock apartment houses, and behind them the teepeelike *ghers*, also known by their Russian name, *yurts*. It is in these round tents—made of woolen felt and canvas covering a latticed wood frame—that most Mongolians live. A pictorial map of the city portraying Ulan Bator at the turn of the century shows that it once consisted mostly of *ghers* and magnificent complexes of Buddhist temples and monasteries. At the time of the Mongolian revolution in 1921 there were said to have been almost a thousand monasteries in the country and 120,000 lamas—roughly 40 percent of the mature male population at that time.[14] Because a fourth of the country's population lives in the major city, Ulan Bator, many of the temples were located there.

Almost all these magnificent old temple buildings—some constructed in a circular, Mongolian style, and others in an elaborate Tibetan fashion—came tumbling down as the entire downtown area of Ulan Bator was leveled, and sturdy Soviet-style monoliths were constructed in their place. The only temple complex to escape the Soviet wrecking ball was the Gandan Tegchinlen Monastery, the center of Mongolian Buddhism, which is located on a knoll on the outskirts of the Ulan Bator valley. Even there, the population of monks shrank from several hundred to under a hundred, and during Stalin's most repressive assaults against religious institutions throughout the Soviet world, the monastery virtually closed its doors.

Now the Gandan monastery is open again, packed with worshipers on weekends and holy days; the number of lamas expanded from 100 to 250 in less than two years. Many of the newcomers are "hidden lamas," men who had been lamas years ago and were forced to go back to ordinary society when their monasteries were closed, and young monks who have been ordained in secret. In fact, more new lamas are demanding a place in the monasteries than the monasteries have room for, and newly organized neighborhood monasteries are springing up all over the country. These new lamas include women as well as men, although the authorities are as yet undecided about whether to give the women full monastic ordination. In general, the authorities at Gandan are concerned about quality control in these new organizations. A council has recently been instituted to set standards for monastic life and to decide where new monasteries should be located.[15]

The rise of monastic organizations and the resurgence of Mongolian nationalism are related to one another. "Mongolian identity and its religion cannot be separated," the deputy head lama of Gandan monastery remarked to me in a matter-of-fact way.[16] Although no one in Mongolia would doubt this assertion, it strikes the outsider as being a little odd: the religion of Mongolia, after all, is Tibetan—the "yellow-hat" school of Vajrayana, or Tibetan, Buddhism—and one of the standards of monastic life is the ability to function in Tibetan as the canonical language of the tradition. Every major temple in Mongolia has a throne for Tibet's exiled leader, the Dalai Lama, to sit on, and when he does—as he has on three visits to the temple of the Gandan monastery—the seat becomes blessed.

The highest spiritual authorities in Mongolia, therefore, come from outside the country. In 1989, shortly before the political climate rapidly changed, the Indian government attempted to help the Mongolian Buddhist authorities bring a famous Tibetan spiritual leader into the country. He was an incarnate spiritual being, a bakula, and the last of a lineage of seventeen. He was living in India, and the socialist authorities of Mongolia would not allow him a visa. The Indian government officials hit on a clever scheme, however: they made him the Indian ambassador to Mongolia, which enabled him to enter the country with diplomatic privileges. He has lived in Ulan Bator ever since, where he holds spiritual court every Saturday in the Indian Embassy and helps to provide religious guidance for the country's expanding Buddhist institutions.[17]

What makes the country's Buddhism distinctively Mongolian, therefore, is not the tenets of the faith but the history of its religious institutions, which is intertwined with Mongolia's national history. The people of Mongolia are ethnically mixed, but their language, and probably their basic ethnic stock, is Altaic and can be traced to a culture that stretches from Turkey to Manchuria, a cultural band that separates the Euro-Russians in the Northwest from the Han Chinese in the Southeast. Their religion, however, they acquired on their own.

According to the traditional history as recalled by the monks in Ulan Bator, Mahayana Buddhism came to Mongolia via the Silk Road in the century before the time of Christ.[18] Over the centuries other religious influences followed the same route. Each of these religious traditions left its mark: Manicheanism, Nestorian Christianity, and Islam. The arrival of Tibetan Buddhism in the thirteenth century is attributed by the monks to the great Mongolian ruler Genghis Khan (1162–1227), whose adventures took him throughout Central Asia.[19] Later in the thirteenth century one of Genghis Khan's descendants, Kublai Khan, ruled from China to Russia and named a lama in Beijing as the head of the Buddhist faith for Tibet, Mongolia, and

China.[20] In the seventeenth to nineteenth centuries, when the tables were turned and the Manchu Ch'ing dynasty dominated Mongolia, the Mongolians held to Tibetan Buddhist tradition as a bulwark against Chinese cultural influences.

The departure of the Manchu governor in 1911 from what was then called Urga (Ulan Bator) marked the beginning of modern, independent Mongolia.[21] It also marked the advent of Mongolia's brief experiment with theocracy. On December 16, 1911, Mongolia's hereditary Buddhist leader, Bogda Gegeen Javdzandamba Hutagt, was proclaimed the new khan of Mongolia. Like the Dalai Lama in Tibet, he was regarded as possessing both secular and spiritual authority. Although the local leaders of the section of Mongolia that lay to the southeast of Ulan Bator, across the Gobi desert, preferred to unite with their kinfolk under the leadership of the Bogda Khan, both Russia and China wished to keep independent Mongolia as small as possible, and the southeastern part of Mongolia—Inner Mongolia—remained, as it does today, a part of China.[22]

In the northern, independent part of the country—Outer Mongolia—the Bogda Khan's theocratic rule was short-lived. It was preoccupied with a military threat from the Chinese, who in 1919 set up a command post in Ulan Bator. Help appeared to come from a White Russian cavalry unit, which entered Mongolia with Japanese support and attempted to oust the Chinese and reinstall the Bogda Khan. But the picture was complicated by yet another group of Mongolians attempting to defeat the Chinese and set up its own secular, working-class rule. These Mongolian revolutionaries, led by Sühbaatar, were no friends of either the Bogda Khan or the White Russians; they were supported by the new Communist government in Moscow.

Ultimately the new group—the Mongolian People's Revolutionary Party (MPRP)—won this three-way tussle. However, the intervention of the Red Army was necessary. With its help, the MPRP drove the Chinese back across the Gobi, and the White Russian cavalry was defeated. On July 11, 1921, the new government came to power, and that date has been proclaimed Mongolian National Day. One of the first acts of the new government was to request the Russian troops to stay on for a while to help restore order.

Needless to say, the Russian troops managed to extend their stay for another seventy years. At first the religious institutions of the country were respected, and the Bogda Khan retained his title, although little of his secular power. When the Bogda Khan died in 1924, his palace across the river from the center of Ulan Bator was turned into a museum, and the country was proclaimed a republic. The new leader of the MPRP, Choybalsan, was a more determined socialist than his predecessor had been and began to turn the country in a distinctly Stalinist direction. The 1926 Law of Separation of Religion from the State called for protection of the Buddhist faith, but it also aimed to "liberate the population from religious prejudice."[23] Mongolia became de facto a part of the Soviet Union. During the so-called Leftist Deviation of 1929–32, Choybalsan and his colleagues appropriated many of the huge monastic properties— *jas*—and suspended the operations of many other religious institutions as well. Atheism became a state policy.

Choybalsan's long career came to an end at his death in 1952. He was succeeded by Tsendenbal, who enforced one aspect of Stalin's Russification program that had heretofore been resisted in Mongolia: the use of the Russian Cyrillic alphabet rather than the strange, vertical cursive script used for centuries by the Mongolians, who had borrowed it from the Uigurs in the thirteenth century. In other ways, however, Tsendenbal was a rather bland, bureaucratic leader, and although he carried out Khrushchev's antireligious campaigns in the 1960s, his focus was more on "superstitious" religious folk practices than on Buddhist organizations; in 1979 he allowed the Dalai Lama to make a brief but triumphant visit to Ulan Bator.[24] By 1984, when Tsendenbal was succeeded by Batmönh, the leadership was facing a rising swell of nationalism and religious resurgence at home, and the beginnings of Gorbachev's restructuring in the patron state to the north.

The old system began to crumble in December 1989.[25] Massive demonstrations in the main square in front of the parliament building in Ulan Bator were followed in February 1990 with hunger strikes by ardent young activists who demanded the democratization of Mongolia. In March 1990, to everyone's surprise, the government capitulated and called for open elections in June of that year. As the MPRP reorganized to meet the election challenge, it removed virtually every senior party leader and government official from power. The new leader of the party, D. Bayambsuren, who advocated democratic reform, economic opportunity, and human rights, was overwhelmingly elected.[26]

The party lived up to its promises. In the two years that followed, a rash of new political parties were formed, newspapers were allowed to openly criticize the government, the old Mongolian script was back in fashion, and, most important, a new constitution guaranteed these freedoms and allowed for democratic elections and private ownership. Long before the Russian government adopted the idea, the Mongolian government instituted a system of vouchers, which were distributed equally to all its citizens, allowing them to "purchase" stocks in formerly state-owned companies or in private businesses, thereby, as one of Mongolia's economists described it, "creating an economic system from nothing."[27]

In 1991, in a burst of democratic enthusiasm, a crowd of young people attacked and destroyed a statue of Stalin, replacing it for a time with a talismanlike stone, which some regarded as having spiritual powers. This act was symbolic in several ways. The most obvious was the replacement of the most vicious symbol of Russian colonialism with a natively Mongolian symbol. Moreover, two other nearby statues were ignored. In the central square, the statue of Sühbaatar, the founding leader of the MPRP, is unblemished. Directly in front of Mongolia State University—a particularly vulnerable location—the statue of Choybalsan, "Mongolia's Stalin," is largely untouched as well. From time to time, I was told by university officials, graffiti and spray paint mar the statue's base, but for the most part students leave it alone.[28] Even though Choybalsan was excessive, he was still a Mongolian, and for that reason, if for none other, he deserves respect.

This same spirit of nationalism pervades the new constitution (the Yassa) ratified early in 1992. Its preamble contains some familiar phrases, but it carries a distinctively nationalist slant: "We, the people of Mongolia, cherishing human rights, freedoms, justice, and the national unity; inheriting the national statehood, the traditions of its history and culture; strengthening the independence and the sovereignty of the nation; respecting the civilization of mankind; and desiring to develop a humane and democratic society in the land of Mongolia, hereby proclaim the State Yassa as the Constitution of the State."[29]

The drafting committee seriously considered a clause that would have proclaimed Buddhism the state religion but ultimately rejected the idea in favor of the more vague wording respecting "the traditions of [Mongolia's] history and culture." Despite this show of support for traditional religion, the constitution explicitly prohibits monasteries from assuming political power. Presumably this clause is intended to guard against the resumption of the sort of theocratic power once enjoyed by the Bogda Khan.

There is good reason to be concerned. A new Bogda Khan was identified some years ago by the Dalai Lama and today lives in New Delhi.[30] Quite a few Mongolians are ready to vault him back into power, and many of them demand that the government allow him to take up residence in Ulan Bator. "We need a spiritual center," one Buddhist activist explained, "and even if he is not yet allowed to have political power, he will give spiritual direction to the nation."[31] The government, however, is not eager to deal with the potential political consequences of such a significant immigrant. It already has its hands full with the explosion of religious activity throughout the country.[32]

In the past, the government controlled religion by allowing a moderate expression of it in the Gandan monastery and by setting up a showcase international Buddhist organization, the Asian Buddhist Conference for Peace (ABCP), the headquarters of which were located in the monastery. The general secretary of the organization, G. Lubsantseren, is a scholar of Buddhist philosophy who is also a member of the MPRP. He once wrote articles offering a Marxist critique of Buddhism.[33] Today, however, the government funding for ABCP has been drastically reduced, and its offices have been moved from Gandan monastery. Lubsantseren, who claims that he was never really an atheist, is considering new projects, such as founding an international institute of Buddhist studies.[34]

Such government-sponsored Buddhist organizations as ABCP became obsolete as the traditional centers of Buddhism flourished after 1990. The number of lamas in Gandan monastery doubled from 1990 to 1992. The monastery, however, continues to play a moderating role in Buddhist affairs. Choiyal, the one lama elected in 1990 to the Mongolian parliament, the Great Hural, is a member of Gandan. He ran on an independent slate and is said to enjoy the ruling party's confidence.

The growth of new monastic organizations outside Gandan's au-

thority has tested it more than the government. Many of these
upstart monasteries are nothing more than small neighborhood
clubs, the *gher* equivalents of storefront churches. A more serious
challenge has come from the former deputy head lama of Gandan
monastery, C. Dambajav, who hurried back to Ulan Bator from
Dharamsala, India, where he had been studying with the Dalai
Lama during the time of the 1989–90 uprising, to found his own
separate monastic organization.

Dambajav located several old monastic buildings in the heart of
Ulan Bator that had somehow escaped the Soviet wreckers. These
round, tent-like wooden buildings situated behind several high-
rise apartment buildings had fallen into disrepair. Two were used as
storage facilities; a third had become the training gymnasium for
young aspirants to the Mongolian circus. Dambajav set up an office
adjacent to the circus gymnasium and began transforming the storage buildings into Tibetan Buddhist temples. His Tashichoeling
Monastery now has a hundred lamas, and he plans to make room
for many more. Conveniently located in the heart of the city and
run in an enthusiastic, youthful style, the monastery has become
popular among the urban faithful. Considering its rate of growth, it
could overtake Gandan in size and popularity. Dambajav told me
that Buddhism in Mongolia was "a sleeping giant" that was only
beginning to realize its potential.[35]

Both Gandan and government authorities have been concerned
about Dambajav's own potential, however, and have taken steps to
channel his power. Through the mediation of the Indian ambassador cum rinpoche, various Buddhist leaders were brought together
late in 1991, including Dambajav and the Gandan hierarchy, to
form a governing council—or rather a series of regional councils,
each of which would be represented on the national council.
Dambajav was appointed head of the Ulan Bator division, which
thereby gave him a seat on the national panel, of which the head
lama of Gandan monastery was appointed chair. Thus both leaders
received status and a hierarchical relationship.

As far as secular politics is concerned, Dambajav has been cir-
cumspect about the role that monasteries should play. He told me
that he has not ruled out political involvement for lamas. Ordinarily, however, he feels that Buddhism as a religion has only two
roles to play in Mongolian political life: it provides "social values,"

and it gives a locus of "national identity."[36] Any sincere Buddhist layperson—even a member of the MPRP—can bring these characteristics to public life. As long as they support Buddhist nationalism there is not yet a need for a separate Buddhist political party.

Other Buddhists, even more radical than Dambajav, disagree. Many of them may be found outside the main gate of Gandan monastery, where a rough wooden-plank fence demarcates a section of bare earth on which a cluster of felt and canvas-covered *ghers* have been constructed. These serve as the headquarters of the Association of Buddhist Believers and its allied political arm, the Mongolian Buddhist Party. Their founder, Bayantsagaan, graduated from the theological seminary of Gandan monastery in the late 1970s, but because opportunities to become a monk were limited in those days, he became a research scholar in Buddhist philosophy for the Institute of Oriental Studies in the state's Academy of Sciences. In 1990, when Mongolia was undergoing its political changes, he heard reports of new Islamic and Christian religious parties being formed in other former Soviet states and felt that the time was ripe for a similar, Buddhist party to be established in Mongolia.[37]

Bayantsagaan claims over a hundred thousand registered members in the association and its political party. In a nation of two million, this is not yet enough to constitute a serious electoral threat. Shortly before the June 28, 1992, elections, he told me that he hoped his party would gain three or four seats out of the seventy-six contested, but in fact the party failed to gain any at all. Despite this personal defeat, Bayantsagaan was pleased with the modest success of several democratic opposition parties with which he is allied; they won five seats.[38] And he has no regrets for the time spent campaigning. He feels that the 1992 electoral campaign helped him build an audience for his message, which, simply put, is one of Buddhist political power. Until the last vestige of the old secular socialism is rooted out, he feels that Buddhism will be in danger and that is the reason Buddhist politics is so necessary.

When I asked him whether he longed for the restoration of the Bogda Khan in all his imperial power, Bayantsagaan responded, "Of course." Realizing this was not an immediate possibility, however, he stated that as many religious people should be elected to parliament as possible: preferably "half the deputies in the Great Hural," he said, "should be lamas."[39] Eventually, however, a Buddhist state would not need such devices as parliaments. The lamas could rule directly. "This would not constitute a theocracy, however," he hastened to explain, in answer to my query, "because Buddhism is by nature democratic." When I pressed him on this point, he explained that democracy essentially means "respect of man for others," and in that sense "Buddhism is the highest form of democracy."[40] Because the 1990s promises to be the decade of revival for both Buddhism and democracy in Mongolia, it remains to be seen just how compatible the two will be.

Islamic Nationalism in Central Asia

Shortly after April 25, 1992, when Kabul, the capital of Afghanistan, fell to Islamic guerrilla fighters associated with the Jamiat-i-Islami (Islamic Society), the Hezb-i-Islami (Islamic Party), and other rebel cadres known collectively as the Mujahadin (Fighters), the country was proclaimed an Islamic republic, and the crowds in the streets roared their approval with the cry "God is great."[41] From the rebels' point of view, they had finally been successful in ousting the secular communist leaders who at one time had been propped up by Soviet colonial military forces. Islam had won. An Islamic scholar, Sibghatullah Mojaddidi (Mojadedi), was installed as the interim president, and although rival Muslim groups continued to struggle for power with one another after the coup, the new government was able to begin the process of Islamicizing the Afghani legal code: it promulgated a series of laws enforcing Muslim customs, including a ban on alcohol, the requirement that women wear veils in public, and the use of flogging, amputations, and other forms of punishment prescribed by Islamic law.[42]

Perhaps nowhere was the news from Kabul greeted with greater trepidation than in the capitals of the Central Asian republics—Uzbekistan, Turkmenistan, Kazakhstan, Tajikistan, and Kyrgyzstan—and in areas west of the Caspian Sea, including Azerbaijan and Russia's Dagestan and Tatar.[43] Everything that the Muslim rebels in Afghanistan said about their country could be said about theirs. Like the Afghan government, their governments were largely secular and communist, formerly backed by a Soviet military and economic power that is easily characterized as imperial in its attitudes and designs. As in Afghanistan, groups of Muslim nationalists in each of the Central Asian republics and Russian Muslim regions were eager to take the secular leaders' place and create Islamic states.[44]

The fears of the secular leaders were warranted. Less than two weeks after the fall of Kabul, a coalition of democratic politicians and Muslim activists formed a Revolutionary Council and seized power in Dushanbe, the capital of Tajikistan. On May 7, 1992, the old Communist leader, Rakhman Nabiyev, barricaded himself inside the KGB headquarters and the new leaders proclaimed Tajikistan a democratic Muslim state. Again, as in Kabul, the crowds roared in response the slogan, *Allahu akbar,* "God is great."[45]

Islamic rule is no stranger to the vast region of Central Asia to the south of Russia, which is home to some fifty million Muslims. These Muslims were all but ignored by the outside world during the heyday of the Soviet Union, even though their numbers made the Soviet Union the fifth largest Muslim nation in the world (following Indonesia, Pakistan, Bangladesh, and India). Although each of the countries has its own identity—and its own cultural nationalism—the region as a whole is a part of an area known as Turkestan, which briefly in the pre-Soviet era was a nation of its own (not to be confused with Turkmenistan, which is only one of the present-day Central Asian nations). Some Islamic nationalists in the region see the revival of the nation of Turkestan as the wave of the future. The cultural area known as Turkestan reached beyond the boundaries of the five countries currently in Central Asia—the Xinjiang region of China, for instance, is known as East Turkestan—so the attempt to revive the nation would have international implications.

"In my lifetime," the founder of Uzbekistan's Islamic political movement, Birlik (Unity), claimed, "there will be a Turkestan that extends beyond Central Asia."[46] Other Muslim leaders in Kazakhstan and Uzbekistan are said to "dream of a Central Asian empire" united by an "Islamic radicalism."[47] In the Uzbekistan capital of Tashkent, the senior Muslim cleric of Central Asia proposed dismantling borders of the separate states and reviving Turkestan once again.[48] Although Turkestan was only briefly a political entity, the idea of it remains a powerful image of Central Asian unity.

Thus the issue of religious nationalism in Central Asia is really two issues. One is whether Muslim nationalists within each of the five Central Asian nations have sufficient force to challenge the secular order—the order that is often led by old Communists who have adopted a new, democratic posture. The other is whether the various religious nationalists in the region will be able to come together under a common banner, even if it is a loose federation of states.

Both these forms of religious nationalism are fueled by strong feelings of anticommunism. The deep disdain of communism in the region is in part because it oppressed Islam; in part because, despite Lenin's policy of divide and rule, it painted over all the traditional ethnic identities with the same gray Soviet brush; and in part because that imposed Soviet ideology was perceived as being the agent of Russian imperialism. Thus the antisecularism of the region is to a large degree a protest against the years of what is regarded as Russian colonialism.

In a newly opened Islamic school (*madrasah*) in the old Muslim capital of Bukhara in Uzbekistan, several students made explicit the link between communism and Russian colonialism. In Soviet days, they explained, the dead were not allowed to be buried in a shroud. "Why is it communist to be buried in a coffin," one of them asked, "but not in a shroud?"[49] The same pattern of prejudice was to be seen in the restrictions on married women covering their heads, the outlawing of the practice of circumcision, and the encouragement to eat pork. "As is well known," one of the students said sarcastically, "pork is socialist, while *pilaf* [a central Asian rice dish] is not."[50]

Among other reasons, the Uzbek students, and many other citizens of Central Asian nations, disdained Russian colonialism because their own Altaic cultural and ethnic heritage is tied to Turkey (and Iran, in the case of Tajikistan) rather than Russia. At one time, in fact, Central Asia was the cultural seat of an Islamic empire that controlled Russia, and the history of the region is clouded by the competition for domination between Turkic Muslims in the south and Christian Russians in the north.

The early history of the region is complicated. Before the time of Christ the Greeks were aware of a great kingdom, Bactria, in the area that is now Central Asia, and shortly after the time of Christ the Central Asian region, like Mongolia, became subject to a variety of influences from the south. Along the Silk Road that came from India and the Middle East traveled Buddhists, Zoroastrians, Manicheans, and Nestorian Christians, and Central Asia was affected by all of them.

Islam also came to the region from the southwest, arriving from the Middle East in the seventh century.[51] By 639 C.E. Arabs had conquered Azerbaijan, and by 642 Dagestan was Arab territory. In 673, the Arabs crossed the Amu Darya River and laid seige to the city of Bukhara, now in Uzbekistan. During the first decades of the next century the conquests were completed, although it took several hundred years for Islam to take root among the Central Asian masses. From the ninth to sixteenth centuries, Central Asia housed one of the most prestigious cultural centers of the Muslim world. The city of Samarkand—today in Uzbekistan—flourished during the Abassid dynasty, and the great mosques and madrassahs (Islamic schools) of Samarkand and Bukhara served as Islam's easternmost outpost. From there Islam traveled north on the so-called Fur Road along the Volga River, and east via the Silk Road into China. Although the region fell under the hegemony of the Mongol Empire in the thirteenth and fourteenth centuries, the Buddhist Mongols were not able to shake the Central Asians' dedication to Islam, which survived in part through Sufi brotherhoods and lay activities. In the late fourteenth century, Mongol sovereigns of the Golden Horde and the Chagatai Khanate had become Muslim themselves, and Islam again flourished throughout Central Asia and beyond. From the thirteenth to the sixteenth centuries Russia was under Tatar domination—and to this day it is the only Christian nation besides Spain to have been under prolonged Muslim rule.

In the mid-fourteenth century, Moscow began to fight back against the Golden Horde, and by the sixteenth century the Russians were sufficiently free from external domination to attempt to purge Russia of Muslim influences. From 1565 on, Muslims began to be converted to Christianity by force. The major departure from this anti-Muslim stand of Russian rulers was provided by Catherine II, who in the eighteenth century protected the Volga River Tatars from persecution and encouraged the spread of Islam in the outlying regions, where, she felt, it helped to civilize such people as the Bashkir and Kazakhs. Most areas of Central Asia, including the regions around Chimkent, Tashkent, and Bukhara, were brought under Russian control in the latter half of the nineteenth century, but there was no significant attempt to Christianize or Russify the population at that time. The region became known as Russian Turkestan.[52]

After the Bolshevik revolution, leaders of the region imagined that they could now be free from Russian control, and in 1918 they declared a new state, the Turkestan Independent Islamic Republic. Needless to say, the new Communist government had no intention of letting any republic in the union, much less an Islamic one, remain autonomous, and by 1925 the independence movement was crushed. The region became firmly a part of the Soviet system, and Russian Turkestan was transformed into the five republics of Soviet Central Asia.[53]

Initially, many Muslim leaders joined the Communist cause, but after 1928, when antireligious policies were promulgated throughout the Soviet Union, Islam and Marxism parted ways, and Muslim clergy were imprisoned. During the war, when Stalin relaxed his repression against religion, Islam experienced a temporary revival. From 1959 to 1964, however, Khrushchev's offensive against religion was a serious blow to Central Asian Islam. The number of mosques dropped to fewer than 500 in 1968; at one time, in 1912, there had been over 26,000. From 1982 to 1985, Central Asian Muslims suffered yet another wave of anti-Islamic sentiment because of the Soviet Union's war in Afghanistan. The end of the war and the ascendance of Gorbachev to power in 1985 brought significant changes. From 1988 on, Islam underwent an enormous revival throughout Central Asia, spurred on by the breakup of the Soviet Union and the creation of new, independent states in Central Asia in 1991–92.

The expansion of Islam after 1988 was built on an Islamic organizational framework created during the Soviet era. During the 1940s, two spiritual directorates were created to lead Muslim religious organizations throughout the Soviet Union. One was established in Ufa (in Bashkir) to cover European Russia, and another in Tashkent (in Uzbekistan) for Central Asia. A few years later, two more directorates were created: one in Baku (in Azerbaijan) for Transcaucasia (administering both Sunni and Shi'a congregations), and another in Makhachkala (in Dagestan) for the northern Caucasus region. Each of these directorates was led by a mufti—or, in the case of Baku, a sheik. The mufti of Tashkent was de facto the leader of them all. In 1956 an Islamic school was opened in Bukhara, in Uzbekistan; and in 1971 another was opened in Tashkent.

The tentative revival of Islam after 1988 had turned by 1992 into a torrent of new Islamic activities: the establishment of mosques, seminaries, Islamic courts, and political parties. In Uzbekistan there were only eighty mosques in the whole of the country in 1988. By the end of 1991 there were several thousand—over 1,000 in one of the country's twelve regions alone. According to some estimates, on average ten new mosques were opened every day in 1991 throughout Central Asia.[54]

The official spiritual directorates have not fared well in this revival. In Tashkent, a new chief mufti of the directorate established his own television show in 1990 to promote Islamic teachings.[55] But he was also accused of selling for profit some of the one million Korans that had been donated to his office by Saudi Arabia for free distribution.[56] His fellow mullahs attempted to oust him from office, and the qazi of Alma Ata in Kazakhstan defied his authority and set himself up as the grand mufti of Kazakhstan.[57] The Communist government in Uzbekistan, fearing the rise of more militant new Islamic leaders, kept the Tashkent mufti in office. This government support did little to shore up his credibility among the masses, who already regarded many of the old-guard Muslim officials as colonial Russian errand boys.

The Communists' fear of Islam is understandable. When a Muslim leader in Tajikistan asserted that his country had entered into an "ideological struggle" between Islam and communism, he was referring to the efforts of the secular government—led by reformed Communist leaders—to keep Islamic political parties from seizing power.[58] Islam is a serious threat to the secular governments of Central Asian nations, for without the ideological underpinnings of Marxist theory and the military and economic support of the Soviet Union, they have little on which to base their political power. Some of the old Communists have turned to nationalism as a basis of support, but the boundaries of the five nations of Central Asia were loosely drawn and encompass a variety of ethnicities. For that reason it is difficult to establish what is specifically Uzbek about Uzbekistan, for example, as opposed to what is Tajik or Kyrgyz.

Islam appears to unite all Central Asians, but it also divides them along the various lines within the religion, for the revival of Islam mixes easily with populist politics. National identities are linked to particular forms of religious identities—Shi'ite, Sunni, Sufi—all of them Muslim. Even some of the old Communists claim to have renewed their affiliations with their Muslim heritage. "In the past," a Muslim leader in Kyrgyzstan complained, "they lectured on atheism, but now they wear turbans and have become mullahs."[59] Most Islamic politicians were Muslims before they became politicians, however, and their religious politics are extensions of their anti-Communist and anti-Russian attitudes. Most of them are also ethnic nationalists, and they are not necessarily rushing to re-create the old, united Turkestan. Instead, the Muslim activists of Central Asia have attempted to use their new political power to build a nationalist constituency in each of the five emerging nation-states.

In Uzbekistan, the most populous country in the region, the government has taken the threat of Islamic activists seriously and banned all religious political parties.[60] Although Uzbekistan's president, Islam Karimov, attempted to woo Muslim support by allying with the discredited head mufti of Tashkent, the Muslim masses are not easily impressed with this attempt at cooptation. Instead, many of them support the popular Birlik movement, which regards itself as an Islamic democratic movement, and the Islamic Renaissance Party, which calls for the overthrow of communism and the creation of an Islamic republic. According to one of its members, it seeks to establish "a theocratic state run by the clergy" but also insists that it, like Birlik, is in favor of "an Islamic democracy."[61] Since the 1970s underground Islamic groups have been organizing against the government, but they remained outlawed until October 1991, when Uzbekistan relaxed the ban slightly, allowing Birlik and other groups to be legally registered as religious organizations. Yet the government still prohibits it and the Islamic Renaissance Party from running candidates for office. For that matter, Uzbekistan bans all clergy of whatever faith from running for office regardless of which party endorses them.

In adjacent Tajikistan, prior to the 1992 coup, Islamic political parties were also banned.[62] The Communist leader there, Rakhman Nabiyev, a party boss during the Brezhnev era who was edged out of power in 1985, returned to leadership in 1990 and was again hounded out of office in September 1991—this time by means of public demonstrations held in front of the parliament and involving the building of a tent city with materials supplied by the central mosque. Two months later open elections allowed a variety of parties, including some Islamic groups, to contend for the first time: among them were the secular Democratic movement, a moderate Muslim movement known simply as the Renaissance, and Tajikistan's version of the radical Islamic Renaissance movement. The Islamic Renaissance received support from militant Islamic leaders of the Mujahadin movement across the border in neighboring Afghanistan.[63] Despite accusations of voter fraud, Nabiyev was reelected by a 57 percent majority, and some speculated that in order to win he must have made a deal with the Islamic parties.[64] Whether he did or not, the Muslim politicians were biding their time for a more propitious moment to strike for political power.

Their time came in May 1992, with a wave of public demonstrations against the government. A Muslim guerrilla band was formed to counter the Tajik army, and the majority of the members of Nabiyev's own Council of Ministers abandoned him for the opposition. The triumphant rebel coalition, led by the Islamic Renaissance Party and secular democrats, hastily formed a Revolutionary Council. But as the year wore on, the confrontation between Islam and communism became part of a civil war between competing regions in the southern part of the country.

The Islamic revolution in Tajikistan turned out to be short-lived. By December 1992, pro-communist leaders associated with the Kulyab region took control and purged the capital of Islamic political activists. In 1993 the backlash against the Islamic opposition was so violent that Muslim leaders, fleeing to Russia and Afghanistan, described it as "genocide."

One of the key leaders in Tajikistan's brief Islamic revolution was Qazi Hajji Akbar Turadzhonzoda, a thirty-seven-year-old activist who operated out of his office in the main mosque of Dushanbe, utilizing a cellular phone and a fax machine.[65] A pragmatist, the qazi stated that although Islam would play a role in the new government, it would be a limited one; he did not want Tajikistan to become a new Iran. Even though Tajiks are ethnically linked with Persians, the qazi explained, they are sunni rather than shi'a, which means that it is "very difficult for a Khomeini-style figure to impose his views on everyone else."[66] Moreover, he said, he wanted to work in harmony with "the entire free world."[67] On an earlier occasion he explained that he did not want "the same thing to happen to the Islamic revolution that happened to the Communist revolution." By that he meant that he did not want his state to become "isolated" from the rest of the world.[68]

In the other three Central Asian nations, Islamic politics are more subdued. In the vast region of Kazakhstan in the north, where almost as many residents are ethnically Russian as are Kazakh, and the old Communist Party (now called the Socialist Party) holds 338 of the 358 seats in parliament, one small Islamic political party, Alash, yearns for a government based on Islamic law.[69] Although it is not banned, it is barred from running candidates for office, and seven of its leaders were arrested in March 1992 for "insulting" Kazakhstan's president, Nursultan Nazarbayev.[70]

In Kyrgyzstan, near the Chinese border, the reformed branch of the Communist Party, led by President Askar A. Akayev, is outspokenly in favor of the democratic system and has joined forces with moderate Muslims in the non-communist Democratic Movement to defeat Communist hardliners.[71] A more radical Islamic movement remains in the background: the outlawed Sufi order known as the Hairy Ishans, who live in the lush Fergana Valley of Kyrgyzstan, and who have fought against communist influences in the region for most of this century.[72]

In Turkmenistan, the desert region of western Central Asia, Islam is a potent force in the countryside, but the prevailing Communist Party has managed to contain all efforts, Islamic or otherwise, at organizing an opposition to its rule. Because the country shares a long border with Iran, it has reason to be concerned about the potency of religion, and with that danger in mind Turkmenistan's president, Sapurmarad Niazov, has himself embraced Islam. He has also organized religious elders in helping to improve the social mores of the Turkmenistan population.[73]

Throughout Central Asia the stage is set for confrontation between secular politicians, many of them former Communists, and popular new Muslim leaders. However, the diverse Muslim political sentiments have not coalesced into a single Islamic position in any one of the five republics, much less throughout the whole region.[74] The Islamic Renaissance parties of Uzbekistan and Tajikistan and the Alash party in Kazakhstan called for a theocratic state run by the clergy, as did the Muslim seminary students in Tashkent. Yet other Muslim activists called for an Islamic democracy.

Some want to follow the Iranian model of Islamic revolution; others do not. Moderate Islamic leaders, such as the qazi in Tajikistan, called for Islamic social mores and Islamic nationalism in a non-theocratic state and, citing pragmatic considerations and ethnic differences within the Central Asian region, rejected the goal of Turkestan.

Yet a great many Muslim activists, spurred on by a revival of Turkish influence in the region, yearn for the union of Central Asia under the banner of an Islamic Republic of Turkestan. It is this specter, more than any other potential effect of Islamic domination, that secular nationalists in the region fear, for it would not only undercut their own power but also have ramifications outside the region: it would alter relationships with neighboring China, Afghanistan, and Iran. These fears have not prevented secular leaders from joining Islamic political alliances however. In February 1992 an economic-cooperation organization—nicknamed "the Islamic Common Market"—was formed by Iran, Turkey, Pakistan, Azerbaijan, and four of the Central Asian countries: Uzbekistan, Kyrgyzstan, Tajikistan, and Turkmenistan. Although it is doubtful whether this organization will be the precursor of an Islamic supernation—a united sphere of Islamic cultural and political hegemony in the region—it is certainly a sign of the hospitality and deep kinship that exists among proud but separate Islamic nations.

The Religious Rejection
of Socialism in Eastern Europe

In the Soviet republics of Eastern Europe and in the Eastern European nations under Soviet control, religion has also played a role in the resurgence of national identities. When I asked the official in charge of religious affairs in the Ukrainian government why it and so many of its neighboring states have turned to religion in their rejection of Soviet control, he explained that "it is due to a failure of ideology." Marxist and other secular ideologies have "failed," he explained, for they are not able to "touch the heart" the way ethnic and religious identities do.[75]

Whether or not Marxist ideology "failed," it is clear that it became unhappily tied to what was perceived as Russian imperialism. The liberalization of Soviet policies in the 1980s opened the floodgates for a lively expression of ethnic loyalties in Eastern Europe that only intensified after the end of the Soviet Union on New Year's Day in 1992. In such diverse locations as Lithuania, Armenia, East Germany, Poland, and Ukraine, religious movements were at the forefront of opposition to Soviet control and the emergence of new nationalisms. In a sense, these are old nationalisms; they trace their identities at least to the nineteenth century and in most cases much earlier. In their present form, however, these national identities are new: their combination of democratic popularism and cultural nationalism is a distinctive feature of the present age.

In the nations of Eastern Europe and the European republics of the former Soviet Union the patterns of religion and nationalism vary. In Romania and Hungary, for instance, despite the involvement of some rebellious young priests in nationalist movements, the church has been largely supportive of the authorities, not the dissidents.[76] In Romania, a group of young priests in the Romanian Orthodox Church helped lead the movement that toppled Nicolae Ceausescu in December 1989. In 1991, however, charges were made that the new spirit of Romanian nationalism was so closely identified with the Romanian Orthodox Church that members of the Catholic minority in the Romanian Uniate Church were suppressed; anti-Semitism was also on the rise.[77] In Czechoslovakia there has been no religious nationalism, in part because there has been no united Czechoslovakia.

In what used to be Yugoslavia, the confrontation among the Serbs, Croats, and Slovenes in 1991 and 1992 involved, among other things, a clash of religious loyalties. The Serbs are largely Orthodox Christians, and the Croats and Slovenes, Roman Catholics.[78] Priests in the Croatian Catholic Church have been at the forefront of the separatist movement in Croatia. To further complicate matters, the region of Bosnia-Herzegovina comprised an incendiary mixture of Serbs, Croats, and Muslims, which ignited into a bloody conflagration in 1992. The capital, Sarajevo, was a Muslim outpost under siege by the surrounding Serbs, and Muslims throughout the region were targets of "ethnic cleansing" by Serbs. Serbian leaders claimed that if Bosnia were allowed to become independent, its 44-percent-Muslim population would create a "fundamentalist state."[79]

In other Eastern European countries as well, national and religious identities have coalesced. In Albania, Muslim and Christian movements were part of the resurgence of an Albanian nationalist identity that began in 1990. In Latvia, a statue of Jesus Christ was installed in the space where a statue of Lenin had stood before being smashed to pieces in a mass rally shortly after the failed Soviet coup in August 1991.[80] Latvians, along with Estonians, have traditionally been Lutherans. Lithuanians identify with the Western-rite Catholic form of Christianity. The ambit of Eastern Orthodox Christianity contains many regional variations—the Georgian Orthodox Church, the Armenian Apostolic Church, and the like—and these have been involved in the nationalist movements in their countries. In other areas non-Orthodox Christianity has played that role. In Poland and Ukraine, for instance, local forms of Catholicism have played major roles in nationalist struggles against Moscow's hegemony.

In Poland, the Roman Catholic Church has historically been supportive of the Polish national cause—even more so after the Soviet occupation of Poland, when Polish nationalism and the religious rejection of socialism became allied. "Next to God," Poland's Stefan Cardinal Wyszyński proclaimed, "our first love is Poland."[81] This affection is reciprocated by the Polish people. When workers marched on the headquarters of the Communist Party in Poznan in 1956, they demanded "God and bread."[82] Their desire for economic security and religious freedom often expressed itself in support for the Church as a symbol of national independence and prosperity.

The Polish Church was linked with Polish national identity virtually from the beginning. It was founded in 966, when Duke Mieszko I, who had married a Czech princess from a Christian dynasty in Bohemia, embraced the faith himself and used it as the means to culturally unify the new entity of Poland, which he had created by consolidating several tribes into a new state. Significantly for the independence of the Polish Church, it was directly related to the Holy See in Rome rather than being affiliated with the episcopate based in Germany. During the eighteenth and nineteenth centuries, when Poland's territory was carved up and controlled by three neighboring powers, the Polish Church was one of the primary purveyors of the spirit of Polish nationalism. Its central role was especially evident during the czars' attempts to Russify the areas of Poland they controlled by forcing the churches to embrace the Orthodox faith. These unsuccessful attempts reinforced the image of the Polish Church as a bulwark of Polish nationalist culture.

After World War II, when Poland came under Soviet occupation, the state attempted to subjugate the power of the Church. In addition to limiting and controlling the clergy, the state attempted to rewrite history books to play down the role of the Church in Poland's history, an attempt that was attacked by the Church in a series of pastoral letters, sermons, and public statements. Cardinal Wyszyński became a symbol of the resistance. He was imprisoned for a period of time for refusing to follow the dictates of the government, and this refusal to capitulate strengthened the image of the Church as the patient guardian of Poland's independent nationalist interests.

At the outset of Soviet occupation the Church overtly supported opposition parties. It endorsed the Labor Party of Karol Popiel and supported attempts to create a confessional political party in opposition to the Communists. These attempts were stiffled by the government, which was determined that the Church have free reign only in matters of individual faith. The Church for its part was forced temporarily to retire from politics, and it concentrated instead on the celebration of its thousand-year anniversary in 1966.

The election of a Polish bishop as pope in 1978 was the occasion for a renewed emphasis on the political importance of the Polish Church. Almost at the same time the Solidarity labor movement emerged as a new mass base of power counterposed against the government. Although the Church was clearly supportive of Lech Walesa and his Solidarity movement, its independent stand allowed it to play a mediating role between the movement and the government during critical moments of confrontation. The government increasingly relied on the Church as a buffer against the most severe of the labor movement's actions; the labor movement, for its part, relied on the Church as its interpreter and defender vis-à-vis the government.

After Solidarity became established as an official party in 1980, Walesa and his colleagues became the vehicle of opposition against the government, rather than the Church. The Church continued to support Solidarity, however, and it developed new forms of resistance to what it regarded as an occupying Soviet colonial government. Outside of Poland, the Vatican's John Paul II was conspiring with President Ronald Reagan to keep Solidarity alive and to destabilize the Communist government.[83] Inside of Poland, new movements for liberation were forming within the Church. One of these, Wolnosc i Pokoj (Freedom and Peace), was founded in 1985 to encourage a new generation of Catholics to reject Soviet influence. It began with the refusal of a young Catholic to take the military oath, which included a pledge of loyalty to the Soviet Union. A band of his friends undertook a hunger strike at a church near Warsaw, and the new organization was formed. It based its ideas on the teaching of Pope John Paul II and put forward a broad platform of social reforms and pacifist ideals in addition to opposition to Soviet control.

The liberalization of Soviet policies, the withdrawal of the Soviets from Poland, and the new democratic elections in 1990 were rewards for the Church's patience. One of the leaders of Solidarity, Bogdan Cywinski, described the Polish Church as a "Julian Church," drawing a parallel with the Christian community that persevered during the persecutions of the Roman emperor Julian the Apostate.[84] After 1990, however, the Church became part of the establishment. The new government that swept into power with Walesa's victory voiced its indebtedness to the Church's support and pledged to support the Church's central role in Poland's national life. The Church has not achieved all its political objectives—the Polish legislature rejected a Church-supported bill that would have banned abortion—but in other matters, such as a new requirement that public schools must teach courses in religion, the Church has prevailed.

Ironically, once the nationalist aspirations of the Church were realized, the institution itself became increasingly peripheral to public life.[85] The Church faced rising anticlericalism in society and the implicit suggestion that with the triumph of nationalism the Church had shifted its allegiance from the oppressed to the new authorities. Yet the very openness of the new politics meant that the Church was not the only vehicle in Polish society for expressing feelings of nationalism and opposition to oppression. It retains that potential, however, and lies in wait for an opportunity sometime in the future to again play that role.

In Ukraine, Catholicism also played a role in the country's rejection of Russian domination and Soviet control, and the Church there continues to be at the forefront of nationalist causes. The religious culture of Ukraine is more complicated than that of Poland, but the Ukrainian Church has also traditionally resisted the imposition of religious control from Moscow, and, like the Polish Church, it has helped to lead the region's movement for liberation. The statement declaring Ukraine's independence on August 24, 1991, claimed "a thousand-year-old tradition of building statehood," which originated in the tenth century, when Vladimir the Great created a separate Ukrainian Church.[86]

This link between Ukrainian nationalism and religion has persisted to the present day, especially in Western Ukraine. The eastern part of the country contains a large percentage of Russians, most of whom are nominally Russian Orthodox. The residents of Western Ukraine have traditionally been Catholics—members of the Uniate Church, a Ukrainian branch of Catholicism—or members of a distinctly Ukrainian form of Orthodoxy. In Western Ukraine, therefore, the present religious competition is among three groups: Russian Orthodox, Ukrainian Orthodox, and Uniate Catholic.[87]

During the harsh years of Soviet repression of Ukrainian nationalism, Ukrainians in the western part of the country resisted not only the secular state but the Russian Orthodox Church, which was perceived by many Ukrainians to be an agent of Russian colonialism. An uprising against the Russian Orthodox Church in Ukraine in 1990 was regarded by the church hierarchy as motivated by "an underlying nationalist cause," as one Russian Orthodox archbishop scornfully put it.[88] The Russian Orthodox Church's metropolitan of Kiev warned that "a handful of people" were trying to use Gorbachev's "democratization process" in order to set up a "national church" in the Ukraine that would "estrange Ukrainians from Russians."[89] Many Western Ukrainians would agree. They feel, however, that their estrangement from Russians occurred decades— even centuries—ago and that the responsibility for the schism was as much Russian as it was Ukrainian.

The main opponents to the Russian Orthodox Church in Western Ukraine are those clergy and laity who identify with the "Uniate Church"—the Ukrainian Catholic Church. It is called the Uniate Church because it dates from the union of the Ukrainian Orthodox Church with the Roman Catholic Church in 1596. Christianity had come to the region in 988, when Vladimir the Great became Christian, and in the great division between Rome and

Constantinople, the Ukrainian region fell on the Orthodox side. For that reason the Uniate Church, which is dominant in the two western regions of Ukraine—Galicia and Transcarpathia—is very much Orthodox in its practices and beliefs. Its clergy are married, for instance, as Orthodox clergy are. Since the 1596 union, however, it has recognized the patriarchy of Rome and used this connection to assert its independence from the Russian Orthodox Church. Members of the Russian Orthodox Church in the eastern part of Ukraine also support Ukrainian nationalism, but they recognize the primacy of the patriarch of Moscow.

When Ukraine was made a part of the Soviet Union in 1923, the role of the Uniate Church became uncertain. The Marxist government, especially under Stalin, had no use for any sort of religion, but in its efforts to undercut the Russian Orthodox Church it at first took a permissive position toward regional forms of the faith, such as the Uniate and the Ukrainian Orthodox churches. During the Second World War, however, Stalin felt that latent nationalist sentiments in Ukraine were being spurred on by the Uniate Church and were keeping Ukrainians from being as supportive of the war effort as they might have been. When the war ended, therefore, Stalin attempted to make Ukraine in every way a seamless part of Russia. In the Synod of Lvov in 1946 the Uniate Church was abolished. The property of some 3,000 churches was transferred to the Russian Orthodox Church, and the former Uniate clergy were forced either to join the Orthodoxy or to leave the church altogether. Some who stayed remained true to the Uniate confession but practiced their faith in secret. Nuns who adopted civilian clothes and worked as teachers and nurses were often dressed in their identifying religious habits only after their deaths when they were laid to rest in their coffins.

In 1988, with the increase of religious freedom throughout the Soviet Union, formerly Russian Orthodox clergy proclaimed their true Uniate identities, and a new movement developed in Western Ukraine to reestablish the Uniate Church. It became fashionable in some urban intellectual circles to join the Uniate confession largely for nationalist reasons.[90] By 1990 several hundred Orthodox churches had been converted back to Uniate congregations, in some cases by force, and in 1991 the seventy-six-year-old head of the Uniate Church, Cardinal Miroslav Lubachivsky, re-

turned to the cathedral of Lvov in glory from an exile that had
been imposed on him since 1938. Cardinal Lubachivsky had spent
seventeen of his forty-five years abroad serving as a parish priest
in Cleveland, Ohio. Between 1988 and 1991 over a thousand
clergy professed to be Uniate rather than Russian Orthodox. The
Orthodox patriarch in Moscow vigorously protested these conversions, claiming that the churches had functioned as Russian Orthodox congregations for half a century and that many, if not most, of
the members were now truly Orthodox in belief rather than Catholic. Moreover, he argued, the prime motive of most of the Uniate
leaders in reclaiming their churches was political, not spiritual:
they wanted to reestablish the cultural base for an independent
Ukrainian nation. The patriarch's disdain of Ukrainian nationalism, however, did not prevent him from changing the name of the
Orthodox Church in the Ukraine from the Russian Orthodox to
the Ukrainian Orthodox Church.

In 1989, yet another contender entered this Orthodox/Uniate
controversy—a group of formerly Russian Orthodox clergy and laity
who wanted to revert to the "true Ukrainian church." They had in
mind, however, not the Uniate Church but an earlier form of Ukrainian Orthodoxy that had existed before the union of 1596 and that
paid homage to neither the pope nor the patriarch of Moscow nor the
patriarch of Constantinople. It had its own head and was therefore
known as the Ukrainian Autocephalous Orthodox Church.[91] It had
been established in 1921 as a nationalist movement, and Stalin allowed it to flourish briefly before crushing it in 1930. By 1991, the
revived form of the Autocephalous Church had attracted only a
relatively small number of clergy and had even fewer congregations,
but it had created a great deal of public controversy. It was virulent
in its attacks on the Russian-related Ukrainian Orthodox Church and
was even more nationalist than the Uniates. It competed with them
over which form of religion truly represented the Ukrainian nationalist cause. The Uniate Catholics claimed that because the Autocephalous were Orthodox, they were somehow identified with Russia, and the Autocephalous claimed that because the Uniates were
Catholics, they were somehow linked with Poland.[92] In December
1991 members of the Autocephalous Church staged a hunger strike
in Saint Sophia's Cathedral in Kiev to reclaim the Byzantine church
they said was theirs.[93]

In January 1992 Metropolitan Archbishop Mstislav Skrypnyk, who lived in the United States for more than forty of his ninety-three years, returned to Kiev in order to take up his post as patriarch of the Ukrainian Autocephalous Orthodox Church. Although he came to the United States in 1950, he never took out U.S. citizenship, and he was elected patriarch by a synod of bishops in Kiev in 1990. Patriarch Skrypnyk stated that he intended to live half of each year in Kiev and the other half in his headquarters in South Bound Brook, New Jersey.

The fact that the heads of both the Uniate and Autocephalous Ukrainian churches had lived in the United States was taken as a symbol of the nationalist spirit of the religious movements. A priest who supported the Autocephalous cause compared his leaders with "the founding fathers of America." Like them, he said, the Autocephalous leaders have "embarked upon the difficult road leading to self-determination which sooner or later must be accepted and recognized."[94] He went on to say that the members of his church desire nothing more than "their inalienable, divinely given rights of life, dignity, liberty and the pursuit of happiness."[95]

It is something of an irony that the Russian Orthodox Church, which suffered greatly under Stalin and Khrushchev, came to be regarded as the persecutor in Ukraine. But, as the minister of religious affairs in Ukraine explained to me, the leaders of the new independent Ukrainian churches are young and remember only the recent history of attempts to Russify Ukrainian culture through the imposition of the Russian Orthodox faith.[96] These members of a new generation see the Uniate Church and the Ukrainian Autocephalic Orthodox Church as pioneers in a renewed cultural nationalism aimed at establishing an independent Ukraine. The Ukrainian churches may quarrel with one another, but they are united in their support for a Ukrainian nationalism free from any latent cultural ties to the old Soviet state with its secular socialist ideology and its Russian colonial rule.

The Ambivalent Relationship of Religion and Socialism

These movements of religious rebellion in socialist states raise the question of when religious movements are compatible with socialism and when they are not. One answer is related to nationalism: when socialism is touted as being transnational, it is often rejected by proponents of particular local cultures. Because local cultures are usually defined by religion, international socialism—like the international secular nationalism of the West—is seen as an enemy of religion. The great socialist empires of the twentieth century, the Soviet Union and the People's Republic of China, are portrayed as colonial conquerers by local leaders of the regions within their borders, and when these leaders assert the distinctiveness of their regions' religious identities, they make a powerful political statement: they claim a cultural autonomy that could be the basis for a separate nation.

In China, as in the former Soviet Union, movements for regional autonomy often have had a religious dimension. On the border between China and Kazakhstan, the Kirghiz and Uigur people of Kashgar in Xinjiang, who rioted against the Chinese authorities in 1990, have been involved in a struggle for what they hope will become an independent Islamic Republic of East Turkestan. Tensions between Tibetan Buddhists and the Chinese have likewise erupted into violence. In the late 1980s the Chinese government attempted to suppress several uprisings that supported the Dalai Lama and Tibetan Buddhist rule. The bloodiest encounter occurred in March 1989, leaving as many as seventy-five dead and scores wounded. Thousands of Tibetans in Lhasa poured into the streets for three days of protests at the central Jokhang Temple led by young Buddhist monks and nuns. The protests escalated to rioting against Chinese and Chinese-owned businesses, and the Beijing government sent an estimated 2,000 troops to quell the riots. The Dalai Lama, in a conciliatory gesture, announced from his government in exile in India that he deplored the violence and assured the Chinese government that he had no ambitions of returning to power in Lhasa. He did, however, propose a five-point basis for peace talks, which included the idea of semiautonomous political status for Tibet.[97]

In two other socialist states in Asia, Vietnam and North Korea, religion has also played a role in national identity. In Vietnam, both Buddhist and Catholic leaders were politically active in the 1960s and have been regarded as potential leaders of resistance to the socialist government since. After massive Vietnamese emigration in the 1980s, the importance of religious institutions has increased because they provide a link between the Vietnamese at home and those in exile throughout the world. In North Korea, where Buddhism and Christianity are closely controlled, the ideology of the leader, Kim Il Sung, has taken on a religious character. Kim's doctrine of self-reliance, *Juche* thought, contains elements of Marxism, Confucianism, and Korean shamanism, and North Koreans have told me proudly that it is superior to orthodox Marxism.[98] Moreover, it is uniquely Korean. It allows North Korea to be culturally and intellectually independent from its powerful Chinese and Soviet patrons.

In nonsocialist parts of the world, however, the shoe is on the other foot. There, capitalism rather than socialism is seen as the main transnational ideology. When a country's secular government is tied to an international entity through its economic and political affiliations, it is perceived as being colonial or neocolonial, and the movement against it has often been both socialist and religious. This was the case in Sri Lanka, where Buddhist monks who loathed the secular nationalism propagated by the Colombo government advocated "Buddhism socialism" and aligned with Marxists in the JVP movement.[99] The monks regarded the Marxists, who identified with rural communities and poorer sections of the cities, as closer to the grass roots of Sinhalese society than the urban secular elite.

This has also been the case in parts of Latin America, including El Salvador, Guatemala, and especially Nicaragua, where American political influence and economic domination had so closely bound the Somoza government to the United States that the movement against it was largely an attempt to liberate the country from foreign domination. It was an anticolonial struggle with both cultural and political elements, and for a while it welded together popular religion and social revolution. "The Revolution and the Kingdom of God," proclaimed Ernesto Cardenal, a priest who was a cabinet member in Daniel Ortega's revolutionary government, "are the same thing."[100] This point of view was echoed by many other devout Christians who took part in Nicaragua's decade of revolution, which lasted from the overthrow of the Somozan dictatorship in 1979 to the election of Violeta Chamorro in 1990.

Although Ortega and his Sandinista party were portrayed in the

American press as Marxist and were excoriated by Nicaragua's Archbishop Miguel Obando y Bravo as being hostile to the faith, the revolution was to a remarkable degree a religious movement. It was conducted not only with a religious zeal but also with specifically Christian imagery. Moreover, it appealed to a large number of socially concerned clergy and other devout Christians, who often regarded their participation in the revolution as a religious act. [101] A priest in Managua told me that he was so impressed with the revolution's call for social service that he turned his badly attended church building into a warehouse for food grains and held mass on the streets. [102] One of the leaders of the Sandinista movement proclaimed that she was in the revolution because of her Christian faith, explaining that it helped her to "live the gospel better."[103] Carlos Tuennermann, minister of education in the Ortega cabinet, also joined the revolution as the result of "a Christian decision."[104]

One of the reasons the revolution had such a religious flavor—and a specifically Catholic one at that—is that the Nicaraguan national identity is in some measure linked with the Church. A visit to the great cathedrals at Granada and Leon is like a visit to a national museum, and the walls of churches bear the scars of great and violent moments in Nicaragua's history. Nicaraguan nationalism is characteristic of both the Church's conservative leadership and its rebels. [105] For this reason, a genuine Nicaraguan nationalist revolution, one touted as being by and for the people, as the Sandinistas claimed theirs to be, had to be in some sense linked with the Church. Thus, in Nicaragua the socialist revolution was also a religious revolution.

Even though religion allied itself with socialism in Central and Latin America, and opposed it in Eastern Europe and Central Asia, religion has joined forces with nationalism in each of these locales as it has elsewhere in the world. What is striking is how unanimously religious politicians—be they Christians in Eastern Europe, the former Soviet Union, and Latin America; Muslims and Jews in the Middle East and Central Asia; or Sikhs, Hindus, and Buddhists in South and Southeast Asia—reject Western-style secular political ideologies, in part because they reject their claims of universality. By implication a transnational ideology—such as international socialism or secular nationalism—denies the value of what is unique in particular cultures. To counteract the alienation and dehumanization that allegedly accompany a bland universal secularism, proponents of religion offer a powerful antidote: the symbols and communal pride related to particular people in particular places. Even the grand religious traditions, such as Christianity and Islam, that seem transnational by nature are reduced to particular allegiances in particular places: it is the Ukrainian Church and Algerian Islam that Ukrainians and Algerians, respectively, embrace. For that reason socialism is an ally of religion when it joins forces with it against a transnational foe; it is religion's enemy when it is itself that foe.

Patterns of Religious Revolt

In this chapter and the two preceding it I have concentrated on confrontations involving revolutionary religious movements in formerly socialist states and in what used to be called Third World countries. They provide the most obvious examples of religious nationalism in the contemporary age. By concentrating on these cases, however, I do not mean to leave the impression that the industrialized nations of Europe, Asia, and America are immune to religious-nationalist sentiments. In the United States, for instance, American patriotism is often fused with biblical images and Protestant Christian rhetoric, creating a "civil religion" that is as nationalist in its own way as the Muslim Brotherhood in Egypt or the RSS in India. The involvement of evangelical and fundamentalist Protestant groups in American politics in the 1980s revealed the political power that is potentially at their command.[106] From time to time in American history, separatist movements supported by native peoples have also utilized symbols from their religious heritage to define a national identity of their own.[107]

These forms of religious nationalism may be found in other industrialized countries as well. In South Africa, Christian nationalism is the avowed aim of the Reconstituted National Party.[108] In the United Kingdom, the separatist movement of the Irish Republican Army (IRA) in Northern Ireland, while not religious in motivation or ideology, is characterized by religious identity—Catholics fighting against Protestants—and it can be regarded as one of the last anticolonial struggles against what little is left of the formerly vast British Empire. Some scholars see the conflict among the IRA, the

Irish Protestant militants, and the British government as being, on some level, religious.[109]

The rise of National Socialism in Germany earlier in this century, while not explicitly religious, carried overtones of millenarian Christianity. Heinrich Himmler and other formulators of Nazi ideology relied on a mixture of religious images and ideas, including the Knights Templar symbol from the Crusades; nature worship from the German folk movement of the 1920s; the notion of Aryan superiority from, among others, the Theosophists; and a fascination with the occult from a certain strand of German Catholic mysticism. To the degree that the Nazi movement was religious, then, one could consider World War II as a war of (or from the Allies' point of view, against) religion.[110]

Germany's ally, Japan, also engaged in the war with a religious zeal. Among the neglected aspects of the war were Japanese religious concerns related to the honor of the emperor, who was regarded as both a political and a spiritual leader. Likewise, in contemporary Japan a religious dimension may be found in the revived emperor cult. Several of the new religious movements in Japan carry strongly nationalist overtones, including the Institute for Research in Human Happiness, led by Ryuho Okawa, who claims to have sold thirty million copies of his anti-American and pro-Japanese books of prophecy and spiritual mysticism. Okawa, recalling Moses, asserts that the Japanese are the new chosen people.[111]

These strands of religious nationalism in industrialized societies, like those in the areas of South and Central Asia and the Middle East that I described earlier, follow several general patterns. In the beginning of Part 2 of this book, I described these as defining characteristics of movements of religious revolution. For each of these characteristics, however, I have found significant variations.

Rejection of Secular Nationalism

Virtually all the religious nationalists I have studied are articulate about what they are against—more so, in fact, than what they are for. They have been able to unite a regime's opponents by criticizing the government, even though often they have given hardly a clue as to what would replace it. Although some, such as Sikh militants and

Islamic revolutionaries in Palestine, oppose their religious rivals as fiercely as they war against the secular state, the latter is the easier target. How well they unite their constituencies against this secular foe depends in part on how weary the populace is of the secularism of the prevailing order. It is fair to say that the longer the period of secular nationalism, the more strident and united are the religious-nationalist opponents. This relationship held in the shah's Iran before the revolution, in Nehru's India and Nasser's Egypt before the rise of significant forms of religious nationalism in those countries, and in the client states of the former Soviet Union.

The main exceptions to this rule have been the nations of North America and Europe and other Europeanized nations—the very archetypes of secular nationalism—which have failed to produce coherent and credible movements of religious nationalism in response. This anomaly is explained, in part, by the arguments presented earlier in this book regarding the Christian character of Western secular nationalism; but even if one does not accept these arguments, it is clear that Christianity (along with most other religious communities in America and Europe) has accommodated the Western nation-state. Not even the most pious Christians in America—even those who disdain everything about secular culture—would care to reject the humanistic tenets of secular nationalism. The same is true of religious persons in the other industrialized states of Europe. For that reason, the threat of religious nationalism there is fairly slight.

Anti-Western and Anticolonial Posture

Only some of the movements I have mentioned can be said to be anticolonial in a direct way. The movement in Northern Ireland is anticolonial, and those who regarded the Soviet empire as a latter-day example of imperialism would see the movements in the former Soviet states and the Eastern European countries as anticolonial as well. In other cases the movements were responding to what they regarded as cultural and ideological vestiges of a previous colonial era: the British presence, for instance, in India, Sri Lanka, and Egypt. In still other cases, the "colonialism" was metaphorical: American influence in Nicaragua, Israel, and Iran was real enough, but the involvement was through military support, economic ties, cultural domination, and ideological examples, rather than through formal political control.

Hostile and Violent Stance

Because religious nationalists have been so strident and their critique so fundamental, they have often not been welcomed in the councils and chambers of secular states. The degree of their hostility, however, has been directly related to the ability of such states to accept contrary points of view: the more dictatorial the regime, the broader the violent response. The rigidity of the shah in Iran, Somoza in Nicaragua, and the Israeli occupation forces in Palestine has invited broad-based violent responses. In Israel itself, most parts of India, and to a large extent Egypt, the electoral process has been able to reflect strongly divergent views—including those of political parties that embrace religious nationalism—and large-scale violence or civil war has been avoided, even though secular leaders remain vulnerable to terrorist attack.

The situations in Sri Lanka and the Punjab would appear to be exceptions to this rule because in both cases massive violence has broken out despite a strong tradition of pluralist electoral politics. The religious militants in these two areas, however, perceived the electoral system to be either ineffective or inaccessible to them. For that reason, they turned against electoral politics and political parties as savagely as they fought against the secular rulers in power. Why religious movements are particularly susceptible to violence is a matter I discuss in the next chapter.

Religious Rhetoric, Ideology, Leadership

In some ways it is misleading to describe all these movements as religious, for in only a few cases are they linked with mainstream religious organizations and leadership. Only in Iran, Algeria, Afghanistan, and Tajikistan, has the official religious leadership unequivocally joined the revolution. In Egypt, Sri Lanka, Israel, and India, although some clergy have been involved, the leadership of the religious-nationalist movements has come largely from the laity. Many leaders, such as the Hindu nationalist Advani, are not particularly pious or religiously observant. They are, however, fiercely loyal to their religious communities.

In many cases the activists rely on theology to elaborate their political ideologies. In Egypt and Palestine, religious nationalists look to the theological writings of Mawdudi and Qutb; in Israel, Jewish radicals heed the theological insights of Kuk; in Latin America, activists follow the writings of liberation theologians; and in India, the BJP leans toward the positions of V. D. Savarkar and M. S. Golwalkar. Two of the religious-nationalist leaders—Khomeini in Iran and Bhindranwale in Punjab—are now regarded as theologians in their own right, and their speeches and writings continue to be studied by activists who are looking for a link between political strategy and theological explications of the nature of the world. Although theology is an arcane and little studied field in Western universities, it is still the queen of the sciences in those parts of the world where a divine order is presumed to underlie reality, including the everyday realities of society and politics.

Religious Alternative
to the Secular Nation-State

Although most religious-nationalist movements eschew a theocracy, they envision a new political and economic order born out of a religious revolution. But what kind of order? Sinhalese activists in Sri Lanka see it as vaguely socialist, perhaps something like the Sandinista rule in Nicaragua. For Muslim activists in Egypt, Palestine, Central Asia, and elsewhere, the model is less clear, but it seems to contain elements of socialism, popular democracy, and small-scale capitalism. Some Jewish revolutionaries say they have no use for Western-style democracy, but almost all other religious activists regard democracy as necessary for a modern state. The constitution of the Islamic Republic of Iran and the political platform of the religiously based BJP party in India appear remarkably similar to the political ideals that have become commonplace in the West. This similarity would seem to indicate that religious revolution and democratic values can be compatible. In fact, the pattern of political change followed by most religious revolutionaries fits exactly the guidelines for "democratizers" that Samuel Huntington, an American political scientist, offers as the prescription for democratically overthrowing authoritarian regimes.[112] The main concern that most secular nationalists have about the religious nation-state is that individual and minority rights will not be protected, but even here there may be more latitude for tolerance than initially meets the eye. The sort of new political order appropriate and possible in a religious nation-state will be discussed later in this book. First, however, I must turn to a topic that is perhaps more pressing: the subject of violence and why it seems to be such an integral part of religious revolutions.

Part Three

The Problems Ahead

Chapter Six

Why Religious Confrontations
Are Violent

The bombing of the World Trade Center by militant Muslims in 1993 brought home to millions of Americans the potential for violence in religious confrontations. In fact, some religious activists seem to advocate it. The Sikh leader Bhindranwale praised his young lieutenants for hijacking an airplane and called for full concessions to his demands from India's political leaders "or their heads."[1] Iran's Khomeini said he knew of no command "more binding to the Muslim than the command to sacrifice life and property to defend and bolster Islam."[2] A right-wing Jewish leader in Israel told me in passing, "Of course we have no problem with using force to win our religious goals."[3] Not only have a number of political leaders fallen at the hands of religious assassins in recent years, but so have thousands of defenders of both the secular states and the religious revolutions.

Revolutionaries of all kinds are violent, and it is not surprising that religious revolutionaries are as well. Yet the ferocity of some religious nationalists is jarring: they seem to be even more violent than necessary, and they cloak their violence in religious rhetoric. The question for this chapter is whether there is a special relationship between religion and violence that makes this ferocity possible and gives an added impetus to the violent behavior of religious revolutionaries.

Even ordinary religion contains a strand of violence. Some of the world's most significant religious symbols are stained with blood. The savage martyrdom of Husain in Shi'ite Islam, the crucifixion of Jesus in Christianity, the sacrifice of Guru Tegh Bahadur in Sikhism, the bloody conquests detailed in the Hebrew Bible, the terrible battles celebrated in the Hindu epics, and the religious wars described in the Sinhalese Buddhist Pali Chronicles—all these events indicate that in virtually every religious tradition images of violence occupy a central place. For that reason, any attempt to understand the violence of religious nationalism must begin with an understanding of the violent nature of religion in general.

A spate of studies attests to the fact that the seeming ubiquity of these symbols of religious violence is not coincidental. The authors of these studies, including René Girard, Walter Burkert, and Eli Sagan, give social and psychological reasons for the virtual universality of violence in religion.[4] According to Girard's thesis—probably the most articulate and most widely discussed explanation—violent religious symbols and sacrificial rituals evoke, and thereby vent, violent impulses in general. Girard is here following the lead of Sigmund Freud, but unlike Freud Girard pinpoints as the root cause of violence "mimetic desire"—the desire to imitate a rival— rather than sexuality and aggression. Girard thinks ritualized violence performs a positive role: by allowing members of societies to release their feelings of hostility toward members of their own communities, it enables groups to achieve increased social cohesion. "The function of ritual," claims Girard, "is to 'purify' violence; that is, to 'trick' violence into spending itself on victims whose death will provoke no reprisals."[5] Those who participate in ritual are not consciously aware of the social and psychological significance of their acts, for Girard claims that "religion tries to account for its own operation metaphorically."[6]

Much of what Girard says about the function of symbolic violence in religion is persuasive. Even if one questions, as I do, Girard's idea that mimetic desire is the driving force behind symbols of religious violence, one can still agree with him that, in most religions, sacrifice occupies a central place and that the ritualized acting out of violent acts plays a role in displacing feelings of aggression, thereby allowing the world to be a more peaceful place in which to live.[7]

But what about real acts of religious violence? The death squads of Sikh and Sinhalese revolutionaries, the terrorists among militant Lebanese and Egyptian Muslims, and the religious soldiers pledged to Jewish and Christian causes are all engaged in violence in a direct and nonsymbolic way. At first glance their actions do not appear to fit

Girard's theories, nor do they result in the peaceful displacement of violence that ritualized forms of religious violence are supposed to produce.

On closer inspection, however, some of these real cases of violence do seem to fit the pattern after all because the violence is committed in an almost symbolic way.[8] The acts themselves—such as the hijacking of American planes by Muslim terrorists and the murder of a busload of Hindu pilgrims in the Himalayan foothills by a band of radical Sikh youth—are performed dramatically. They are illegal, abnormal, and shocking acts, carried out with the intention of vividly displaying the destructive power of violence. All acts of killing are violent, but these are even more violent than death inflicted during warfare or through capital punishment, in part because they have a symbolic impact. They are deliberately designed to elicit feelings of revulsion and anger in those who witness them.[9] In some cases the killing takes the form of religious sacrifice. Martin Kramer has demonstrated that when the Lebanese Hizbollah group of terrorists chose one of their own to be a martyr/victim to lead a suicide attack against Americans and Israelis, their choice had all the characteristics of a sacrificial victim in traditional religious rites.[10]

Still, most real acts of religious violence do not easily fit the Girardian scheme. The reason, I believe, is that most acts of religious violence are less like sacrifice than they are like war. One can think of religious warfare as a blend of sacrifice and martyrdom: sacrificing members of the enemy's side and offering up martyrs on one's own. But behind the gruesome litany is an idea that encompasses both sacrifice and martyrdom and much more: the dichotomy between the sacred and profane. This great encounter between cosmic forces—an ultimate good and evil, a divine truth and falsehood—is a war that worldly struggles only mimic.

When Americans sent troops to the Saudia Arabian desert following Hussein's invasion of Kuwait in 1990, a communiqué issued by the Palestinian Islamic movement, Hamas, declared it to be "another episode in the fight between good and evil" and "a hateful Christian plot against our religion, our civilization and our land."[11] I have heard or read similar comments from Egyptian, Iranian, Israeli, Sikh, Sinhalese, and Algerian religious activists, and the vocabulary of cosmic struggle is found in the rhetoric of virtually all the religious revolutionaries I have studied.

Elsewhere I have shown how the language of warfare—fighting and dying for a cause—is appropriate and endemic to the realm of religion.[12] Although it may seem strange that images of destruction often accompany a commitment to realizing a harmonious form of existence, there is a certain logic at work that makes this conjunction natural. Because, as we discussed in Chapter 2, religion may be defined as the language of ultimate order, it has to provide those who use it with some way of envisioning disorder, especially the ultimate disorder of life: death. Believers must be convinced that death and disorder on an ultimate scale can be encompassed and domesticated. Ordinarily, as Girard has eloquently argued, religion tames death and disorder through images projected in myth, symbol, ritual, and legend. The cross in Christianity is not, in the eyes of most believers, an execution device but a symbol of redemption; similarly, the sword that is the central symbol of Sikhism is worn proudly by the most pious Sikhs not as a weapon of death but as a symbol of divine power.

Thus violent images can be given religious meaning and domesticated. But an awful thing can also happen: conceptual violence can be identified with real acts of violence. These acts, although terribly real, are then sanitized by becoming symbols; they are stripped of their horror by being invested with religious meaning. They are justified and therefore exonerated because they are part of a religious template that is even larger than myth and history: they are elements of a ritual that makes it possible for people involved in it to experience the drama of cosmic war.

The Rhetoric of Cosmic War

Soon after the outbreak of the Gulf War on January 16, 1991, religious television programs throughout the United States capitalized on the warfare theme and drew parallels between the conflict and the spiritual struggle of everyday life. One television evangelist dressed up in desert battle fatigues and stood in front of a battle bivouac set. "There is a war going on," he sternly warned his viewers, explaining that "the devil has invaded our minds and hearts with bad thoughts and fear of the unknown."[13] Only a full-fledged spiritual assault comparable to that of the allied forces in Desert Storm, he implied, can liberate the soul.

This television evangelist is hardly an anomaly among preachers of most religious faiths. The rhetoric of warfare is as prominent in modern religion as is the language of sacrifice, and virtually all religious traditions are filled with martial metaphors. The ideas of a Salvation Army in Christianity and a Dal Khalsa (Army of the Faithful) in Sikhism, for instance, are used to characterize a disciplined religious organization. Images of spiritual warfare are even more common. The Muslim notion of jihad is the most notable example, and Protestant preachers everywhere encourage their flocks to wage war against the forces of evil. Their homilies might be followed with hymns about becoming "Christian soldiers," fighting "the good fight," and struggling "manfully onward."[14]

In a Th.D. dissertation submitted to Harvard University, Harriet Crabtree surveys the images in the "popular theologies" projected in the hymns, tracts, and sermons of modern Protestant Christianity. She finds the "model of warfare" to be prominent.[15] What is significant, Crabtree states, is that the image is meant to be taken in a more than metaphorical way. When the writers of hymns urge "soldiers of the Cross" to "stand up, stand up for Jesus," this call is interpreted as a requirement in situations of real, albeit spiritual, combat. Preachers and religious writers such as Arthur Wallis claim that "Christian living *is* war." Wallis explains that the warfare is not "a metaphor or a figure of speech" but a "literal fact"; the character of the war, however—"the sphere, the weapons, and the foe"—is spiritual rather than material.[16]

In earlier times images of warfare were at least as common in religion as sacrificial rites, perhaps more so. Whole books of the Hebrew Bible are devoted to the military exploits of great kings, their contests related in gory detail. Though the New Testament does not take up the battle cry, the later history of the Church is, in fact, a Christian record of bloody crusades and religious wars. In India, warfare contributes to the grandeur of mythology. The great epics, the *Ramayana* and the *Mahabharata,* are tales of seemingly unending conflict and military intrigue, and, more than Vedic rituals, they define subsequent Hindu culture. The legendary name for India, Bharata, comes from the epics, as does the name Sri Lanka. The epics continue to live in contemporary South Asia. As mentioned, a serialized version of the epics produced in the mid-1980s was the most popular television series ever aired in India (and, considering that country's vast population, perhaps the most widely watched television series in history).

Even cultures without a strong emphasis on sacrifice have persistent images of religious war. In Sri Lanka, for example, the legendary history recorded in the Pali Chronicles, the *Dipavamsa* and the *Mahavamsa,* has assumed canonical status. It relates the triumphs of battles waged by Buddhist kings.

The interesting thing about the battles of the *Mahavamsa,* the Bible, and the Hindu epics is that they are generally not moral struggles; these battles testify to an ultimate encounter different from the Manichaean notion of a cosmic conflict between good and evil. The motif that runs through these mythic scenes of warfare is the theme of us versus them: the known versus the unknown. In the battles described in the Bible and in such epics as the *Ramayana,* the enemies are often foreigners from the shady edges of known civilization: places like Canaan, Philistia, and Lanka. These foes often embody the conceptual murkiness of their origins: that is, they represent what is chaotic and uncertain in the world, including those things that defy categorization altogether.

In cases where the enemy possesses a familiar face—as in the *Mahabharata,* where war is waged between sets of cousins—chaos is embodied by the battle. It is the wickedness of warfare itself that the battle depicts, as the mythic figure Arjuna observes at the outset of his encounter with Lord Krishna on the battlefield.[17] To fight in such a circumstance is to assent to the disorder of this world, although the contestants know that in a grander sense this disorder is corrected by a cosmic order that is beyond killing and being killed. Such is the message of Lord Krishna in his address to Arjuna, the *Bhagavad Gita.*[18] Ultimately such struggles are battles against the most chaotic aspect of reality: death.[19]

Crabtree asserts that the image of warfare is attractive because it "situates the listener or reader in the religious cosmos."[20] This assertion is true, but the opposite is also the case: the sense of being situated in a religious cosmos leads naturally to images of warfare. This is so because, as I argued in Chapter 2, religious rhetoric affirms the primacy of order. To affirm the primacy of order, disorder must be conquered, and in so doing violence must be quelled as well, for it is the main perpetrator of disorder. Thus religious harmony and violent disruption are themselves locked together in a cosmic struggle. Religion must deal with violence not only because violence is unruly and has to be tamed but because religion, as the ultimate statement of meaningfulness, always has to assert the primacy of meaning in the face of chaos. For that reason, also, religion is order-restoring and life-affirming even though it may justify the taking of life in particular instances, as when a heroic or sacrificial act is seen as tipping the balance of power and allowing a struggle for order to succeed.

Religious images are mechanisms through which peace and order conquer violence and chaos; so it is understandable that the violence religion portrays is in some way controlled—for instance, in the normalcy with which the Christians' eucharist is eaten and their blood-filled hymns are sung. In ritual, violence is symbolically transformed. The blood of the eucharistic wine is ingested by the supplicant and becomes part of living tissue; it brings new life. In song a similarly calming transformation occurs as the images are absorbed aurally, for, as Christian theology explains, in Christ violence has been bridled. Christ died for death to be defeated, and his blood is sacrificed so that his faithful followers can be rescued from a punishment as gruesome as that which he suffered.

Other religions deal with violence in much the same way. In the Sikh tradition, for instance, the image of the two-edged sword is an example of the domestication of violence. This familiar symbol is worn on lockets and proudly emblazoned on shops and garden gates. It stands in front of Sikh *gurdwaras*, where it is treated as reverently as Christians treat their own emblem of destruction and triumph, the cross. Other images of violence in Sikhism also function like their counterparts in Christianity: the gory wounds of Sikh martyrs, like those of Christian saints, bleed on in calendar art, reminding the faithful that because their blood was shed, the faithful need fear no harm. Sikh theologians and writers, like their Christian counterparts, are eager to explain the meaning of such symbols and stories allegorically. They point toward the war between belief and unbelief that rages in each person's soul. In a somewhat similar way, interpreters of Jewish and Islamic culture have transformed the martial images in their traditions. The chroniclers of the Hebrew Bible saw acts of war as God's vengeance. So too have Muslim historians; some Islamic mystics even speak of the true jihad as the one within each person's soul.

Rituals of sacrifice fit into this general pattern of religious rhetoric: they are enactments of cosmic war. Like the enemy in a religious battle, the sacrificial victim is often categorically out of place and is therefore a symbol of disorder. Animals used for sacrifice, for instance, are usually domesticated beasts in the ambiguous middle ground between the animal kingdom and the human. If the victims are human, they are frequently also from an uncertain category. The young men chosen by the Hizbollah sect in Lebanon to be sacrificed as martyrs in bombings of American and Israeli targets were no longer children but not yet married; they were members of the community but free from family responsibilities; and they were pious but not members of the clergy.[21] In the sati of Indian widows, the victims are anomalies: married women bereft of living husbands. Sometimes it is God Himself or Herself who is offered up, or a divinely inspired person such as Jesus or Husain, whose very existence is extraordinary. It is not their sacrifice that makes them divine; rather, their almost unhuman holiness is precisely what makes them candidates for sacrifice.[22]

Thus images of sacrifice, like other symbols of violence in religion, are ordinarily symbols of a violence conquered—or at least put in place—by the larger framework of order that religious language provides. But if religious images are supposed to conquer violence, one must ask the obvious but difficult question: Why and how are these symbolic presentations of violence occasionally linked to real acts of violence? Ordinarily they should prevent violent acts by allowing the urges to conquer and control to be channeled into the harmless dramas of ritual. Yet we know that the opposite is sometimes the case: the violence of religion can be savagely real.

When Cosmic War Becomes Real

When Bhindranwale exhorted his militant Sikh followers to action, his rhetoric was crowned with the image of struggle: a "struggle . . . for our faith, for the Sikh nation, for the oppressed."[23] On the personal level it was a tension between faith and lack of faith; on the cosmic level it was a battle between truth and evil. Often his rhetoric was vague about who the enemy really is. "To destroy religion," Bhindranwale informed his congregation, "mean tactics have been initiated," and they come from "all sides and in many forms."[24] But rather than explain what these forces are, who are behind them, and why they would want to destroy religion, Bhindranwale dwelled instead on what the response should be: a willingness to fight and defend the faith—if necessary, to the end. "Young men: with folded hands, I beseech you," Bhindranwale implored, reminding them that the ultimate decision for truth or evil was up to them.[25] Because the cosmic war is waged against disorder, it is understandable that the foes are amorphous; they are, in fact, symbols for amorphousness itself.

This link between a worldly struggle and the cosmic one is found in the rhetoric of other religious activists as well. "Life is faith and struggle," said Khomeini, indicating that the notion of fighting is basic to human existence and on a par with religious commitment.[26] Khomeini's one-time associate Bani-Sadr wrote at some length about the notion of struggle in Islam, explaining how, although the monotheism of Islam will not allow for a struggle between the world and the spirit—for it does not recognize that duality—it does allow for a struggle against duality itself.[27] When Khomeini and Bani-Sadr talked about the struggle against evil and injustice in these vague terms, they were at home with preachers in every religious tradition who speak about the need to struggle against a generalized sense of falsehood and unbelief.

What made the language of Bani-Sadr and Khomeini different from the language used by many of their fellow preachers in Islam and elsewhere is that they saw the struggle occurring on a social and political plane. When Khomeini prayed to his "noble God for protection from the evil of every wicked traitor" and asked Him to "destroy the enemies," he had particular traitors and enemies in mind.[28] His list of the "satanic" forces that are out to destroy Islam included Jews but also the even "more satanic" Westerners. When he referred to these evil Westerners, Khomeini was not speaking of Christians, particularly, but of merchants, politicians, and corporate leaders with "no religious belief" who see Islam as "the major obstacle in the path of their materialistic ambitions and the chief threat to their political power."[29] Before the Iranian revolution, the shah was supposedly a companion of these satanic forces and a tool of colonialists.[30] Like the radical Sikhs' enemies, the ayatollah's foes were often vaguely described.

The interesting aspect of the ayatollah's diatribes was that they identified American colonialism as a threat to the Islamic faith as well as to social and political interests: not only were "all the problems of Iran" due to the treachery of "foreign colonialists" but so were all the problems of Muslims everywhere.[31] On another occasion, the ayatollah blended political, personal, and spiritual issues in generalizing about the cosmic foe—now described as Western colonialism—and about "the black and dreadful future" that "the agents of colonialism, may God Almighty abandon them all," had in mind for Islam and the Muslim people.[32]

Christians supporting the Sandinista revolutionary struggle in Nicaragua also perceived their opponents as being more than political enemies: they were cosmic foes (and often vaguely described). A fight against such a foe is not just an ordinary political conflict, the Christian revolutionaries implied, but one that has sacral dimensions. Ernesto Cardenal explained that the revolutionary struggle in Nicaragua was "totally different from the case of political parties that are all trying to come to power" in what he described as "a normalized, organized country." Cardenal searched for biblical metaphors in explaining what made the revolution in Nicaragua different: "We're taking sides, yes—with the good Samaritan." He went on to say that "here you have to take sides, you have to be partisan. Either you're with the slaughtered or you're with the slaughterers. From a gospel point of view I don't think there was any other legitimate option we could have made."[33]

In Sri Lanka, the metaphors of sacred struggle are drawn from Buddhist theology. "We live in a time of *dukkha*," a militant bhikkhu explained.[34] As he elaborated this point it became clear that he was not simply restating the first of the Four Noble Truths, that all life is suffering. In the bhikkhu's mind the concept of suffering—*dukkha*—had a definite social significance. "We live in an immoral world," he stated, using the term *adhammic*, which can also be translated as "disorderly" or "irreligious." Behind the notion is the conflict between dhamma and adhamma—order and disorder, religion and irreligion—and, by invoking that image, he couched the political concerns of himself and other Buddhist activists in sacred terms.

Right-wing Jewish activists in Israel have also used the images of cosmic war to justify their actions. Kahane, for instance, spoke of

God's vengeance against the Gentiles, which began with the humiliation of the Pharaoh in the exodus from Egypt over 3,000 years ago and continues in the present with the humiliation of the Gentiles that resulted in the creation of Israel.[35] "When the Jews are at war," Kahane said, "God's name is great."[36] An Israeli activist who was once arrested for his participation in a plot to blow up the Dome of the Rock in Jerusalem echoed Kahane's words and explained to me that "God always fights against His enemies"; he added that activists such as himself "are the instruments of this fight."[37] Although he tended to blame secular Jews as much as Muslims for exacerbating the cosmic struggle, the identity of the enemy—like the cosmic foe itself—is beyond any easy description or demarcation.

Religious Sanction for the Use of Violence

The language of cosmic struggle is easily exploited by political activists who want to give sacred legitimacy to worldly causes. Sometimes they do so only for the sake of public relations. In other instances it is for a much more important purpose: empowerment. Because religion has the ability to give moral sanction to violence, and violence is the most potent force that a nonlegal entity can possess, religion can be a potent political tool.

The Sikh case is an interesting example of religious legitimization. Among the Sikh concerns are a number that most people in India would regard as perfectly legitimate—the inadequacy of Sikh political representation and the inequity of agricultural prices. These issues did not need the additional moral weight of religion to give them respectability. In fact, the Sikh businessmen and political leaders who were primarily concerned about such issues were seldom supporters of Bhindranwale and his militant followers, at least early on. Even when they were later drawn into his campaign, their relation to him and his strident religious language remained ambivalent.

One political demand, however, was not widely supported at the outset, and it desperately needed all the legitimization that it could get, including the legitimacy it could garner from religion. This was the demand for Khalistan, a separate Sikh nation. Although it was seen initially as a political solution to the Sikhs' desire for a separate identity, it soon became a religious crusade. Separatist leaders such as Jagjit Singh Chauhan appealed to Bhindranwale for support and were greatly buoyed when he said, "I have always expressed myself in favor of mobilising the entire Sikh world under one flag."[38] They cheered when he stated further that he would fight for a separate identity for the Sikhs, "even if it demands sacrifice."[39]

Despite these fighting words, Bhindranwale never explicitly supported Khalistan. "We are not in favor of Khalistan nor are we against it," he said, adding that "we wish to live in India" but would settle for a separate state if the Sikhs did not receive what he regarded as just respect.[40] Whatever his own reservations about the Khalistan issue, his appeal to sacrifice made his rhetoric attractive to the separatists. It also suggested another, potentially more powerful result of the sacralization of political demands: the prospect that religion could give moral sanction to violence.

Even though virtually all religions preach the virtues of nonviolence, it is their ability to sanction violence that gives them political power. The Sikh tradition, for instance, ordinarily applauds nonviolence and proscribes the taking of human life.[41] Even Bhindranwale acknowledged that "for a Sikh it is a great sin to keep weapons and kill anyone." But he then went on to justify the occasional violent act in extraordinary circumstances and said that "it is an even greater sin to have weapons and not to seek justice."[42] Many other religious leaders, be they Christian or Muslim or Native American, agree. They believe that the rule against killing may be abrogated in unusual circumstances when social or spiritual justice is at stake.[43]

Killing is often justified during a "just war"—a conflict that is deemed appropriate because the end merits it and the means to achieve it may in fact moderate the violence that existed before the conflict. First stated by Cicero, the theory of just war was developed by Ambrose and Augustine into a Christian doctrine that was later refined by Aquinas. It has analogues in Jewish, Islamic, and many other traditions as well. Christians supporting the liberation struggle in Latin America have speculated that there can be a "just revolution" as well as a "just war."[44]

A similar question was raised by Kahane regarding his own movement for establishing a religious state in Israel and the West Bank. According to him, Jewish law allows for two kinds of just war: obligatory and permissible. An obligatory war is required for defense, while a permissible war is allowed when it seems prudent. The determination of when conditions exist for a just war is to be made by the Sanhedrin or a prophet (in the case of permissible war) or a Halakhic state (in the case of obligatory war). None of these religious entities exists in the present day. In the absence of such authorities, the existence of the necessary conditions is to be determined by any authoritative interpreter of Halakha, such as a rabbi.[45] Kahane was himself a rabbi and perhaps for that reason felt free to pass judgment on the morality of his own movement's actions.

Kahane called on the people of Israel to rise up and reclaim the West Bank in a just war. He argued that defense was not the only religious basis for warfare: national pride was also a legitimate reason.[46] He reminded the Jews that their claim to the West Bank came from a 2,000-year-old vision that originated when the Jews came "out of the fear and shame of exile." And now, he asked them, "what about our national pride?"[47] He pointed out that Jews were afraid to go to the Mount of Olives, much less to Judea and Samaria. He urged them to fight to retain their self-esteem and pride.

Kahane also justified acts of violence as expressions of the war that is already raging but that is seldom seen—the battle for the reestablishment of a Jewish state, the enemies of which are both Arabs and secular Jews. "Every Jew who is killed has two killers," Kahane explained: "the Arab who killed him and the government who let it happen."[48] This logic exonerated Kahane's use of force not only against Arabs but against his own people.

In using violence against cosmic foes, the lives of individuals targeted for attack are not important. "We believe in collective justice," a right-wing Jewish leader explained.[49] By that he meant that any individual who was part of a group deemed to be the enemy might justifiably become the object of a violent assault, even if he or she were an innocent bystander. In a cosmic war, there is no such thing; all are potentially soldiers. "War is war," Kahane explained.[50] One of the purposes of violence against civilian Arabs is to "scare them" and not let them assume that they can live in Israel peacefully or normally.[51]

Some of Kahane's Arab opponents made precisely the same argument in justifying their struggle against the Israelis. The Palestinian leader Sheik Yassin, in defending the *intifada,* explained that it is necessary in order to show the Israelis that the Palestinian situation is intolerable and should not be treated as ordinary. "There is a war going on," the sheik explained, implying that the *intifada* is simply an expression of a larger, hidden struggle.[52]

Sheik Yassin justified his people's use of violence through the Islamic sanction for violence in the case of self-defense. He expanded the notion, however, to include the defense of one's dignity and pride as well as one's physical self.[53] One of Yassin's colleagues, Sheik 'Odeh, explained that the Islamic *intifada* is different from the *intifada* waged by secular supporters of the PLO in that the Islamic struggle is a moral struggle as well as a political one and comes from religious commitment. It is also part of a tradition of Islamic protest against injustice.[54] The *intifada* is a "sign from God," the sheik proclaimed, indicating that "the people need Islam as a center."[55]

The *intifada* is sometimes described as a holy war but not always. The concept of jihad, although important, is not central to the thought of all Islamic nationalists. Defense of the faith— including the traditional mores of the faith—is a sufficient basis for political action. In Egypt, in part because of the influence of the writings of Faraj, the "neglected duty" of jihad has increasingly been applied to political and paramilitary struggle as well as to military combat. Even in a political context, however, Muslim activists stress that jihad has a wider meaning than violent encounters with an enemy. At Cairo University, Professor Ibrahim Dasuqi Shitta explained that the "neglected duty" is a call for a general engagement against the forces of evil in the world, a battle that can be waged through economic policies and social service as well as through political and revolutionary action.[56]

Most religious nationalists are able to find within their religious traditions an existing justification for violence that they then apply to their own revolutionary situations. Buddhist activists find themselves in an interesting position in this regard because their tradition proscribes any sort of violence, including the killing of animals. One might think that the doctrinal commitment to *ahimsa* would prevent both monks and the laity in Buddhist societies from accepting the idea that violence could be morally approved or justified as an act of sacred war.

Yet in Sri Lanka some bhikkhus have explained the violence of Sinhalese activists in religious terms. Some monks told me that they actively participated in violence because there was no way to avoid violence "in a time of *dukkha*."[57] In such times, they said, violence naturally begets violence. Politicians who are violent and are seen as an enemy of religion might expect violence in return as a sort of karmic revenge.[58] During such times evil rulers are always overthrown. "We believe in the law of karma," one of the bhikkhus added. "Those who live by the sword die by the sword."[59]

The killing of Sri Lanka's prime minister by a Buddhist monk in 1959 underscores the seriousness of the monks' involvement and the degree to which they, like their clerical counterparts in every other religious tradition, are able to justify violence on moral—or, rather, supramoral—grounds.[60] Like violent actors in Sikhism, Islam, and Christianity, Buddhist militants have identified their political targets as enemies of religion and have thus been given sanction to take their lives. Those who want their use of violence to be morally sanctioned but who do not have the approval of an officially recognized government find it helpful to have access to a higher source: the metamorality that religion provides. By elevating a temporal struggle to the level of the cosmic, they can bypass the usual moral restrictions on killing. If their struggle is part of an enormous battle of the spirit, then it is not ordinary morality but the rules of war that apply.

Empowering Marginal Peoples

The empowerment granted by religious violence is especially appealing to those who have not had power before. The Iranian revolution is a potent example. Beneath the clerical exclusivism of the ayatollah's regime was a genuine social revolution, one that has had an effect on all levels of Iranian society.[61] It is incorrect to think of the Iranian revolution as simply a reversion to an earlier form of Islamic government. Traditional Islamic government has often been monarchic: rule by a caliph, a king, or some other singular power holder. The revolutionary government of Iran has a parliament and all the accoutrements of Western democracy. More to the point, it has the active participation of hundreds of lower-echelon mullahs throughout the country. These kinds of religious functionaries have never held power before—neither in Iran nor in any other Islamic regime in the world.

Much the same can be said about many of the other movements of religious nationalism, including the one that received overwhelming electoral support in the 1991–92 elections in Algeria. There the Islamic opposition to the secular National Front Party was fueled by a 20 percent inflation rate, a 25 percent unemployment rate, and a young population—70 percent of which was under twenty-five years of age—who could not hope for marriage, an apartment, or a job given Algeria's economic circumstances.[62] In Sri Lanka, a similar desperate situation prevailed, especially in the countryside. There an antipathy to the relatively wealthy urban middle class was expressed in religious differences: the rural people rejected the middle-class "Protestant Buddhism"—which eschews traditional and folk forms of Buddhism and is ambivalent about the leadership of the monastic orders—and instead rallied around the monks.[63] They also provided the mass base of support for the Sinhalese nationalist involvement in the revolutionary JVP.

The phenomenon of marginal groups rising to power by means of violent religious nationalism was also a feature of the Sikh revolution in the Punjab. Bhindranwale's call to take up arms to defend the faith had a particular appeal to those who greatly wanted to be associated with a core group within Sikhism: Sikhs who were socially marginal to the community, including Sikhs from lower castes and those who had taken up residence abroad. Some of the most fanatical of Bhindranwale's followers, including Beant Singh, the assassin of Indira Gandhi, came from untouchable castes (Beant Singh was from a sweeper caste), and a considerable amount of money and moral support for the Punjab militants came from Sikhs living in such faraway places as London, Houston, and Los Angeles.

These Sikhs gained from their identification with Bhindranwale a sense of belonging. The large expatriate Sikh communities in England, Canada, and the United States were especially sensitive to his message that the Sikhs needed to be strong, united, and defensive of their tradition. Many of Bhindranwale's supporters in the Punjab, however, received a more tangible benefit from associating with his cause: politically active village youth and religious functionaries were able to gain a measure of popular support. In that sense Bhindranwale was fomenting something of a political revolution, and his constituency was not unlike the one acquired by the Islamic revolution in Iran. Insofar as Bhindranwale's message was taken as an endorsement of the killings that some of these fundamentalist youth committed, the instrument of religious violence gave power to those who had little power before. In the Punjab it was not the established leaders who encouraged violence but a lower level of leadership—a younger, more marginal group for whom the use of violence was enormously empowering. The average age of Sikh extremists killed by police was quite low. The largest group was young men in their twenties; most were sons of small farmers with little education. [64]

The male composition of the violent Sikh cadres is worth noting. This gender bias is found in many other activist movements as well, including groups of Hindu nationalists and rural Sinhalese nationalists, and Muslim movements in Egypt, Palestine, Algeria, and elsewhere. [65] The activists often refer to the need to properly clothe and respect women, and to keep them in their place. During the 1991– 92 Muslim uprising in Algeria, Ali Belhaj, one of the Islamic Front leaders, said a woman's primary duty was to "bear good Muslims"; and Sheik Abdelkhader Moghni, another Islamic Front leader, complained about women working and taking jobs away from men. Women, he said, just "spend their salaries on makeup and dresses, they should return to their homes." [66] A businesswoman in Algiers responded by saying she feared that if the Islamic Front succeeded, it would usher in a reign of "pig power." "They're all male chauvinist pigs," she explained, adding, "believe me, we are worried." [67]

In India, Bhindranwale addressed his congregations as if the men (especially the young men) were the only ones listening, encouraging them to let their beards grow in the long Sikh fashion and describing their acts of cowardice in the face of the government opposition as "emasculation." One senses in this longing for a recovery of virility expressed by Bhindranwale and the other religious activists a strange, composite yearning that is at once sexual, social, and political. [68] The marginality of such persons in the modern world is experienced by them as a kind of sexual despair. It could almost be seen as poignant if it were not so terribly dangerous.

Perhaps these men found that their power had eroded in modern society and for that reason were attracted to militant cadres. Violence is empowering. The power that comes from the barrel of a gun is direct; the indirect, psychological dimension of this power may be even more effective. As Frantz Fanon argued in the context

of Algeria's war of independence some years ago, even a small
display of violence can have immense symbolic power by jolting
the masses into an awareness of their own potency.[69] In this sense
there are in the Punjab, as in Sri Lanka and elsewhere in the
world, aspects of social revolution embedded in violence that at
first glance seems to be only religiously inspired.

It can be debated whether Bhindranwale succeeded in jolting
the masses in the Punjab into an awareness of their own capabili-
ties, but the violent actions of the militants among them have
certainly made the masses more appreciative than they were of the
militants' power. Militants were treated as if they possessed an
authority rivaling that of the police and other government officials.
One of the problems in the Punjab was that villagers in the so-called
terrorist zones around Batala and Tarn Taran were unwilling to
report terrorist activities to officials. The radical youth even set up
their own courts and governmental offices.

By being dangerous, these young religious radicals have gained a
certain notoriety, and by clothing their actions in the moral garb of
religion they have given those actions legitimacy. Because their
activities are sanctioned by religion, they are not just random acts
of terror but are strategic political actions: they break the state's
monopoly on morally sanctioned killing. By putting the right to kill
in their own hands, the perpetrators of religious violence are making a daring claim to power on behalf of those who previously had
been impotent and ignored by those in power.

For these reasons it is not surprising that many radical movements for religious nationalism have been accompanied by violence. What is surprising is how many of them have not turned in a
violent direction—even those that are as committed to their ideals
and are as revolutionary in their goals as the violent ones. Although
religious revolutionaries of all persuasions see a cosmic struggle
emerging between the old order they wish to bury and the new
religious nations they are pledged to create, a sizable number of
them subscribe so deeply to democratic procedures and human
rights that the violent potential of their struggle is tempered.

Chapter Seven

Democracy, Human Rights,
and the Modern Religious State

A propensity toward violence may be the matter that most immediately alarms outsiders about religious revolutionary movements,
but in the long run observers are often even more concerned about
the restrictions on freedom that might be imposed in religious
states. Because there have been so few attempts to create a religious state in modern times, it is easy to conclude that such an
entity would be old-fashioned: it would be dogmatic, repressive of
differences, and intolerant of diversity. Unfortunately, the stories
that have circulated about life in the Islamic Republic of Iran have
done little to dispel these impressions; and because Iran was the
first religious state to have come into existence in this generation, it
serves as the example of what religious nationalists must want
everywhere. Fortunately, however, not all religious nationalists see
Iran as the ideal model—Sheik Yassin in Palestine and Qazi
Turadqhonqodz in Tajikistan, for example, have adamantly rejected
the Khomeini position. And, for that matter, the Iranian case is
often exaggerated. Yet the image persists of religious nationalists
being horribly out of step with modern times.

Several scholars in India, for instance, who viewed with dismay
the remarkable rise of religious nationalism in that country in 1991,
rushed into print a volume of essays analyzing the controversy over
the mosque at Ayodhya and lamenting the inability of Indian politics to stay free from the scourge of religion. The editor of the
volume, Sarvepalli Gopal, claimed that the very reputation of India
as a modern nation was at stake. To his mind, "the separation of the

State from all faiths" was a fundamental attribute of modernity and was characteristic of "a modern outlook anywhere." Only "secularism of this type," he claimed, was appropriate for "an egalitarian, forward-looking society."[1]

Are his assumptions correct? Let us, for the moment, delay the question of whether a religious state could be considered modern and begin with the issue of whether religious nationalists have a propensity toward dictatorship and an opposition to human rights. From what I have said previously in this book about religion as an ideology of order, it follows that movements with a strong religious vision will indeed have a tendency toward firm leadership and internal discipline. As a result, they are often autocratic. A Muslim leader in Algiers buttressed his opinion that the place of women is in the home with the statement, "It is not I who demand this, but God."[2]

Having a strong religious vision often also means settling on a single figure as the authority for the entire movement. In India, for example, the Hindu nationalist movement, the RSS, claimed that its "skilled and efficient leadership" should not only be obeyed but revered, just as a guru in traditional Hinduism is revered, even worshiped.[3] In Iran, some thought Khomeini led his country with divine providence. In other revolutionary religious movements throughout the world Khomeini has been an object of admiration, even by those who disagree with his ideology and religious point of view. Even though Sheik Yassin regarded the Iranian revolution as "an experiment that failed," he "admired Khomeini."[4] From the opposite camp in Israel, Kahane also professed an admiration for the Iranian leader and led his own movement as Khomeini led his—autocratically, with virtually no rivals.[5] Religious activists from Egypt to Indonesia have admired in the Khomeini style the order and certainty that come with a clear religious vision and unchallenged authority.

Although religious movements tend to be authoritarian, the same is true of secular nation-states, which, like religion, uphold ideologies of order and are pledged to maintain society's mores. In some cases the authoritarianism of secular nationalism has resulted in dictatorships as brutal as any that religious nationalism has produced; that of the Soviet Union's Stalin is one example; Germany's Hitler (if we accept National Socialism as secular) is another. In most secular nation-states, however, strong central authority has been transferred from single commanding leaders to a system of authority involving an elected parliament of representatives and an independent judiciary. Most secular nationalists refer to this system when they speak of democracy. The question, then, is whether religious nationalism can embrace a democratic system.

Theocracy or Democracy?

The rhetoric of many religious nationalists suggests that they are remarkably enthusiastic about democracy. Even those activists most opposed to the secular state affirm the importance of the democratic spirit in politics. Sheik Yassin, for instance, told me that "Islam believes in democracy."[6] One of his Buddhist counterparts in Sri Lanka said that Buddhism also "is democratic by its nature."[7] A member of the Muslim Brotherhood in Egypt told me that "democracy was the only way" for an Islamic state.[8] A leader of Israel's Gush Emunim said that "we need democracy," even in "a religious society."[9] The Central Asian religious nationalists echo this desire for democracy in a religious state.

Some of this enthusiasm for democracy is self-serving. If democracy simply means majority rule, then it means letting the people have what they want; and if the people want a religious society rather than a secular one, then they should have it. "Since 80 percent of the people in Egypt are Muslims," one Muslim activist explained to me, "Egypt should have a Muslim state."[10] The same line of reasoning has been used in Sri Lanka and in Punjab, where Sinhalese and Sikh activists, respectively, think that democracy legitimizes a rule by whichever camp has the preponderance of the population on its side. In these cases, democracy means simply "the will of the majority."

It is possible that the will of the majority could be discerned by an insightful leader, who need not trouble himself or herself with such details as elections and parliaments. Religious activists who come to this conclusion can affirm the general idea of democracy but reject its specific procedures. This position is not frequently taken, however, for even religious activists who interpret democracy solely as majority rule stress that this control should not come about by fiat. "The decision to have an Islamic state," Sheik Yassin argued, "should come about through democratic vote."[11]

Ultimately, however, it is not the will of the people that matters in a religious frame of reference but the will of God. For that reason, religious nationalists often state that good leadership involves the ability to discern what is godly and truthful in a given situation. But, as Rabbi Kahane said, "you don't vote on truth."[12] Most religious nationalists agree; they regard the discernment of truth as ultimately beyond the democratic process.[13] Thus the normal way of transacting politics in democratic states—through voting, political bartering, and the interplay of competing interest groups—is seen as irrelevant and perhaps even contrary to a higher morality. In an interesting moment in my conversations with a Buddhist bhikkhu in Sri Lanka, he cited as an example of the immorality of secular government its tendency to pander to the self-interests of contending parties. That, however, is precisely what democratic politics in the United States and elsewhere in the West is supposed to do: distribute the largess of the state as widely as possible and supply the greatest amount of happiness to the greatest number of people. But that is a morally insufficient notion of government from the bhikkhu's point of view. He wanted the government to adopt a larger vision of ethical order and uphold dhamma (virtue).[14]

To a remarkable degree, the bhikkhu's position on democracy and truth echoed Plato's in *The Republic*. There Plato characterized democracy as a "charming form of government, full of variety and disorder," which leads naturally to tyranny.[15] Plato feared that if people were allowed to make decisions collectively, they would simply endorse their own self-interests, which would result in policies that were nothing more than the lowest common denominator of individuals' greed and desire for personal security. What was needed, Plato decided, was leadership that could rise above self-interest and provide a broad vision for the whole. This decision led him to the idea of a philosopher-king: leadership in the hands of someone trained in the art of political insight.

Democratic theory as propounded by Locke and other eighteenth-century rationalists countered Plato's objections to democracy in two ways. First, proponents of the theory had considerable faith in the ability of individuals to surmount self-interest in their collective decisions and to vote for the welfare of the whole. Second, democratic theorists conceived that elected representatives would have a double role: they would be both mouthpieces of their constituencies and independent judges of what was appropriate for the welfare of the wider community.[16] These two roles may clash, and much of the discussion at the time of the writing of the American Constitution had to do with structuring the Congress in such a way that these two roles were balanced. The creation of two houses of Congress, a House of Representatives to represent the people and a Senate to represent the states, was part of this compromise.[17]

Many religious nationalists challenge Locke's assumptions. They do not have the rationalists' faith that reason alone is sufficient for finding the truth, nor do they feel that unbridled self-interest is an adequate moral base for a political order. This view puts the religious nationalists back in Plato's position: unhappy with a democratic rule of the mobs and eager to find a philosopher-king.

Religious nationalists have one advantage over Plato: they are more certain than he about where truth may be found. For most religious activists their tradition provides a framework of religious law that is considered normative for human activity. Because religious law is the only certain repository of social and ethical truth, they reason, it should be the basis of politics. According to some activists, the establishment of religious law is the primary—some would say the sole—aim of religious-nationalist movements. Religious leaders in Egypt, for instance, explain that the main problem with the Sadat and Mubarak government is that it ignores shari'a and does not make it the law of the land. They resent the fact that the government prefers Western law instead. "Why should we obey Western laws when Muslim laws are better?" one of them asked me.[18]

This sentiment is echoed in Israel, where Jewish nationalists feel that the Knesset gives more credence to Gentile laws than to Jewish ones, even though, as one of them put it, "Jewish law was formulated long ago when the Gentiles were still living in the bushes."[19] The same speaker, on another occasion, told me that Israel should strive for "Torahcracy" rather than democracy.[20] He has developed a constitution for the State of Israel based entirely on Halakhic laws, but, significantly, except for the slightly archaic language, it looks much like a modern constitution based on Western secular law. The Torah constitution, for example, grants individuals freedom of expression. The main deviation from a Western secular constitution is its provision of an ultimate arbiter of what is good for society: the council of judges, the Sanhedrin.

The constitution of the Islamic Republic of Iran is also, to a remarkable extent, similar to the constitutions of most modern Western countries. It contains guarantees of civil rights and minority rights and prescribes three branches of government—executive, judicial, and legislative—and the balances of power among them. The president and the members of the legislature are to be elected by the people for fixed periods of time. The only unusual features of the constitution, from a secular Western point of view, are the insistence on Islamic law as the basis from which all principles of law are to be derived and the role of Islamic clergy in telling the lawmakers which laws are appropriate. The constitution also establishes an unusual role of "leader"; initially this role was delegated specifically to the Ayatollah Khomeini. The leader appoints the council of clergy who pass judgment on Islamic law, appoints the Supreme Court and the commanders of the army, leads the National Defense Council, and declares war and peace. Interestingly, the leader does not have the power to appoint the president of the country, but the leader can withhold signing the decree approving the election of the president if the leader chooses. The leader can also dismiss the president but only if the Supreme Court convicts the president of "failure to fulfill his legal duties," or the National Consultative Assembly testifies to "his political incompetence."[21] Similarly, the leader has the power to pardon convicts or reduce their sentences, but only after receiving a recommendation to that effect from the Supreme Court. Thus the Iranian constitution has provided the country with an Islamic version of Plato's philosopher-king—but it has placed this leader within a modern parliamentary system.[22]

Even in Iran, then, the power of the clergy is limited.[23] At the beginning of the revolution the mullahs were slow to become involved in politics, and a number of American scholars concluded that the clergy would "never participate directly in the formal government structure" because they lacked the intelligence to do so or the interest.[24] Most of the mullahs would have been satisfied with a return to the democratic constitution of 1906, which allowed for a review process to ensure that laws were enforced according to

Islamic principles. Khomeini, however, insisted on the more active involvement of the clergy and a more complete break from the old system of politics.[25] Some of the Western-trained politicians who led the government soon after the revolution, including Bani-Sadr, Bazargan, and Sadeq Qotbzadeh, were replaced with clergy who had little familiarity with the West. But even with their involvement, Iran was far from being a theocracy, and following Khomeini's death the number of clergy involved in politics dropped dramatically. Some of the most vicious, including "Judge Blood"— Hojat-ol-Eslam Sadeq Khalkhali—fell into disfavor. In October 1991 Khalkhali and several other radical clergy were not even allowed to run for seats in the Assembly of Experts because the ulama jurists (doctors of Muslim religion and law) in the Council of Guardians failed them during what one scholar called a "humiliating examination in Shi'ite jurisprudence."[26]

In other movements of religious nationalism, the clergy has also played a limited role. In Israel, Palestine, and the Punjab, the leadership of the movements has included rabbis, sheiks, and other religious figures, but they have not been the sole leaders.[27] Sheik Yassin, for instance, claimed that the leadership of an Islamic political movement should be open to all and the clergy should not be forced into political activity if they were not interested in it.[28] In Sri Lanka, Nicaragua, and Ukraine, monks and priests have joined revolutionary movements as active partners without being the primary leaders. A bhikkhu in Sri Lanka told me that it was not necessary to have monks in power as long as government officials are mindful of consulting with religious leaders: "They should seek their advice."[29] In Egypt and India, the religious-nationalist movements are generally not led by clergy. In Egypt, a Muslim activist said that the clergy should be teachers of religious principles rather than politicians.[30] In India, where large numbers of sadhus (religious ascetics) have worked to bring out the votes for the Hindu-nationalist BJP, the leaders of the party have given public assurances that the sadhus will not exert a significant influence on party policy. Although the party has allowed some sadhus to run for office under the BJP banner, they are unlikely to become a significant bloc within the party leadership. In virtually every movement for religious nationalism the idea of theocracy—rule by the clergy—is rejected.

In fact, as long as religious law is affirmed as the basis for political action, the method for discerning that law and the procedure for choosing leaders who will carry it out can be democratic: the system can rely on ballots and elections. "These days we expect our governments to be democratically elected," a bhikkhu explained to me in Sri Lanka, indicating that democracy is consistent with Buddhist principles as long as the leaders are mindful of the fact that they are upholding dhamma (divine order).[31] In Egypt, some religious activists feel that only through the democratic process will the legitimate religious parties succeed.[32]

Most movements for religious nationalism also follow democratic procedures within their own organizations. Even though Rabbi Kahane advocated an autocratic rule for Israel, he endorsed democratic procedures for the committee he set up to establish an independent state of Judea.[33] Revolutionary committees from Sri Lanka to Algeria, and from Palestine to Ukraine, have been chosen democratically.

The implication is that the electoral process, as a means of choosing leaders and making decisions, has become well established throughout the world, including places where revolutionary movements for religious nationalism are on the rise. If this process is the hallmark of democracy, religious nationalists are as democratic as any secular politician. Religious nationalists are concerned not with the process but with the purpose: from their point of view, the political system exists ultimately only for divine ends, to make certain that human activity is consonant with the fundamental moral order that undergirds it. Religious nationalists break with democratic theorists primarily over the issue of whether the democratic system can legitimate itself: religious nationalists deny the possibility. A democratic gang of thieves, they argue, is still a gang of thieves. For the process to be morally valid it must be put to noble purposes, and that is why religious law must be the basis for any moral state.

The Protection of Minority Rights

In many parts of the world, minority communities have watched the rising tide of religious nationalism with great apprehension.

Their misgivings, often exacerbated by the warnings of secular nationalists, center around the concern that a state supported by religious nationalism will favor the majority religious community at the expense of the minorities.

This apprehension is warranted, for at the very least religious nationalists want the symbols and culture of their own religious communities to be glorified as part of the heritage of the nation. Most members of minority communities can live with reminders that they are residents of a nation dominated by another religion if it is simply a matter of putting up with the Sinhalese lion or the phrase *Allahu Akbar* ("God is Great") on their national flag, as they do in Sri Lanka and the Islamic Republic of Iran, or a matter of enduring a string of national holidays that celebrate someone else's faith. Minorities, however, are concerned about two, more problematic, possibilities: the potential for preferential treatment of majority community members in government hiring and policies, and the possibility that the minorities will be required to submit to religious laws that they do not respect. Beyond these concerns is a third, more apocalyptic, fear: that they will eventually be driven away from their own homelands, or persecuted or killed if they remain. These matters are not the concern solely of members of minority communities. They are also the subject of much discussion among religious nationalists.

Before I describe how religious nationalists deal with these potential problems, though, I should point out that the problem of minority rights and the assertion of minority identities are not peculiar to religious nationalists; they are fundamental problems in secular societies as well. In fact, secular nationalism is unable to deal easily with any kind of collective identity except those defined by geography. African Americans in the United States, for instance, constitute over 10 percent of the population but do not supply 10 percent of the representatives to Congress because not all of them reside in one place. A system that is set up to represent people on the basis of where they live almost invariably fails to represent equally the groups that people identify with, unless the groups happen to be coextensive with the geographical boundaries of a city or state.

In India, the British recognized this flaw in the Western system of democratic representation and tried to correct it with the device of "reserved constituencies"—a system that allowed only members of certain minority communities (Muslims and members of untouchable castes, for instance) to run as candidates in selected constituencies. In most cases, however, secular governments have dealt with the political representation of minority communities by denying that a problem exists—that is, they have held to the illusion propounded by democratic theory: that all people are equal, and for that reason discrimination should not occur among groups. The illusion is reinforced by law: if people are, in fact, found to be discriminating on the basis of communal distinctions, they will be punished. Thus the myth of equality is enforced.

By using the phrase *the myth of equality* I do not mean that this ideological position of democratic theory is untrue or morally insufficient. Just the opposite may be the case: as with religious myth, secular myth can convey great images of the moral potential of humanity. The term *myth*, however, suggests that equality is an ideal condition—one that is desired, and not one that is necessitated by nature. The conviction of religious nationalists that people are defined fundamentally by their affiliation with cultural groups is also a myth, and the competition between religious and secular nationalists is to some measure a contest to see which myth will prevail. In the Europeanized West, to a large extent the myth of equality has won, as public attitudes have been molded by the laws established to enforce it and by the political, economic, and social structures designed to promote it.[34]

Yet communal identities continue to exist in Europe and the Europeanized countries of the Western world, just as they continue to exist elsewhere. What makes religious nationalists shockingly out of step with most secular governments is their recognition that communal identities persist and that secular politics has failed to change what they would regard as natural religious loyalties. Their recognition of these loyalties makes them both dangerous (if one feels that communal identities are immoral in a healthy society) and honest (if one believes that these identities exist, whether or not one wants them to).

Some religious nationalists think that honesty about communal identities is an advantage in dealing with minority groups. In India, for example, the BJP claims that tensions between the government and the unhappy Muslim and Sikh minorities would be eased if government leaders appreciated communal identities and tried to find a way of integrating Muslims and Sikhs into society as Muslims and Sikhs rather than as faceless individual members of a secular state. For this reason, Advani, the BJP leader, said that if his party came into power, "the Muslims will be happy" within "a couple of months."[35] In Israel, similarly, Rabbi Kahane told me that when his group fought for its own religious rights, it became more sensitive than it had been to Muslim groups who were fighting for theirs.[36] In Iran, one of the early leaders of the revolution, Bani-Sadr, argued that every group should have rights—minority groups as well as majority ones. "Considering one's identity and rights as one's own and someone else's as his own is an Islamic idea," he claimed; "therefore, we have no quarrel with those who say: our rights belong to us."[37]

The question, however, is how religious nationalists should deal with the issue of minority rights if and when a religious state is established. In general, they have proposed two solutions. One is to provide a separate status (or even a separate state) for minority communities—essentially the British solution of providing reserved constituencies for minorities in India. The other solution is to accommodate the communities within the prevailing ideology—primarily by regarding the dominant religious ideology as a general cultural phenomenon to which a variety of religious communities are heir. This is the approach of the BJP in India, which claims all of Indian tradition—including Sikhism, Buddhism, and Jainism—to be Hindu tradition and which allows the religions from outside India, such as Christianity and Islam, to be affiliated with Hinduism as syncretic Christian-Hindu and Muslim-Hindu branches. In Sri Lanka, efforts have been made to create a Buddhist "civil religion" that would incorporate various strands of the country's religious traditions.[38]

The first solution—separate status—is problematic in that it requires finding an appropriate status or place for the minority groups. Whereas the British could provide separate electoral positions in parliament, most religious nationalists are required to come up with a much more substantial peace offering—land—for minorities. Land is significant because religious nationalism is often rooted in a particular place. Judaism is intimately connected with biblical locations, many of which are on the West Bank of the

Jordan River in Palestine. The religious nationalists of Sri Lanka insist on the political integrity of the whole of the island; and the Hindu nationalism of the BJP glorifies all of India. There is not much room in these positions for granting separate territory to minority communities. For that reason, religious nationalists who want to solve the minority problem through separatism might be forced to return to the British solution of separate political representation after all.[39]

The second solution—accommodation of cultural differences— also has its problems, but it provides a more flexible range of options. One of the more promising is an idea that I first heard discussed by Muslim activists in Egypt, and then again in an entirely different context, among Muslim leaders in Gaza.[40] These Muslim leaders insisted that Egyptian and Palestinian nationalism should subscribe to Islamic shari'a, but they indicated that there are two kinds of shari'a, or rather two levels of it: at a general cultural level there are social mores that are incumbent on all residents of the nation, regardless of their religious affiliations. This general level of shari'a is much like what passes for law-abiding, civilized behavior everywhere. At a more particular level, however, are detailed personal and family codes of behavior that are required only of Muslims. This formulation is similar, they said, to patterns they had experienced while traveling abroad. When in England or North America they were expected to obey the laws and standards of Western civilization in public, but privately they followed Muslim, rather than Western, customs.[41] They would expect Christians to return the favor when visiting, or living in, Muslim countries.

The two-level–shari'a solution is a promising one and has parallels in other traditions. In India, as I have mentioned, the BJP leader Advani insists that on one level Hinduism is simply another name for India's national cultural identity, and one of his party's slogans is that while other parties play off caste and ethnic groups against one another, the BJP "unites the country with its cultural heritage."[42] In Sri Lanka, proponents of the Jatika Chintanaya movement claim that Sinhala Buddhist culture is all-embracing and that Tamils are Sinhalese Buddhist Tamils and Muslims are Sinhalese Buddhist Muslims. Even some Christian leaders have described the Sinhalese culture as part of the background of all religious traditions represented in the country, including their own. Anglican and Catholic priests in Colombo have encouraged Christians to be in touch with the Buddhist dimension of their culture in order to be true Christians.[43] The two-level–shari'a solution also has parallels in earlier periods of Islamic history. The Delhi Sultanate in fourteenth-century India, for instance, allowed non-Islamic behavior, including the maintenance of Hindu temples and priests, as long as Islam was recognized as the state religion.[44] The Mogul Emperor, Akbar, is fabled for his tolerance of non-Muslim religions, and although scholars dispute just how open-minded he was, Akbar is familiarly portrayed in art surrounded by religious counselors of various faiths, including a Jesuit.

The two-level–shari'a solution will not work, however, if it implies that members of minority communities are second-class citizens. Members of the dominant community may not be able to show sufficient sensitivity or be willing to provide the legal safeguards to prevent this implication. If members of minority communities feel that they are treated badly, leaders of religious states may face the same sorts of political strategies that they themselves have used against the secular state. There is reason to hope that a form of the two-level–shari'a solution might work in some of the cases discussed in this book; in others one wonders whether a solution to longstanding ethnic and cultural differences will ever be found.

In Iran, there is some reason for hope. The leaders have allowed a limited number of minorities to pursue their own domestic codes of behavior as long as they behave with a propriety consistent with Muslim standards in public. The constitution of the Islamic Republic of Iran guarantees "equal rights" not only to every "ethnic group or tribe" but to "Zoroastrian, Jewish, and Christian Iranians" as "recognized minorities."[45] Some groups, such as the Baha'is, however, are regarded as heretical Muslims rather than as genuine minorities, and they have only two options: to revert to the true faith or leave. Those that have done neither have been persecuted.[46]

In Egypt, the Coptic Christian community is the major minority and can claim a more ancient link with Egyptian culture than the Muslims can. It traces its roots to the fifth century, when a central idea of the Monophysite branch of Christianity—that Christ had a single, divine nature, not two, a human and a divine one—was rejected by the Council of Chalcedon. The patriarch of Alexandria, a Monophysite, led his branch of the church in its own direction, relying on a liturgy written in the Coptic language, which is based on the ancient script of Egypt. Today there are some three million Copts, most of whom live in Egypt, where they constitute only a fraction of the population. They tend to reside in urban areas, and they have prospered as businessmen and professionals. Their prosperity is a cause for some resentment from their Muslim neighbors, and the perception that they were favored during the Nasser regime has been the cause of some hard feelings as well. Nonetheless, the antiquity of their tradition brings them respect, and even members of the Muslim Brotherhood acknowledge that the Copts are as Egyptian as any Muslim citizen.[47]

For that reason, any plan for Muslim nationalism in Egypt invariably provides exceptions for the Copts, such as in the two-level–shari'a solution. Some Muslim leaders have suggested that the Copts be given their own representation in parliament. If they were, the Muslim leaders told me, the Copts would be "better off" than they are under the secular government, which, because it does not recognize religious differences, does not provide political concessions for religious minorities.[48] Other Muslims say that the Copts should wear distinctive clothing, or some other sign, that would indicate that they were allowed to keep their own customs. The Copts themselves continue to be suspicious of this accommodationist rhetoric however. Although they confirm that many Muslim leaders are sensitive to their situation, they fear "Muslim fanatics."[49] One scholar in Cairo said that, with the rise of Islamic nationalism, Copts have been made to feel "less Egyptian."[50]

In Israel, the Palestinian Muslim minority is less easily accommodated than the Coptic community in Egypt. The secular Jewish state gives citizenship to Muslims but on secular terms: the state tolerates Muslim nationalists even less than they abide Jewish ones. Jewish nationalists have no problem with Muslim nationalism—as long as it is not practiced in Israel, including especially the wider Eretz Yisra'el described in the Bible, which includes most of the West Bank. For that reason, the most extreme Jewish nationalists in Israel call for a direct solution to "the Arab problem": they should leave. Jordan and Saudi Arabia are the most frequently suggested destinations. If they wish to stay, Rabbi Kahane told me, they could be treated as "resident guests" but not as full citizens.[51] At the same time, Kahane said, he could not imagine why self-respecting Muslims would want to stay in a place where they were treated as second-class citizens. Out of "respect for them" and not wanting them to "live in disgrace in an occupied land," Kahane explained, he felt that "they should go."[52]

Jewish nationalists such as Kahane have not been willing to accept the idea that Palestine is as sacred to Muslims as it is to Jews, and they regard the Muslim reverence for the Dome of the Rock and other sites in Palestine as "recent affectations" professed "for political reasons."[53] As a result, it is unlikely that a Jewish state can easily accommodate its Muslim minority. The solution of a separate location—an independent Palestine—may in time prove to be the only viable one.

Separation is a solution that is increasingly accepted throughout the world as large, unwieldy nations have fragmented into federations of smaller, more ethnically homogeneous ones. The idea that India might break into smaller units was unthinkable during the Nehru era, when large national units such as the United States and the Soviet Union were the models for modern nation-states. Now that the Soviet Union has broken into smaller, ethnic-based entities, the fissiparous ethnic tendencies of the Sikhs and other groups in India do not seem so ominous. The same can be said of Sri Lanka. Even though Buddhist leaders there have invited the Tamils to remain a part of a united Sri Lanka—as long as they accept the condition that Sri Lanka is culturally a Sinhalese Buddhist nation—many Tamils want a separate homeland of their own. Increasingly many Buddhists in Sri Lanka see this as a viable solution. The separatist solution works best when the minority community resides in a distinct region that can be given a measure of autonomy in a federal state. When the minorities are dispersed throughout society—as the Copts are in Egypt and the Muslims are in India—the accommodation approach is more viable.

Could the accommodation approach work with secular minorities? Even in traditional religious cultures there are people who were raised in religious households but who, through travel, education, or association with modern urban culture, have lost interest in religion. Should there not be a safe cultural haven for such people in a religious society, just as the cultures of Copts and other minorities are maintained as islands in seas of religiosity? From most religious nationalists to whom I posed the question, the answer was a resounding no.[54] They could accept the idea that other religious traditions provide valid alternatives to their own religious law but not secular culture: it has, in their eyes, no links with a higher truth. From their point of view, it is simply antireligion. Some religious nationalists found it difficult to accept secularism even in Europe and the United States, where, they felt, Christianity failed to keep its backsliders in line.[55] Still, it seems to me that the logic of the two-level–shari'a admits at least the possibility of islands of secular culture within a religious state.

The Protection of Individual Rights

Behind the question of minority rights is a more fundamental issue: the protection of individuals. Terms such as *separate status* and *accommodation* ultimately are important only insofar as they define how persons are treated. If a separate status for minority groups leads to new political positions or a semiautonomous state through which individuals may express their needs and concerns, that is one matter. If it leads to oppression and ostracism, that is quite another.

The term that has evolved in the West to indicate resistance to oppression and respect for people is *human rights.* It has come to have a host of meanings, from legal due process to equal opportunities for women to freedom of the press. At the very least it means the right that Amnesty International watches out for: the right to live free from physical intimidation and incarceration on account of one's political positions or ethnic and religious affiliations. At the very most it means a libertarian attitude toward any expression of an individual's tastes, feelings, or desires.

Before we can ask whether traditional religions embrace human rights, we have to be clear about what we mean by the term.[56] Not only is the phrase fuzzily defined in English, it does not easily translate into other languages. The minimum definition of human rights—the notion that people should be able to reside peacefully alongside each other in dignity and with personal security—is embraced by virtually every religion, albeit in its own terms. For example, one might find, as one Western scholar has, "deep and surprising parallels" between Islamic notions of religious tolerance and one's own.[57] The problem that Islam and many other religious traditions have is with the notion of rights: the idea that individuals possess on their own some characteristics that do not come from the community or from God.

When rights are conceived as being held by individuals rather than groups, some religious nationalists feel this definition connotes the unacceptable idea that a society is made up of persons who are granted authority and independence—their rights—at the expense of the integrity of the communal whole. Rather than using the term *rights*, then, most religious nationalists would rather describe the relationship between the individual and society as one of moral responsibility. As one of them put it, "We have no rights, only duties and obligations."[58]

This reluctance to embrace the term *rights* and the individualism that is perceived as standing behind it is not confined to religious critics in non-Western societies. Their concerns are echoed by some clergy in the United States and Europe, and increasingly by liberal intellectuals. The sociologists who coauthored the surprisingly popular critique of American individualism, *Habits of the Heart*, saw the commitment and communal identity of religion as a vital counterbalance to the isolation and competitiveness of American individualism.[59] In a similar vein, Alasdair MacIntyre has suggested a recovery of virtue in the classical sense as an antidote to what he regards as an excessive preoccupation with individual rights.[60]

In a way the controversy over rights makes little difference as long as societies respect the personal security and dignity that is at the heart of both human rights and the moral values of all religious traditions. In Egypt, for instance, Muslim nationalists speak ardently about the "uplift of the oppressed."[61] In Sri Lanka, religious nationalists insist that one of the prime purposes of a nation is to uphold free expression and personal dignity—the sorts of "rights" listed in the United Nations Universal Declaration of Human Rights—but they describe them as Buddhist values rather than as secular humanistic ideals.

The constitution of the Islamic Republic of Iran affirms that one of the purposes of an Islamic republic is to protect the "exalted dignity and value of man, and his freedom, joined to responsibilities, before God."[62] The constitution describes the protection of this dignity in terms that echo constitutions everywhere: the language of human rights. These are, however, the rights of "the people" rather than of individuals. The constitution contains a whole chapter—some twenty-one articles—devoted to the "rights of the people," including equal protection under the law, the equality of women, freedom to express opinions, freedom from torture or humiliation while in incarceration, and freedom to hold "public gatherings and marches," with the condition that "arms are not carried and that they are not detrimental to the fundamental principles of Islam."[63] The constitution also goes beyond the usual list of human rights and includes the right to being provided with "basic necessities," including housing, food, clothing, healthcare, education, and employment.[64]

The only part of the Iranian constitution's list of rights that would give a Western advocate of human rights pause is the occasional use of the phrase "subject to the fundamental principles of Islam." This wording, for example, accompanies Article 24, freedom of the press. It also accompanies the last article of the constitution, regarding mass media: Article 175 guarantees that the media, especially radio and television, will be dedicated to "the free diffusion of information and views" but "in accordance with Islamic criteria."[65]

Is this caveat about Islamic principles the loophole through which massive violations of human rights can enter Iranian society? The answer to that question depends on how much one trusts the Iranian leaders to be true to their word and on how much one believes that the fundamental principles of Islam are consistent with human rights. A good many Muslims outside of Iran think that the Ayatollah Khomeini and his "Judge Blood" comrades took liberties in interpreting Islamic principles and gave Islam the image of being narrow and intolerant. Even Sheik Yassin, the Palestinian Muslim leader, disapproved of taking Americans hostage and said that Khomeini "went too far" in bridling freedom of speech.[66] Yassin and other Muslim leaders think that Khomeini's actions contradicted his own constitution, which on the face of it seems as dedicated to human rights as any created by a secular state.

The Islamic version of human rights is not, however, ultimately the same as the humanistic secular version. From the point of view of traditional religious cultures, stark individualism and a laissez-faire attitude toward personal expression run fundamentally counter to the collective loyalty and disciplined demeanor typically found in the religious life. It is unlikely, therefore, that religious nationalists will ever fully support a libertarian version of individual rights, even though in many other ways they may look and talk like human-rights advocates anywhere in the world. The fact is that most religious nationalists would carry the values of communal life to an extreme that would be uncomfortable even for the most sympathetic Westerner—a Bellah or a MacIntyre. The basic difference between the role of an individual in Western "individualistic" society and in non-Western "communitarian" religious ones stands behind much of the talk about the protection of human rights. That difference is so deep and abiding that it will not be easily resolved.

Modernity and the Religious State

When critics sometimes cite religious nationalism as being out of step with modernity, they often have in mind this inability to enshrine individualism as an ultimate value. Or they may be thinking of a related matter: the familiar religious limitations on freedom of expression. Strong restrictions of this kind are also to be found in a secular nation when it is seized with a sense of ideological purpose— in a period of revolutionary change, for instance, or in the midst of war. The dismal American press coverage of the Gulf War in 1991 is ample testimony to that fact.

Yet although similar restrictions often accompany movements of religious nationalism, the logic of religious nationalism does not, in itself, require close-mindedness.[67] In fact, most movements of religious nationalism are remarkably unspecific about how far a government—even one that exemplifies moral virtue—can go in limiting personal freedom. Should government legislate morality? Most religious nationalists would say "Yes, up to a point." But this point may vary.

In India, for example, Hindu nationalists make a distinction between nation and state, claiming that as long as the country has a clear sense of national identity and moral purpose, the specific policies of the state matter little.[68] The policies proposed by the Hindu BJP during the 1991 election campaign were remarkably similar to those of secular political parties; it stated that despite its affirmation of Hinduism as the ideological glue that holds the na-

tion together, it had no intention of "running a Hindu government."[69] In this case, the role of religion in the political process is
primarily in formulating a national identity; as long as government
leaders are "in touch with the God behind the justice and the truth
that the government espouses," as one religious nationalist put it,
they will be satisfied.[70]

When movements of religious nationalism are open to a diversity
of members, they are likely to be more tolerant. In Iran, as I have
noted earlier, the influence of the clergy in the government has
waned somewhat since the mid-1980s, and the leaders now come
from a wider spectrum of the population. In India, there is a tension between the often ragtag band of religious mendicants who
help get out the vote for Hindu parties and the middle-class urban-
ites who lead them. Among the urban leaders are those whom the
Indian press during the 1991 elections referred to as Scuppies—
saffron-clad yuppies; they are successful businessmen and administrators who see in Hindu political parties a stabilizing influence on
the country and not a narrow dogmatism.[71]

In other movements of religious nationalism one can also find
this Scuppie pattern of an educated, urban religious elite linked
with a large, disenfranchised rural constituency. In Sri Lanka, for
instance, groups of uneducated rural youth have urban student
allies. In Sudan, where the Islamic regime is based on the support
of the uneducated masses, the leadership is well educated; the
Muslim leader, Hassan Abdullah Turabi, studied in Paris at the
Sorbonne. Many Palestinian Muslim leaders were also educated
and trained abroad. The same is true of the Islamic Front in Algeria, where participants in the 1991–92 uprising included many
highly educated doctors, scientists, and university professors. According to one of them, Fouad Delissi, a forty-year-old party leader
in the popular quarter of bab al-Oued who worked as a maintenance director for Algeria's petroleum-products retailing company,
"If there are people who consider themselves democrats, . . . it's
us." A majority of the Muslim leader's circle of comrades had studied in the United States or in France, and their interest in being
involved in the Islamic political movement was to help "guide the
country in a scientific, normal, modern way."[72]

As they appear to have a broad outlook on their own society and
its role within the larger international context, can we take these

Algerian religious nationalists at their word and accept them as "modern"? The answer to that question depends in large measure on what is meant by the term. As I mentioned in the Introduction, a number of scholars have insisted on distinguishing between *modernity*, largely defined as the acceptance of bureaucratic forms of organization and the acquisition of new technology, and *modernism*, described as embracing the ideology of individualism and a relativist view of moral values. This distinction allows us to observe that religious nationalists are modern without being modernists.[73] Although they reject what they regard as the perverse and alienating features of modernism, they are in every other way creatures of the modern age.

In Anthony Giddens's frame of reference, their situation is perhaps inevitable. Nationalism, from his point of view, is a condition for entry into a modern world political and economic system based on the building blocks of nation-states.[74] It is unthinkable that a political or economic entity can function without some relationship to large patterns of international commerce and political alignment, and this relationship requires strong centralized control on a national level. Because movements for religious nationalism aim at strengthening national identities, they can be seen as highly compatible with the modern system.

Religious nationalism, then, may be viewed as one way of reconciling heretofore unreconcilable elements—traditional religion and modern politics. Those religious movements that are not nationalist and not political have been hostile to the nation-state; and as Gerald Larson has suggested, they can legitimize the views of those who oppose the notion of a global nation-state system.[75] In a similar vein, Wilfred Cantwell Smith contended in the mid-1950s that there was a fundamental opposition between Islam and modernity, by which he meant not only the attributes of modernism that Bruce Lawrence has mentioned but also the fact that the transnationalism of Islamic culture has mitigated against the nation-state in the manner suggested by Larson.[76] Movements of Islamic nationalism, however, are particular to individual nation-states and provide a remarkable synthesis between Islamic culture and modern nationalism. As one observer of the Iranian revolution remarked, it has "no precedent" in modern history.[77] Since the revolution, however, there have been a number of attempts in other parts of the world to achieve the kind of synthesis between traditional culture and modern politics to which the Iranian revolution aspires. It is ironic, but not wholly surprising, that such attempts would be dubbed anti-modern by secularists who have become accustomed to thinking of modern politics as their private domain.

Conclusion:
Can We Live
with Religious Nationalism?

Will the confrontation between religious and secular nationalism harden into a new Cold War? That depends, in part, on how religious nationalism behaves, and in part on how it is perceived. What once appeared to many Westerners as an anomaly and an annoyance is now often seen as a global foe.

In the early months of the Iranian revolution, some American scholars refused to accept it as genuine. They thought it was only "an unfortunate interruption of the historical process" that they believed had been leading Iran inexorably toward a Western-style liberal political system.[1] Many Westerners still believe that and are waiting for Iran to return to its senses. Yet, in the Muslim world, Iran's revolution is seen quite differently: it is viewed as part of the "march of history" that Muslim nationalists in Algeria proclaimed in celebrating their own successful elections in 1991.[2] For them, history culminates in a world filled with religiously oriented nations. Perhaps neither their vision nor the expectations of the American scholars will be completely realized, but even if the Muslims' prophecy is only partially fulfilled, it will shatter the old illusion— the global vision of Hans Kohn and Rupert Emerson and other scholarly supporters of secular nationalism—that the world is destined inexorably to be more and more like us.

Just when it appeared that the surge of religious revolutions that started in the 1980s might be receding, a whole new outburst of cultural nationalism occurred in Eastern Europe and the former

Soviet Union in the 1990s. In the early 90s, Islamic nationalism
gained strength in areas far from the Middle East: In Afghanistan, in Algeria and elsewhere in Africa, in Mongolia, in Tajikistan,
and in other Central Asian countries of the Commonwealth of Independent States. New leaders rode the crests of power provided by
these movements, and they are likely to continue to find in religion
a useful support for some years to come. Increasingly the world is
forced to come to terms with the possibility that the ayatollahs, the
radical bhikkhus, the Bhindranwales, the Kahanes, and the liberation priests will not quickly fade from the scene. The critical question is whether we can live with what appears to many secular
Westerners to be a hostile force, as alien as the communist ideology
of the old Cold War.

It is no mystery why religious nationalism has become so popular at
this moment in history. In times of social turbulence and political
confusion—which the collapse of the Soviet Union and the decline
of American economic power and cultural influence have created
around the world—new panaceas abound. It was inevitable that
many of these would involve religion, sometimes perceived as the
only stable point in a swirl of economic and political indirection.
Moreover, as nations rejected the Soviet and American models of nationhood, they turned to their own pasts and to their own cultural re-
sources. The material expectations offered by secular ideologies often
cause frustration because they cannot be fulfilled in one's own lifetime; the expectations of religious ideologies do not disappoint in the
same way because they are not expected to be fulfilled in this world.

Religious nationalism raised new hopes, and it also came along in
time to rescue the idea of the nation-state. The political organization of a modern nation must somehow be justified, and in many
former colonial countries new generations of leaders found increasing difficulty in rallying support from the masses on the basis of a
vision of society that mirrored that of the failing old colonial powers. Many of these countries might have descended to anarchy,
might have been conquered by neighboring states, or might have
come under the hegemony of a large international power if it were
not for the insulation provided by religious nationalism. In Eastern
Europe and the former Soviet Union, religious and other forms of
ethnic nationalism might well have blocked Gorbachev's vision of a
new secular, nonsocialist empire to replace the vast Soviet Union.

Although it is understandable, then, that many nations have turned to ideologies of religious nationalism at this point in time, it is not so clear what, if anything, we can or should do about it. Perhaps our first task is coming to terms with the phenomenon itself and accepting the fact that religious nationalism, in one form or another, is here to stay. As one U.S. State Department official put it, "We have to be smarter in dealing with Islam than we were in dealing with communism thirty or forty years ago."[3] If we accept that challenge, our next problem is sorting out which aspects of religious nationalism we should continue adamantly to oppose and which aspects we can coexist with.

If we were to compile lists of those characteristics of religious nationalism we cannot live with and those we can live with, the first list might be quite lengthy. It would surely include the potential for demagoguery and dictatorship, the tendency to satanize the United States and to loathe Western civilization, and the potential to become violent and intolerant. Most Americans, including myself, would agree that these are indeed unacceptable characteristics in any nation that wants to be part of the global community, and we should not have to live with them. Fortunately, many religious nationalists themselves will aver that these tendencies are not essential to their ideology, and they will join in decrying them. For that reason, the most effective ways of countering them may come from within the religious communities themselves: from the critiques of pious Muslims, Hindus, Sikhs, and other religious nationalists who are embarrassed by the misuse of their positions. Undoubtedly, however, the United Nations and other international entities will have to continue to be vigilant about the possibility of abuses of human rights and irresponsible international behavior.

The other list—aspects of religious nationalism that we can live with—would include potentially significant and enduring elements of the movements. Such a list might begin with religious nationalists' appreciation of tradition and historical rootedness, and their insistence on grounding public institutions in morality. The utopian element of Western political theory—the notion that national societies are moral communities—has often been slighted in the rush toward progress and lost among the details of democratic procedure. For that reason there may be some aspects of the religious nationalists' agenda that we cannot only live with but also admire.

They may remind us of a moral dimension in our own political tradition that needs to be revived.

Between these two lists is a third one: it identifies aspects of religious nationalism that we cannot live with easily but that we might have to learn to coexist with. These are basic and persistent differences between our way of looking at nationalism and theirs, and they will continue to be sources of friction in the future. One is the religious nationalists' insistence on divine justifications for human laws and democratic institutions. This idea challenges our notion that reason should reign supreme in public matters. If divine justifications help to give people "the moral motivation" to obey laws, as one Buddhist monk explained, we may agree that they are good.[4] But when religious nationalists refuse to obey secular laws that contradict religious rules—as leaders of the Muslim Parliament of Great Britain advised their constituents to do in January 1992—we are prone to be less enthusiastic.

A second item on the problematic list is the assumption that certain lands are the province of only one religion. In some countries, such as Saudi Arabia and Tibet, this assumption is shared by virtually all their residents. In other countries, however, it is not. As we have seen, the Copts in Egypt, Christians in Iran, Tamil Hindus in Sri Lanka, and Muslims in India have all bristled at the notion that their nations are to be guided by the dominant religious community's ideology, even though they have been repeatedly assured by their respective Muslim, Buddhist, and Hindu compatriots that the dominant community will respect and tolerate them. Even in the best of circumstances, however, they will be made to feel like minorities. Although it may be true that every country, including Western ones, has minorities of one sort or another, a nationalism that is exclusive by its nature will always be difficult for us to accept.

A third problem that will endure is the religious nationalists' exaltation of communitarian values over individual ones. The United States virtually worships its individualists—the cowboy and the lone adventurer. Religious nationalists cherish group loyalties over individual rights and personal achievements. Nowhere are the differences between the two styles more evident than in the area of morality. Western-style governments' easy acceptance of drinking, gambling, and sexually explicit publications is seen by Iranian mullahs, Egyptian sheiks, and Buddhist monks as an example of Western decadence. Another example is Salman Rushdie: the protection the British government has afforded the harried author of *The Satanic Verses* has been seen in the West as a proud demonstration of the value it places on individual rights and freedom of speech; in Muslim countries, it has been seen as an act of social irresponsibility.

Religious nationalists will always be more reluctant than secular nationalists to extend rights to individuals because the notion of individualism goes counter to the logic of religious nationalism: that a nation should reflect the collective values of the moral community that constitutes it. Modern secular nationalism starts from the opposite premise. It sees individuals, who come together in a social compact, as the basis for political order. For that reason the protection of individual rights will always be higher on the secular nationalists' agenda than the preservation of the values of communities.

These differences are deep and abiding, and they indicate that although there can be a certain synthesis between the ideology of religious nationalism and the structure of the nation-state—as I have tried to demonstrate in this book—there can ultimately be no true convergence between religious and secular political ideologies. On the level of ideology, the new Cold War will persist. Over time, however, there might develop a grudging respect between the two and the possibility of mutual coexistence. The extent to which this mutuality of respect develops will depend on whether religious nationalists continue to regard the secular West as the enemy and on whether we continue to regard them the same way. The real question, then, is whether they, and we, can change.

There is some indication of religious nationalists' willingness to be accommodating. The Muslim leaders of Tajikistan's coup in 1992 proclaimed their eagerness to maintain ties with the West, and in Algeria, even in the midst of the celebrations over the electoral success of the Islamic Front early in 1992, a leader of the party assured Western leaders that it would tolerate opposition parties and that it would meet with Western envoys to ensure that trade with Europe continued.[5] Even the most hardened religious revolutionaries sometimes soften: the mellowing of Iran is one example, the release of the American hostages in Lebanon, another. Some observers suggest that in the late 1980s Islamic political activism entered a "new phase," one characterized by an ascription to democratic principles rather than violent confrontation.[6] It would be premature to suggest, however, that movements of religious nationalism follow a predictable life cycle: a burst of rash extremism, for instance, followed over time by a slackening of the brash rhetoric and intolerant behavior. My own tracking of the movements for religious nationalism included in this study shows no simple, predictable trajectory.

For that reason we cannot say what will happen next. At the time of this writing, movements for religious nationalism have had only limited success in providing convincing alternatives to prevailing secular orders. In some cases they have been brutally suppressed. The Sinhalese arm of the radical JVP movement in Sri Lanka was essentially killed off in the 1990 military action against the movement. In India, many rebellious Sikhs have been killed as well, although the efforts to do so turned into a protracted war, which in 1991–92 became even more ugly and violent than before. Elsewhere, in-fighting and factionalism have weakened a good number of movements, including those of Sunni Muslims in Lebanon and rival Muslim factions in Palestine. In Ukraine the opposition of the two nationalist churches to each other is as virulent as their joint opposition to the Russian cultural influences that remain from the days of Stalin and the Soviet Union.

Yet, a number of religious movements succeeded, even though their extreme proponents were crushed, when their ideas were assimilated into the political ideology of the state. In Sri Lanka, for instance, the radical movement could be destroyed in part because moderate religious nationalists had been appeased by the government's policies. In other countries, assimilation has been achieved in the form of political parties—such as the Muslim Brotherhood in Egypt, the Islamic Front in Algeria, and the Hindu BJP in India—that fit into the framework of the existing political system. Yet this political fit has not always been a comfortable one—the parties have been outlawed from time to time—and the assimilationist outcome is only partially successful. Compromise with the secular political order may signal to some religious activists that the nation is not unequivocally grounded in religious principles. For that reason, the next stage of the religious opposition might aim at a more radical transformation of the political order or a more than token intrusion of religion into public life.

Only in Iran, Sudan, Afghanistan, Tajikistan, and Nicaragua have religious nationalists been involved in successful revolutions, and the special circumstances in these places make it difficult to draw generalizations. In some cases these examples raise fears about the dogmatic and authoritarian tendencies of any revolutionary regime, especially a religious one. But at the same time, the course of events in Iran indicates that a state shaped by religious nationalists can accommodate a variety of political points of view, and it can change.

Whether our own attitudes will change is another matter. It is important to recall that much of the passion behind the religious nationalists' position comes as a response to what they perceive as the West's Cold War attitude of arrogance and intolerance toward them. If they could perceive us as changing our attitude—respecting at least some aspects of their positions—perhaps their response would be less vindictive.

It is much more difficult for us to detect our own intolerance, however, than someone else's. At a seminar I attended on the spread of Islamic nationalism in Africa, the former ambassador of Sudan—a Christian, educated in England, a man of great erudition and poise—wished to give an example of the intolerant attitude of Muslim nationalists in his country. One of his compatriots, he said, demanded to know why Sudanese Christians and followers of traditional African religions did not recognize "the superiority of Islam." The tone in the ambassador's voice betrayed his incredulity; Islam could never be superior to secular, Christian, or traditional African values. My own initial response was to share his shocked feelings, until it dawned on me that he and I were guilty of an intolerance of our own—the unfailing assumption that Islam cannot possibly be superior to our own views. If he had told the story to a Muslim audience, they would surely not have shared his and my sense of outrage.

For most of us the difficulty is not only a matter of accepting someone else's religion. It is also a matter of accepting the idea of religious nationalism: the notion that religion has a role to play in defining a nation and in stating its basic values. Although religion is historically part of the background of Western secular nationalism, as we discussed early on in this book, that heritage is largely neglected. If religion were a more vital force in Western societies, perhaps it would be easier for us to accept nations where it is a more dominant presence.

From time to time one hears calls for a more active role for religion in American public life.[7] One of the reasons Mohandas Gandhi appeals so much to the Western imagination is that, without being aggressively religious, he brought a moral and spiritual consciousness into the public sphere. Early in this century he wrote in a treatise entitled *Hind Swaraj, or Indian Home Rule*— arguably Gandhi's only sustained writing on political theory—that modern civilization and its nation-states contained a "sickness" created by the absence of spiritual values in Western political culture.[8] Many Westerners agree. Among them is Reinhold Niebuhr, the American Protestant theologian who influenced the Roosevelt government in the 1940s and who has been respectfully quoted by such diverse American politicians as Jimmy Carter and Jeane Kirkpatrick.[9] One of his central theses had to do with the limited moral ability of nations. They could not be selfless, Niebuhr claimed, because they are by nature nothing more than a collection of the self-interests of all the individuals contained within them. He added, however, that religion can help to transform political organizations and make them more like communities: it can ameliorate some of the harsher characteristics of self-interest and draw people together through a common recognition of "profound and ultimate unities."[10]

Yet both Gandhi and Niebuhr can be faulted for not providing adequate models for the fusion of religion and public responsibility. In Gandhi's case it is said that he went too far: as Ainslie Embree suggests, "Gandhi's use of a religious vocabulary—inevitably Hindu in origin"—may have exacerbated relations between Hindus and Muslims, and in any event his form of cultural politics cannot be transposed easily to the West.[11] In Niebuhr's case, he may not have gone far enough: despite his appreciation of the values that religion provides, when it came to politics he was the consummate secular liberal. His greatest fear was that nations would become too religious and become absorbed with their own illusions of power and grandeur. Niebuhr was deeply concerned about the destructive role that the "illusions" of religion and other moral ideals could play. "Illusion is dangerous," Niebuhr said, because it "encourages terrible fanaticisms." It must, therefore, "be brought under the control of reason."[12] Even so, Niebuhr cautioned against overreacting: keeping religion too far from political life can obscure the positive images of a perfected society that the religious imagination is capable of producing. "One can only hope," he added, "that reason will not destroy it before its work is done."[13]

Is it possible that Niebuhr's dark vision may come to pass, and reason and religion will war with one another on a nationalistic plane? Because there is ultimately no satisfactory compromise on an ideological level between religious and secular nationalism, it is possible to imagine that the current situation could get far worse, and a global state of enmity could settle in, surpassing the hostility of the old Cold War. One can foresee the emergence of a united religious bloc stretching from Central and South Asia through the Middle East to Africa. With an arsenal of nuclear weapons at its disposal and fueled by American fear of Islam, it might well replace the old Soviet Union as a united global enemy of the secular West.

Such a conflict might be compounded by the rise of new religious radicals in Europe and the United States, including not only politically active Christians but also members of newly immigrant communities of Muslims, Hindus, and Sikhs who might support their religious comrades at home. A nascent cult of cultural nationalists in Japan and elsewhere in the Far East might also be in league with what could become the West's new foe.

Barring this apocalyptic vision of a worldwide conflict between religious and secular nationalism, we have reason to be hopeful. It is equally as likely that religious nationalists are incapable of uniting with one another, and that they will greatly desire an economic and political reconciliation with the secular world. In this event, a grudging tolerance might develop between religious and secular nationalists, and each might be able to admire what the other provides: communitarian values and moral vision on the one hand, individualism and rational rules of justice on the other. After all, both are responses to, and products of, the modern age. In Sri Lanka, India, Iran, Egypt, Algeria, Afghanistan, Mongolia, Central Asia, Eastern Europe, and other places where independent nations are experimenting with nationalism of a religious nature, they are doing far more than resuscitating archaic ideas of religious rule. They are creating something new: a synthesis between religion and the secular state, a merger between the cultural identity and legitimacy of old religiously sanctioned monarchies and the democratic spirit and organizational unity of modern industrial society. This combination can be incendiary, for it blends the absolutism of religion with the potency of modern politics. Yet it may also be necessary, for without the legitimacy conferred by religion, the democratic process does not seem to work in some parts of the world. In these places, it may be necessary for the essential elements of democracy to be conveyed in the vessels of new religious states.

Notes

Introduction:
The Rise of Religious Nationalism

1. Interview with Dr. Muhammad Ibraheem el-Geyoushi, dean of faculty of Dawah [Preaching, or Call to Islam], Al Azhar University, in Cairo, May 30, 1990.

2. Interview with el-Geyoushi.

3. Francis Fukuyama, "The End of History," *The National Interest* 16 (Summer 1989): 3–18, and *The End of History and the Last Man* (New York: Free Press, 1992), xi–xxiii.

4. Quoted in Kim Murphy, "Islamic Militants Build Power Base in Sudan," *Los Angeles Times*, April 6, 1992, p. A9.

5. Editor's introduction to Conor Cruise O'Brien, "Holy War against India," *Atlantic Monthly* 262 (August 1988): 54.

6. Imam Abu Kheireiddine, quoted in Kim Murphy, "Islamic Party Wins Power in Algeria," *Los Angeles Times*, December 28, 1991, p. A1.

7. For an analysis of Bhindranwale's sermons, see Mark Juergensmeyer, "The Logic of Religious Violence," in David C. Rapoport, ed., *Inside Terrorist Organizations* (London: Frank Cass, 1988), 172–93.

8. See Mark Juergensmeyer, "What the Bhikkhu Said: Reflections on the Rise of Militant Religious Nationalism," *Religion* 20, no. 1 (1990): 53–75.

9. Dru Gladney, *Muslim Chinese: Ethnic Nationalism in the People's Republic* (Cambridge, Mass.: Council on East Asian Studies, Harvard University, 1991), 113–15 and *passim*.

10. Umar F. Abdallah, *The Islamic Struggle in Syria* (Berkeley, Calif.: Mizan Press, 1983), 23, quoted in Bruce B. Lawrence, *Defenders of God: The Fundamentalist Revolt against the Modern Age* (San Francisco: Harper & Row, 1989), 96.

11. This objection to the comparative use of fundamentalism is also voiced by David Martin, "Fundamentalism: An Observational and Definitional *Tour d'Horizon*," *Political Quarterly* 61, no. 2 (April–June 1990): 129–31.

12. Lawrence, *Defenders of God*, 2. As an alternative to *fundamentalism* I once proposed *heretical modernism* because religious activists, although modern, violate the principles of secularism enshrined in the ideology of modernism (panel, Does Fundamentalism Exist Outside of Christianity?, annual meeting of the American Academy of Religion, Kansas City, November 25, 1991). Hawley, after proposing the phrase *militant antimodern religious activism*, has, for convenience, capitulated to *fundamentalism* after all. John Stratton Hawley, ed., "Introduction," *Fundamentalism and Gender* (New York: Oxford University Press, forthcoming). For a discussion of definitions and a defense of the infelicitous term *fundamentalisms*, see the introduction to Martin E. Marty and R. Scott Appleby, eds., *Fundamentalisms Observed* (Chicago: University of Chicago Press, 1991), viii–x.

13. Lawrence, *Defenders of God*, 27.

14. See Mark Juergensmeyer, *Radhasoami Reality: The Logic of a Modern Faith* (Princeton, N.J.: Princeton University Press, 1991), 4–6.

15. Interview with Sheik Ahmed Yassin, leader, Hamas, in Gaza, January 14, 1989.

16. Similar definitions are given in other studies of nation building and nationalism. See, for instance, Anthony D. Smith, "Introduction," in Anthony D. Smith, ed., *Nationalist Movements* (New York: St. Martin's Press, 1977), 1–2, and Hugh Seton-Watson, *Nations and States: An Enquiry into the Origins of Nations and the Politics of Nationalism* (Boulder, Colo.: Westview Press, 1977), 1–5. In a similar vein, Giddens defines a *nation* as an entity with a political system that administers and has ultimate authority over a distinct territory, and *nationalism* as the subscription of individuals to "a set of symbols and beliefs emphasizing communality among the members of a political order." Anthony Giddens, *The Nation-State and Violence*, vol. 2 of *A Contemporary Critique of Historical Materialism* (Berkeley and Los Angeles: University of California Press, 1985), 215–16.

17. Hobsbawm explains that *nationalism* as a term emerged in the late nineteenth century, replacing *principle of nationality.* I use the term in this nineteenth-century way as the theoretical base on which the notion of a nation rests and a sense of identity with it. Hobsbawm, however, refers to it in an even more subjective manner as the emotional identification of peoples with "their nation" and the ability to be "politically mobilized" under such a rubric. Eric J. Hobsbawm, *The Age of Empire, 1875–1914* (New York: Pantheon Books, 1987), 142. The *nation* he calls "the new civic religion of states" (149). What he calls *nationalism* I might call "extreme

nationalism" or xenophobia; what I call nationalism he might call "national identity" or "national ideology."

18. By *secular* I mean simply nonreligious. I use it to refer to principles or ideas that have no reference to a transcendent order of reality or a divine being. This definition may seem obvious to Americans used to the notion of a secular society, but in some Asian societies, including India, the term is used to refer to religious neutrality—the notion that religion in general may be accepted as true without showing favor to any particular variety of religion.

19. Interview with the Rev. Uduwawala Chandananda Thero, member of Karaka Sabha, Asgiri Chapter, Sinhalese Buddhist Sangha, in Kandy, Sri Lanka, February 2, 1988.

Chapter 1:
The Loss of Faith in Secular Nationalism

1. Quoted in Kim Murphy, "Islamic Party Wins Power in Algeria," *Los Angeles Times*, December 28, 1991, p. A1. In February 1992, after the Islamic Party was crushed, an underground movement called The Faithful to the Promise vowed a jihad against the government that would be "in continuation" of Algeria's 1954 war for independence from France. Kim Murphy, "Algeria Cracks Down, Targets Islamic Front," *Los Angeles Times*, February 10, 1992, p. A10.

2. Hans Kohn, *Nationalism: Its Meaning and History* (Princeton, N.J.: D. Van Nostrand, 1955), 89.

3. Ibid., 16.

4. Ibid.

5. Jawaharlal Nehru, *The Discovery of India* (New York: John Day, 1946), 531–32.

6. Donald Eugene Smith, *India as a Secular State* (Princeton, N.J.: Princeton University Press, 1963), 140.

7. Ibid., 141. Italics in the original.

8. Nehru, *Discovery of India*, 531.

9. Kohn, *Nationalism*, 9. My italics.

10. Kohn, *Nationalism*, 4.

11. Rupert Emerson, *From Empire to Nation: The Rise to Self-Assertion of Asian and African Peoples* (Boston: Beacon Press, 1960), 158.

12. Ibid.

13. Ibid., vii.

14. Giddens, *Nation-State*, 215–16.

15. Arlie J. Hoover, *The Gospel of Nationalism: German Patriotic Preaching from Napolean to Versailles* (Stuttgart: Franz Steiner Verlag, 1986), 3.

16. Carlton J. H. Hayes, *Nationalism: A Religion* (New York: Macmillan, 1960).

17. Ninian Smart, "Religion, Myth, and Nationalism," in Peter H. Merkl and Ninian Smart, eds., *Religion and Politics in the Modern World* (New York: New York University Press, 1983), 27. For another comparison of nationalism and religion, see Hoover, *Gospel of Nationalism*, 3–4.

18. This point is also made by Anderson, who, in observing the ease with which secular nationalism is able to justify mass killings, finds a strong affinity between "nationalist imagining" and "religious imagining." Benedict Anderson, *Imagined Communities: Reflections on the Origin and Spread of Nationalism* (London: Verso, 1983), 18. It has been brought to my attention that other entities, such as the Mafia and the Ku Klux Klan, can also sanction violence; yet it should be pointed out that they are able to do so convincingly only because they are regarded by their followers as (respectively) quasi-governmental or quasi-religious cults.

19. Ibid., 19.

20. W. Howard Wriggins, *Ceylon: Dilemmas of a New Nation* (Princeton, N.J.: Princeton University Press, 1960), 169.

21. Arend Theodor van Leeuwen, *Christianity in World History: The Meeting of the Faiths of East and West*, translated by H. H. Hoskins (New York: Scribner's, 1964), 331.

22. Ibid., 332.

23. Ibid., 334.

24. Ibid., 331.

25. Ibid., 333.

26. Ibid., 418.

27. Ibid., 333.

28. Ibid.

29. Abolhassan Bani-Sadr, *The Fundamental Principles and Precepts of Islamic Government*, translated by Mohammed R. Ghanoonparvar (Lexington, Ky.: Mazda Publishers, 1981), 40.

30. Interview with Essam el-Arian, medical doctor, member of the National Assembly, and member of the Muslim Brotherhood, in Cairo, January 11, 1989.

31. Interview with Ibrahim Dasuqi Shitta, professor of Persian literature, Cairo University, in Cairo, January 10, 1989.

32. Interview with Shitta, January 10, 1989.

33. To some, *Christendom* and *Western civilization* are interchangeable terms (interview with Shitta, January 10, 1989).

34. The terms *Westomania* and *West-toxification* are translations of the Farsi word *gharbzadegi*, coined by Jalal Al-e Ahmad. It is discussed in Michael C. Hillmann, "Introduction," in Jalal Al-e Ahmad, *The School*

Principal, translated by John K. Newton (Minneapolis: Bibliotheca Islamica), 1974.

35. Imam [Ayatollah] Khomeini, "Anniversary of the Uprising of Khurdad 15," in Imam [Ayatollah] Khomeini, *Islam and Revolution: Writings and Declarations*, translated and annotated by Hamid Algar (Berkeley, Calif.: Mizan Press, 1981; London: Routledge & Kegan Paul, 1985), 270.

36. Interview with Uduwawala Chandananda Thero, February 2, 1988.

37. Bani-Sadr, *Fundamental Principles and Precepts of Islamic Government*, 40.

38. Interview with Rabbi Meir Kahane, former member, Knesset, and Leader, Kach Party, in Jerusalem, January 18, 1989; and an article by an anonymous author in the pamphlet *Islam and Palestine*, Leaflet 5 (Limassol, Cyprus, June 1988).

39. Bernard Lewis, *The Political Language of Islam* (Chicago: University of Chicago Press, 1988), 3.

40. Ibid.

41. Interview with Yoel Lerner, director, Sanhedrin Institute, in Jerusalem, January 20, 1989.

42. Interview with Yassin.

43. *Islam and Palestine*. The meaning of this term was pointed out to me by Dr. Ifrah Zilberman, research scholar, Hebrew University, in Jerusalem, May 25, 1990.

44. Interview with Uduwawala Chandananda Thero, February 2, 1988.

45. Interview with Uduwawala Chandananda Thero, February 2, 1988.

46. Interview with Uduwawala Chandananda Thero, February 2, 1988.

47. Quoted from comments of leaders of Egypt's Islamic Labor Party in Gehad Auda, "An Uncertain Response: The Islamic Movement in Egypt," in James P. Piscatori, ed., *Islamic Fundamentalisms and the Gulf Crisis* (Chicago: Fundamentalism Project, American Academy of Arts and Sciences, 1991), 116. The Muslim Brotherhood and Islamic Jama'at voiced similar suspicions about U.S. intentions in the Gulf War. Ibid., 119–20.

48. Hamas communiqué, January 22, 1991, quoted in Jean-François Legrain, "A Defining Moment: Palestinian Islamic Fundamentalism," in James P. Piscatori, ed., *Islamic Fundamentalisms and the Gulf Crisis* (Chicago: Fundamentalism Project, American Academy of Arts and Sciences, 1991), 76.

49. Ayatollah Sayyed Ruhollah Mousavi Khomeini, *Collection of Speeches, Position Statements*, translated from "Najaf Min watha 'iq al-Imam al-Khomeyni did al-Quwa al Imbiriyaliyah wa al Sahyuniyah wa al-Raj'iyah" ("From the Papers of Imam Khomeyni against Imperialist, Zionist, and Reactionist Powers"), 1977, Translations on Near East and North Africa 1902 (Arlington, Va.: Joint Publications Research Service, 1979), 3.

50. Khomeini, *Islam and Revolution*, 28.

51. Interview with el-Arian.

52. Interview with Uduwawala Chandananda Thero, February 2, 1988.

53. Interview with Kahane. A similar remark was made by Rabbi Moshe Levinger, a leader of Gush Emunim, in my interview with him in Jerusalem, January 16, 1989.

54. Interview with Levinger.

55. Jürgen Habermas, *Legitimation Crisis*, translated by Thomas McCarthy (Boston: Beacon Press, 1975), *passim*.

Chapter 2: Competing Ideologies of Order

1. Giddens, *Nation-State*, 4.

2. According to Strayer, secular nationalism was promoted in thirteenth-century France and England in order to buttress the powers of secular rulers after the clergy had been removed from political power earlier in the century. In the fourteenth and fifteenth centuries, there was a reaction against central secular-national governments; the next great wave of laicization occurred in the sixteenth century. Joseph Strayer, *Medieval Statecraft and the Perspectives of History* (Princeton, N.J.: Princeton University Press, 1971), 262–65.

3. Giddens, *Nation-State*, 4. The situation in India prior to the twentieth century was remarkably similar to that in pre–eighteenth-century Europe. See Ainslie T. Embree, "Frontiers into Boundaries: The Evolution of the Modern State," ch. 5 of *Imagining India: Essays on Indian History* (New Delhi and New York: Oxford University Press, 1989), 67–84.

4. Giddens, *Nation-State*, 255ff. This world economic pattern, which Wallerstein calls the "modern world-system," has its roots in the sixteenth century. Immanuel Wallerstein, *The Modern World-System: Capitalist Agriculture and the Origins of the European World-Economy in the Sixteenth Century* (New York: Academic Press, 1974), and *The Modern World-System II: Mercantilism and the Consolidation of the European World-Economy, 1600–1750* (New York: Academic Press, 1980). For the importance of the economic market system in European nation building, see Sidney Pollard, *Peaceful Conquest: The Industrialization of Europe, 1760–1970* (New York: Oxford University Press, 1981).

5. Challenges to the divine right to rule in Europe reach back at least to the twelfth century, when John of Salisbury, who is sometimes regarded as the first modern political philosopher, held that rulers should be subject to charges of treason and could be overthrown—violently if necessary—if they violated their public trust. Along the same lines, William of Ockham,

in the fourteenth century, argued that a "secular ruler need not submit to spiritual power." See Sidney R. Packard, *12th Century Europe: An Interpretive Essay* (Amherst: University of Massachusetts Press, 1973), 193–201; and Thomas Molnar, "The Medieval Beginnings of Political Secularization," in George W. Carey and James V. Schall, eds., *Essays on Christianity and Political Philosophy* (Lanham, Md.: University Press of America, 1985), 43.

6. Because humans are "equal and independent" before God, Locke argued, they have the sole right to exercise the power of the Law of Nature, and the only way in which an individual can be deprived of his or her liberty is "by agreeing with other Men to joyn and unite into a community, for their comfortable, safe, and peacable living one amongst another." John Locke, "Of the Beginnings of Political Societies," ch. 8 of *The Second Treatise on Government* (New York: Cambridge University Press, 1960), 375.

7. According to Rousseau, a social contract is a tacit admission by the people that they need to be ruled and an expression of their willingness to relinquish some of their rights and freedoms to the state in exchange for its administrative protection. It is an exchange of what Rousseau calls one's "natural liberty" for the security and justice provided through "civil liberty." Rousseau implied that the state does not need the Church to grant it moral legitimacy: the people grant it a legitimacy on their own through a divine right that is directly invested in them as a part of the God-given natural order. Jean Jacques Rousseau, "On the Civil State," ch. 8 of *The Social Contract* (New York: Pocket Books, 1967), 23.

8. Strayer, *Medieval Statecraft*, 323.

9. Although the churches supported a number of secular reforms in the nineteenth and twentieth centuries, religion in the West largely fit Whitehead's description: it was what "an individual does with his own solitariness." Alfred North Whitehead, *Religion in the Making*, reprinted in F.S.C. Northrup and Mason W. Gross, eds., *Alfred North Whitehead: An Anthology* (New York: Macmillan, 1961), 472.

10. Alexis de Tocqueville, *The Old Régime and the French Revolution*, translated by Stuart Gilbert (New York: Doubleday, Anchor Books, 1955), 11. See also John McManners, *The French Revolution and the Church* (Westport, Conn.: Greenwood Press, 1969).

11. Ernst Cassirer, *The Philosophy of the Enlightenment* (Boston: Beacon Press, 1955), 171. Among the devotees of deism were Thomas Jefferson, Benjamin Franklin, and other founding fathers of the United States.

12. de Tocqueville, *The Old Régime*, 13.

13. Liberal politicians within the colonial governments were much more insistent on imparting notions of Western political order than were

the conservatives. In the heyday of British control of India, for instance, the position of Whigs such as William Gladstone was that the presence of the British was "to promote the political training of our fellow-subjects," quoted in H.C.G. Matthew, *Gladstone, 1809–1874*, vol. 1 (Oxford: Clarendon Press, 1986), 188. Conservatives such as Benjamin Disraeli, however, felt that the British should "respect and maintain" the traditional practices of the colonies, including "the laws and customs, the property and religion." From a speech delivered after the Sepoy Rebellion in India in 1857, quoted in William Monypenny and George Buckle, *The Life of Disraeli*, vol. 1: *1804–1859* (London: John Murton, 1929), 1488–89. In the end the liberal vision caught on, even among the educated Indian elite, and the notion of a British-style secular nationalism in India was born.

14. Not all missionary efforts were so despised however. The Anglicans were sometimes seen as partners in the West's civilizing role. The activist, evangelical missionaries were considered more of a threat.

15. Larson describes the relation between religion and nationalism as mutually destructive. According to him, the global system relies on autonomous nation-states that need religion for their legitimacy—as long as religion stays in its place. But as religion is drawn into the public arena, the debate over public values is opened up, and religion can then impose itself on political decisions. This "religionization" of politics is a blow to secular nationalism and calls into question the global nature of the nation-state system. Gerald Larson, "Fast Falls the Eventide: India's Anguish over Religion" (Paper presented at a conference, Religion and Nationalism, University of California, Santa Barbara, April 21, 1989).

16. Anderson, *Imagined Communities*, and Ninian Smart, *Worldviews: Crosscultural Explorations of Human Beliefs* (New York: Scribner's, 1983).

17. See Karl Marx and Friedrich Engels, *The German Ideology*, edited by R. Pascal (New York: International Publishers, 1939); and Karl Mannheim, *Ideology and Utopia* (New York: Harcourt, Brace and World, 1936). For a discussion of the contemporary meaning of ideology, see David Apter, ed., *Ideology and Discontent* (New York: Free Press, 1964); and Chaim I. Waxman, ed., *The End of Ideology Debate* (New York: Simon & Schuster, 1964).

18. Richard H. Cox, *Ideology, Politics, and Political Theory* (Belmont, Calif.: Wadsworth, 1969).

19. Quoted in Cox, *Ideology*, 17.

20. Anthony Giddens, *Central Problems in Social Theory: Action, Structure and Contradiction in Social Analysis* (Berkeley and Los Angeles: University of California Press, 1979), 184.

21. Clifford Geertz, "Ideology as a Cultural System," in David Apter, ed., *Ideology and Discontent* (New York: Free Press, 1964).

22. Karl Deutsch, *Nationalism and Social Communication* (Cambridge, Mass.: MIT Press, 1966).

23. Ernest Gellner, *Nations and Nationalism* (Oxford: Basil Blackwell, 1983), 140.

24. Anthony D. Smith, *Nationalism in the Twentieth Century* (Oxford: Martin Robertson, 1979), 3. See also L. Doob, *Patriotism and Nationalism* (New Haven, Conn.: Yale University Press, 1964).

25. Max Weber, "Politics as a Vocation," in Hans H. Gerth and C. Wright Mills, eds., *From Max Weber: Essays in Sociology* (New York: Oxford University Press, 1946), 78. Regarding the state's monopoly on violence, see John Breuilly, *Nationalism and the State* (Manchester: Manchester University Press, 1982); and Anthony D. Smith, *Theories of Nationalism* (London: Duckworth, 1971).

26. Giddens, *Nation State*, 219.

27. Lawrence, for example, describes fundamentalism as a "religious ideology" that emphasizes the maintenance of traditional social values. Lawrence, *Defenders of God*, 90–101.

28. The notion of religion as a conceptual mechanism that brings order to the disorderly areas of life is a theme of such structuralists as Claude Lévi-Strauss and Mary Douglas, and the adherents of René Girard's mimetic theory. For mimetic theory, see Jean-Pierre Dupuy, *Ordres et désordres: Enquêtes sur un nouveau paradigme* (Paris: Editions du Seuil, 1982); and Paisley Livingston, ed., *Disorder and Order: Proceedings of the Stanford International Symposium (Sept. 14–16, 1981)*, Stanford Literature Studies 1 (Saratoga, Calif.: Anma Libri, 1984).

29. Geertz defines religion as "a system of symbols which acts to establish powerful, pervasive and long-lasting moods and motivations in men by formulating conceptions of a general order of existence and clothing these conceptions with such an aura of factuality that the moods and motivations seem uniquely realistic." Clifford Geertz, "Religion as a Cultural System," reprinted in William A. Lessa and Evon Z. Vogt, eds., *Reader in Comparative Religion: An Anthropological Approach,* 3d ed. (New York: Harper & Row, 1972), 168.

30. Robert N. Bellah, "Transcendence in Contemporary Piety," in Donald R. Cutler, *The Religious Situation: 1969* (Boston: Beacon Press, 1969), 907.

31. Peter Berger, *The Heretical Imperative* (New York: Doubleday, 1980), 38. See also Peter Berger, *The Sacred Canopy: Elements of a Sociological Theory of Religion* (Garden City, N.Y.: Doubleday, 1967).

32. Louis Dupré, *Transcendent Selfhood: The Loss and Rediscovery of the Inner Life* (New York: Seabury Press, 1976), 26. For a discussion of Berger's and Dupré's definitions, see Mary Douglas, "The Effects of

Modernization on Religious Change," *Daedalus* 111, no. 1 (Winter 1982): 1–19.

33. Durkheim describes the dichotomy between the sacred and the profane in religion in the following way: "In all the history of human thought there exists no other example of two categories of things so profoundly differentiated or so radically opposed to one another. . . . The sacred and the profane have always and everywhere been conceived by the human mind as two distinct classes, as two worlds between which there is nothing in common. . . . In different religions, this opposition has been conceived in different ways." Emile Durkheim, *The Elementary Forms of the Religious Life,* translated by Joseph Ward Swain (1915; reprint, London: Allen & Unwin, 1976), 38–39.

34. Although I think one can use the term *religion* (as in "the Christian religion") if one is careful to define it, in general I agree with Smith, who suggested some years ago that the noun *religion* might well be banished from our vocabulary because it implies an organized, Christian version of spirituality and that we restrict ourselves to using the adjective *religious.* Wilfred Cantwell Smith, *The Meaning and End of Religion: A New Approach to the Religious Traditions of Mankind* (New York: Macmillan, 1962), 119–53.

35. Weber, "Politics as a Vocation," 78.

36. Stanley J. Tambiah, *World Conqueror and World Renouncer: A Study of Buddhism and Polity in Thailand against a Historical Background* (Cambridge: Cambridge University Press, 1976). For a useful overview of Theravada society, see Donald K. Swearer, *Buddhism and Society in Southeast Asia* (Chambersburg, Pa.: Anima Books, 1981). For the role of monks in Thai politics, see Somboon Suksamran, *Buddhism and Politics in Thailand: A Study of Socio-political Change and Political Activism of the Thai Sangha* (Singapore: Institute of Southeast Asian Studies, 1982); and Charles F. Keyes, *Thailand: Buddhist Kingdom as Modern Nation-State* (Boulder, Colo.: Westview Press, 1987).

37. For the background of religious nationalism in Burma (Myanmar), see Donald Eugene Smith, ed., *Religion and Politics in Burma* (Princeton, N.J.: Princeton University Press, 1965); E. Sarkisyanz, *Buddhist Backgrounds of the Burmese Revolution* (The Hague: Martinus Nijhoff, 1965); and Heinz Bechert, "Buddhism and Mass Politics in Burma and Ceylon," in Donald Eugene Smith, ed., *Religion and Political Modernization* (New Haven, Conn.: Yale University Press, 1974), 147–67. For a somewhat opposing point of view—that there is relatively little Buddhist influence on Burmese nationalism—see the chapter on Burma in Fred R. von der Mehden, *Religion and Nationalism in Southeast Asia: Burma, Indonesia, the Philippines* (Madison: University of Wisconsin Press,

1963), and "Secularization of Buddhist Polities: Burma and Thailand" in Donald Eugene Smith, ed., *Religion and Political Modernization* (New Haven, Conn.: Yale University Press, 1974), 49–66.

38. Donald Eugene Smith, ed., *Religion, Politics, and Social Change in the Third World: A Sourcebook* (New York: Free Press, 1971), 11.

39. See Walter H. Capps, *The New Religious Right: Piety, Patriotism, and Politics* (Columbia: University of South Carolina Press, 1990); Randall Balmer, *Mine Eyes Have Seen the Glory: A Journey into the Evangelical Subculture in America* (New York: Oxford University Press, 1989); and Lawrence, *Defenders of God.*

40. Robert N. Bellah, "Civil Religion in America," *Daedalus* 96, no. 1 (Winter 1967): 1–21, reprinted in Robert N. Bellah, *Beyond Belief* (New York: Harper & Row, 1970).

41. Jaroslav Krejci, "What Is a Nation?" in Peter Merkl and Ninian Smart, eds., *Religion and Politics in the Modern World* (New York: New York University Press, 1983), 39.

42. Krejci, "What Is a Nation?" 39.

43. Interview with Prof. Leila el-Hamamsy, director, Social Research Center, American University, in Cairo, January 10, 1989.

44. Interview with Saad Ibrahim, professor of sociology, American University, in Cairo, January 10, 1989.

45. See Smith, *India as a Secular State*, which details the many concessions the government has made.

46. Ainslie T. Embree, *Utopias in Conflict: Religion and Nationalism in Modern India* (Berkeley and Los Angeles: University of California Press, 1990), 88.

47. Interview with the Rev. Kenneth Fernando, Ecumenical Institute for Study and Dialogue, in Colombo, January 27, 1988.

48. Stanley J. Tambiah, *Sri Lanka: Ethnic Fratricide and the Dismantling of Democracy* (Chicago: University of Chicago Press, 1986), 137.

49. D. C. Vejayavardhana, *The Revolt in the Temple: Composed to Commemorate 2,500 Years of the Land, the Race, and the Faith* (Colombo: Sinha Publications, 1953), reprinted in Donald Eugene Smith, *Religion, Politics and Social Change in the Third World: A Sourcebook* (New York: Free Press, 1971), 105.

50. Ibid., 105.

51. Giddens, *Nation-State*, 71. He goes on to deny that most religions outside the West have much to do with day-to-day morality and the social order (73). Giddens seems unaware of the importance of such ethical and social notions as dharma in Hindu tradition, shari'a in Islam, and li in Chinese religion.

52. Interview with Prof. Abdullah Schleiffer, director, Communications Center, American University, in Cairo, January 7, 1989.

53. Bernard Lewis, *Political Language of Islam*. In a large nation-state such as China, it is "the nation-state apparatus itself" to which minority ethnic groups find themselves in opposition (Gladney, *Muslim Chinese*, 81). When an ethnic group is in the majority, however, it more easily accepts the nation-state.

Chapter 3: Models of Religious Nationalism: The Middle East

1. See Michael Walzer, *The Revolution of the Saints: A Study in the Origins of Radical Politics* (New York: Atheneum, 1974).

2. A stasis-disequilibrium model of society is presumed in the models of revolution developed by social scientists in the 1950s and 1960s. See, for examples, Crane Brinton, *The Anatomy of Revolution*, rev. ed. (New York: Random House, Vintage Books, 1957), 16–17; and Chalmers Johnson, *Revolutionary Change* (Boston: Little, Brown, 1966), *passim*. Arendt maintains a different view of revolutions, arguing that they must always be "something new," aiming at "freedom." Hannah Arendt, *On Revolution* (New York: Viking Press, 1963), 36. She concludes that revolutions are always, therefore, secular.

3. Gary Sick, *All Fall Down: America's Tragic Encounter with Iran*, rev. ed. (New York: Penguin, 1986), 187.

4. I saw this poster in the home of Sheik Ahmed Yassin in Gaza, January 14, 1989.

5. Kalim Siddiqui, "Nation-States as Obstacles to the Total Transformation of the *Ummah*," in M. Ghayasuddin, ed., *The Impact of Nationalism on the Muslim World* (London: Open Press, Al-Hoda, 1986), 1.

6. Ira M. Lapidus, *A History of Islamic Societies* (Cambridge: Cambridge University Press, 1988), 887.

7. Siddiqui, "Nation-States as Obstacles," 11.

8. Ibid., 6.

9. Some observers say that the Gulf War was the final nail in the coffin of the pan-Arab movement. See Auda, "An Uncertain Response," 122.

10. Kim Murphy, "Islamic Militants Build Power Base in Sudan," *Los Angeles Times*, April 6, 1992, p. A1.

11. Ibid., p. A9.

12. Abdelkadir Hachani, quoted in Kim Murphy, "Algerian Election to Test Strength of Radical Islam," *Los Angeles Times*, December 26, 1991, p. A18. After the Front won 55 percent of the vote in local elections in 1990, the army attempted to arrest and intimidate its members, and 4,000 of

them lost their jobs as a result of going on strike against the government in the summer of 1991. The first stage of the national elections, on December 27, 1991, gave the Front 40 percent of the parliamentary seats, and a total of more than 60 percent were expected to be gleaned after the runoff elections on January 16, 1992. The Islamic movement has been a thorn in the side of Algerian nationalists since independence. See John P. Entelis, *Algeria: The Revolution Institutionalized* (Boulder, Colo.: Westview Press, 1986); and Hugh Roberts, "Radical Islamism and the Dilemma of Algerian Nationalism: The Embattled Arians of Algiers," *Third World Quarterly* 10, no. 2 (April 1988): 556–89.

13. Quoted in Robin Wright, "Muslims under the Gun," *Los Angeles Times*, January 28, 1992, p. B1.

14. Kim Murphy, "Revolution Again Echoes through the Casbah," *Los Angeles Times*, March 15, 1992, p. A15. The leader of the Islamic Salvation Front, Abdelkadir Hachani, urged his followers to respond nonviolently to the military and to confine their protests to attendance at mosques, which swelled significantly after Hachani was jailed on January 22, 1992. Robin Wright, "Muslims under the Gun," *Los Angeles Times*, January 28, 1992.

15. Jonathan C. Randall, "Algeria Leader Assassinated during Speech," *Los Angeles Times*, June 30, 1991, p. A1. Boudiaf, a hero of Algeria's war of independence, had openly supported the separation of religion and politics in Algeria and had defended the ban on the Islamic Salvation Front. He was killed in a complicated attack involving bombs and automatic-weapons fire as he was giving a speech in the Mediterranean port city of Annaba. On July 2, he was succeeded by Ali Kafi, another civilian member of the Council of State.

16. The Jordanian government uncovered a cache of weapons allegedly being held for that purpose. See Nick B. Williams, Jr., "Chasm Widening between Amman, Fundamentalists," *Los Angeles Times*, August 8, 1991, p. A4.

17. Raymond A. Hinnebusch, "The Islamic Movement in Syria: Sectarian Conflict and Urban Rebellion in an Authoritarian-Populist Regime," in Ali E. Hillal Dessouki, ed., *Islamic Resurgence in the Arab World* (New York: Praeger, 1982), 138–69.

18. Quoted in R. Stephen Humphreys, "The Contemporary Resurgence in the Context of Modern Islam," in Ali E. Hillal Dessouki, ed., *Islamic Resurgence in the Arab World* (New York: Praeger, 1982), 80.

19. Youssef M. Ibrahim, "Saudi Rulers Are Confronting Challenge by Islamic Radicals," *New York Times*, March 9, 1992, p. A1.

20. Interview with the Ayatollah Khomeini by Prof. Hamid Algar on December 29, 1978, at Neauphle-le-Chateau, France, in Khomeini, *Islam and Revolution*, 323.

21. Ibid., 322.

22. Lewis, *Political Language of Islam*, 2.

23. Ibid., 3.

24. Ayatollah Ruhullah Khomeini, "Muharram: The Triumph of Blood over the Sword," in Khomeini, *Islam and Revolution*, 242. For a general assessment of the ayatollah's politicization of Ashura, see Emmanuel Sivan, "Sunni Radicalism in the Middle East and the Iranian Revolution," *International Journal for Middle East Studies* 21 (1989): 16–17.

25. Sivan, "Sunni Radicalism," 8–11 and note 11 on p. 29.

26. Hamid Algar, "Foreword" to Khomeini, *Islam and Revolution*, 10.

27. Quoted in Sivan, "Sunni Radicalism," 12.

28. A. Ali-Babai, "An Open Letter to Khomeini, *Iranshahr*, June 15–July 16, 1982, quoted in Ervand Abrahamian, *Radical Islam: The Iranian Mojahedin* (London: I. B. Tauris, 1989), 19.

29. Khomeini, *Islam and Revolution*, 334.

30. Ibid., 335.

31. For the U.S. State Department's perspective on the crisis, see the revealing study by Sick, *All Fall Down*.

32. Ibid., 229–30.

33. The early years of the revolution and the mullahs' ascension to power are chronicled in Shaul Bakhash, *The Reign of the Ayatollahs: Iran and the Islamic Revolution* (New York: Basic Books, 1984).

34. Supporters of the moderate Islamic revolutionary movement, the Mojahedin, were especially targeted for repression because of the considerable power and popularity they had gained after the revolution. See Abrahamian, *Radical Islam*.

35. Said Amir Arjomand, "A Victory for the Pragmatists: The Islamic Fundamentalist Reaction in Iran," in James P. Piscatori, ed., *Islamic Fundamentalisms and the Gulf Crisis* (Chicago: Fundamentalism Project, American Academy of Arts and Sciences, 1991), 52.

36. Nick B. Williams, Jr., "Iran's Rafsanjani, Guarding His Political Flanks, Steers a More Militant Course," *Los Angeles Times*, January 13, 1992, p. A3.

37. Robin Wright, "Iran Extends Reach of Its Aid to Islamic Groups," *Los Angeles Times*, April 6, 1993, p. A4.

38. For interesting accounts of life in postrevolutionary Iran, see Robin Wright, *In the Name of God: The Khomeini Decade* (New York: Simon & Schuster, 1989); John Simpson, *Inside Iran: Life under Khomeini's Regime* (New York: St. Martin's Press, 1988); and Roy P. Mottahedeh, *The Mantle of the Prophet* (New York: Pantheon, 1986).

39. For the theological history of the concept, see Abdulaziz Abdulhussein Sachedina, *The Just Ruler (al-sultan al-'adil) in Shi'ite Islam:*

The Comprehensive Authority of the Jurist in Imamite Jurisprudence (New York: Oxford University Press, 1988).

40. Khomeini, *Islam and Revolution,* 342.

41. Ibid., 343.

42. From my informal conversation with a group of journalists in Jerusalem, May 24, 1990.

43. Nejla Sammakia, "Egypt's No. 2 Man Slain by Assassins," *San Francisco Examiner,* October 13, 1990, national edition, p. A16.

44. According to one scholar, "Egypt has been influenced by Arab and Indian subcontinent themes far more than by Iranian ones." Shahrough Akhavi, "The Impact of the Iranian Revolution on Egypt," in John L. Esposito, ed., *The Iranian Revolution: Its Global Impact* (Miami: Florida International University Press, 1990), 138. For a comprehensive analysis of the separation between Sunni and Shi'a radical groups, see Sivan "Sunni Radicalism."

45. Interview with el-Arian.

46. They do, however, occasionally refer to the Iranian revolution in discussing the worldwide development of Islamic political consciousness. See, for instance, the articles from *Al-Hilal,* July 1987, translated into French and summarized in *Revue de la presse égyptienne,* no. 27 (1987).

47. Bakhash, for example, implies that the Iranian revolution provides a model for Muslim radicals in Egypt and elsewhere. Bakhash, *Reign of the Ayatollahs,* 4.

48. For the rise of the Muslim Brotherhood in Egypt, see Charles Wendell, trans., *Five Tracts of Hasan al-Banna (1906–1949)* (Berkeley and Los Angeles: University of California Press, 1978), 40–68, 133–62; Bernard Lewis, "The Return of Islam," in Michael Curtis, ed., *Religion and Politics in the Middle East* (Boulder, Colo.: Westview Press, 1981), 14–16, 55–67, 77–128; Richard P. Mitchell, *The Society of the Muslim Brothers* (London: Oxford University Press, 1969); and Emmanuel Sivan, *Radical Islam: Medieval Theology and Modern Politics* (New Haven, Conn.: Yale University Press, 1985).

49. Interview with Ibrahim.

50. It was published in *Al-Ahrar,* an Egyptian newspaper, on December 14, 1981. An English translation, accompanied by an extensive essay about the document, is to be found in Johannes J. G. Jansen, *The Neglected Duty: The Creed of Sadat's Assassins and Islamic Resurgence in the Middle East* (New York: Macmillan, 1986). I have also found helpful the analysis of this document by David Rapoport in "Sacred Terror: A Case from Islam" (Paper delivered at the annual meeting of the American Political Science Association, Washington, D.C., September 1–4, 1988). Its political implications are discussed in Mohammed

Heikal, *Autumn of Fury: The Assassination of Sadat* (London: Andre Deutsch, 1983).

51. Faraj, par. 84, in Jansen, *Neglected Duty*, 199.

52. In the description of jihad often given by Sunni theologians it applies only to the defense of Islam when it is under direct assault. See Rudolph Peters, *Islam and Colonialism: The Doctrine of Jihad in Modern History* (The Hague: Mouton, 1979), 121–35.

53. Faraj, pars. 102 and 109, in Jansen, *Neglected Duty*, 210–11.

54. Faraj, par. 113, in Jansen, *Neglected Duty*, 212–13; see also par. 109 on p. 211.

55. According to an Egyptian scholar who interviewed in prison members of the group responsible for Sadat's assassination, the writings of Mawdudi were "important in shaping the group's ideas." Saad Eddin Ibrahim, "Islamic Militancy as a Social Movement: The Case of Two Groups in Egypt," in Ali E. Hillal Dessouki, ed., *Islamic Resurgence in the Arab World* (New York: Praeger, 1982), 125.

56. For a discussion of the significance of Sayyid Qutb's life and work, see Richard C. Martin, "Religious Violence in Islam: Towards an Understanding of the Discourse on *Jihad* in Modern Egypt," in Paul Wilkinson and A. M. Stewart, eds., *Contemporary Research on Terrorism* (Aberdeen: University Press, 1987), 54–71; Gilles Kepel, *Muslim Extremism in Egypt: The Prophet and Pharaoh* (Berkeley and Los Angeles: University of California Press, 1986), 36–69; Yvonne V. Haddad, "Sayyid Qutb: Ideologue of Islamic Revival," in John L. Esposito, ed., *Voices of Resurgent Islam* (New York: Oxford University Press, 1983); and Ronald L. Nettler, *Past Trials and Present Tribulations: A Muslim Fundamentalist's View of the Jews* (New York: Pergamon Press, 1987).

57. Qutb studied in Washington, D.C., and California from 1949 to 1951. Haddad, "Sayyid Qutb," 69.

58. Sayyid Qutb, *This Religion of Islam (Hadha 'd-Din)*, translated by Islamdust (Palo Alto, Calif.: Al-Manar Press, 1967), 87.

59. Interview with Prof. A. K. Ashur, dean of the Faculty of Education, Al-Azhar University, in Cairo, May 27, 1990.

60. Interview with Ashur.

61. These points are summarized in Marius Deeb, "Egypt," in Stuart Mews, ed., *Religion in Politics: A World Guide* (London: Longman, 1989), 64.

62. Initially the Muslim Brotherhood condemned Iraq for invading Kuwait, but when the United States became involved, it shifted its condemnation to the United States. This confusion "induced deep ideological and behavioral uncertainty in its ranks." Auda, "An Uncertain Response," 110.

63. Akhavi, "Impact of the Iranian Revolution," 144.

64. Interview with Kahane.

65. Interview with Kahane; see also an interview with Kahane published in Raphael Mergui and Philippe Simonnot, *Israel's Ayatollahs: Meir Kahane and the Far Right in Israel* (London: Saqi Books, 1987), 40–41.

66. Carl E. Schorske, *Fin-de-Siècle Vienna: Politics and Culture* (New York: Knopf, 1980), 165.

67. The best analysis of the new religious politics in Israel may be found in Ehud Sprinzak, *The Ascendance of Israel's Radical Right* (New York: Oxford University Press, 1991). See also Ian S. Lustick, *For the Land and the Lord: Jewish Fundamentalism in Israel* (New York: Council on Foreign Relations, 1989).

68. Alter B. Z. Metzger, *Rabbi Kook's Philosophy of Repentance: A Translation of "Orot Ha-Teshuvah,"* Studies in Torah Judaism 11 (New York. Yeshiva University Press, 1968), 111. See also Jacob B. Agus, *Banner of Jerusalem: The Life, Times, and Thought of Rabbi Abraham Isaac Kuk* (New York: Bloch, 1946).

69. There have been several biographies of Kahane. The most recent is Robert Friedman, *The False Prophet: Rabbi Meir Kahane—From FBI Informant to Knesset Member* (London: Faber and Faber, 1990). For a comprehensive study of the religious right in Israel that puts Kahane's movement in context, see Sprinzak, *The Ascendance of Israel's Radical Right*.

70. Quoted in John Kifner's obituary of Kahane, "A Militant Leader, Fiery Politician and Founder of Anti-Arab Crusade," *New York Times*, November 7, 1990, p. B12.

71. H. K. Michael Eitan's speech to the Knesset Rules Committee in 1984, quoted in Gerald Cromer, *The Debate about Kahanism in Israeli Society, 1984–1988*, Occasional Papers 3 (New York: Henry Frank Guggenheim Foundation, 1988), 37–38.

72. Yair Kotler, *Heil Kahane* (New York: Adama Books, 1986).

73. Interview with Kahane.

74. According to Sprinzak, Kahane did not make the usual nationalist argument that the Jews deserved the land because it was their ancient birthplace; rather, the Jews *"expropriated* it in the name of God and his sovereign will." Sprinzak, *The Ascendance of Israel's Radical Right*, 225; italics in the original.

75. Kahane made this point during a function proclaiming a new state of Judea—one that would be established on the West Bank if and when the Israeli army retreated from those areas (from my notes taken at the function in Jerusalem, January 18, 1989).

76. Interview with Kahane. See also similar comments made by

Kahane in the interview published in Mergui and Simonnot, *Israel's Ayatollahs*, 43, 44, 68, 76–77, 150.

77. Interview with Levinger.

78. See Ehud Sprinzak, "Fundamentalism, Terrorism, and Democracy: The Case of Gush Emunim Underground" (Colloquium paper given at the Woodrow Wilson International Center for Scholars, Washington, D.C., September 16, 1986); revised and expanded version published as "From Messianic Pioneering to Vigilante Terrorism: The Case of Gush Emunim Underground," *Journal of Strategic Studies* 10, no. 4 (December 1987): 194–216 (a special issue entitled "Inside Terrorist Organizations," edited by David C. Rapoport); reissued as a book: David C. Rapoport, ed., *Inside Terrorist Organizations* (New York: Columbia University Press, 1988).

79. The idea that the rebuilding of the Temple will be a part of the messianic age is a common theme in Jewish speculation. See, for example, George W. Buchanan, *Revelation and Redemption: Jewish Documents of Deliverance from the Fall of Jerusalem to the Death of Nahmanides* (Dillsboro, N.C.: Western North Carolina Press, 1978); and Jonathan Frankel, ed., *Jews and Messianism in the Modern Era: Metaphor and Meaning*, vol. 7 of *Studies in Contemporary Jewry* (New York: Oxford University Press, and Jerusalem: Institute of Contemporary Jewry, Hebrew University of Jerusalem, 1991), 197–213 and 34–67. I am grateful to Prof. Richard Hecht of the University of California, Santa Barbara, for bringing to my attention these and other references on Jewish nationalism.

80. Interview with Lerner.

81. Interview with Gershom Salomon, head, Faithful of Temple Mount, in Jerusalem, May 25, 1990.

82. I am grateful to Prof. Hecht for pointing out that the calendar has long been a critical element in clashes between Jews and Muslims at Temple Mount and that conflicts between two different groups of religious nationalists often involve a skirmish over sacred space. See also Bernard Wasserstein, "Patterns of Communal Conflict in Palestine," in Ada Rapoport and Steven J. Zipperstein, eds., *Jewish History: Essays in Honour of Chimen Abramsky* (London: Peter Halban, 1988), 611–28.

83. Although the American television news reports routinely described the incident as unprovoked rock throwing by Palestinians aimed at Jewish worshipers gathered at the Western Wall (directly below the scene of the clash in the Temple Mount area), a fairly full and accurate report of the incident, including the provocation by Salomon and his group, may be found in the October 9, 1990, editions of the *New York Times*, the *Los Angeles Times*, and the *Washington Post*. One of the most complete accounts is Jackson Diehl, "The Battle at Temple Mount: Nei-

ther Palestinian nor Israeli Version Tells Full Story," *Washington Post,* October 14, 1990, pp. A1, A23; and "Special File: The Haram al-Sharif (Temple Mount) Killings," *Journal of Palestine Studies* 20, no. 2 (Winter 1991), 134–59.

84. John Kifner, "Suspect in Kahane Case Is Muslim Born in Egypt," *New York Times,* November 7, 1990, p. B13.

85. "The Legacy of Hate," *New York Times,* November 7, 1990, p. A30.

86. See the essay by Elie Rekhess, "The Iranian Impact on the Islamic Jihad Movement in the Gaza Strip," in David Menashri, ed., *The Iranian Revolution and the Muslim World* (Boulder, Colo.: Westview Press, 1990). An excerpt from this article, under the title "The Growth of Khomeinism in Gaza," was published in the *Jerusalem Post Magazine,* January 26, 1991, p. 12.

87. Legrain, "Defining Moment," 72.

88. Interview with Yassin.

89. Interview with Yassin.

90. Interview with Yassin.

91. Many leaders of the PLO coalition have been eager to avoid a confrontation between religious and secular elements, and to use the ideology of Islam to their own advantage. See, for instance, Matti Steinberg, "The PLO and Palestinian Islamic Fundamentalism," *Jewish Quarterly* 52 (Fall 1989): 37–54.

92. Interview with Dr. Fathi Arafat, president, Palestine Red Crescent Society, in Cairo, May 30, 1990.

93. Interview with Arafat.

94. One poll conducted in 1991 claimed that Hamas was supported by 18 percent of the residents in Gaza, while the support for another militant Muslim group, the Islamic Jihad, garnered another 5 to 10 percent: a total of 25 percent. A Hamas leader described the poll as "nonsense" and claimed 60 percent support in Gaza and 50 percent on the West Bank. "Surveys Show Support for Moslem Hardliners Weaker Than Believed," *Mideast Mirror,* May 7, 1991, p. 3.

95. Interview with Saleh Zamlot, student leader, Fateh, Palestine Liberation Organization, in Al-Azhar University, Cairo, May 27, 1990.

96. Interview with Yassin.

97. See Jean-François Legrain, "Islamistes et lutte nationale palestinienne dans les territoires occupés par Israel," *Revue Française de science politique* 36, no. 2 (April 1986): 227–47; and Ifrah Zilberman, "Hamas: Apocalypse Now," *Jerusalem Post Weekly,* January 12, 1991, p. 11.

98. Jean-François Legrain, "The Islamic Movement and the *Intifada,*" in Jamal R. Nassar and Roger Heacock, eds., *Intifada: Palestine at the Crossroads* (New York: Praeger, 1990), 177, and "Defining Moment,"

72–73. Legrain identifies Fathi Shqaqi, a pharmacist from Rafah, as the military commander of the Islamic Jihad, 'Odeh as the spiritual leader.

99. Legrain, "Islamic Movement," 177.

100. Ibid.

101. Ibid., 176. I am grateful to Dr. Ifrah Zilberman of Jerusalem for showing me a number of copies of *Islam and Palestine*, which he has in his possession.

102. Legrain, "Islamic Movement," 182.

103. Quoted in ibid.

104. Ibid., 183.

105. Reuven Paz, *Ha-'imna ha-islamit umichma'utah 'iyyon rechoni utargum* (*The Covenant of the Islamicists and Its Significance—Analysis and Translation*) (Tel Aviv: Dayan Center, Tel Aviv University, 1988).

106. These rumors were reported to me by Zilberman in my interview with him. See also Legrain, "Islamic Movement," 185. During the first months of 1989 Yassin was allowed to talk to journalists and foreigners such as myself.

107. This ritual, in which the young men were required to sleep beside the Dome of the Rock all night, was described in the newspaper *Al-Sabil*, April 1989.

108. Communiqué #66, October 31, 1990, quoted in Legrain, "Defining Moment," 83.

109. "Israelis Round Up Palestinians in Hunt for Killers," *New York Times*, December 16, 1990, international edition, p. A5. This article reported that an Israeli army spokesman said that the numbers of those arrested, provided by Palestinian sources, were "terribly exaggerated."

110. Ibid.

111. In the year before the Gulf War, Kuwait gave $60 million to Hamas and only $27 million to the PLO. Legrain, "Defining Moment," 79.

112. See "Three Hurt in Muslim-PLO Clash as Internal Feud Turns Violent," *Los Angeles Times*, June 3, 1991, p. A10. Clashes between Hamas and Fateh occurred in the Jabalya refugee camp in Gaza and in Nablus on the West Bank. Also, Hamas began to require women in Gaza to wear the Muslim head scarf (*hijab*).

113. Joel Brinkley, "A West Bank Business Chamber Votes for Islamic Fundamentalists," *New York Times*, June 20, 1991, international edition, p. A10.

114. Daniel Williams, "Arab Revolt: From Rocks to Revenge," *Los Angeles Times*, May 5, 1992, p. H4.

115. Daniel Williams, "The Quiet Palestinian," *Los Angeles Times Magazine*, June 7, 1992, p. 53.

116. Interview with 'Odeh printed in *Islam and Palestine*, Leaflet 5 (Limasol, Cyprus, June 1988).

117. Interview with Yassin.

Chapter 4:
Political Targets of Religion: South Asia

1. After the coup, Pakistan's Prime Minister Nawaz Sharif flew to Kabul, where he praised the new government and rebuked its religious rivals, led by the militant Gulbuddin Hekmatyr, who had been supported by Pakistan's Jama'at-i-Islami (Islamic Party)—which in response withdrew its support from Sharif's coalition government. Mark Fineman, "Worries Rise with Strict Islam Rule in Kabul," *Los Angeles Times*, May 24, 1992, p. A8. For the background of religious politics of Pakistan, see Anwar Syed, *Pakistan: Islam, Politics, and National Solidarity* (New York, Praeger, 1982); Aziz Ahmad, "The Ulama in Politics," in Nikki R. Keddie, ed., *Scholars, Saints, and Sufis* (Berkeley and Los Angeles: University of California Press, 1972); and Mumtaz Ahmad, "Islamic Fundamentalism in South Asia: The Jama'at-i-Islami and the Tablighi Jama'at," in Martin E. Marty and R. Scott Appleby, eds., *Fundamentalisms Observed* (Chicago: University of Chicago Press, 1991), 457–530.

2. Chairman Upadhayay, quoted in Bob Drogin, "Democracy Takes Hold in Himalayan Kingdom," *Los Angeles Times*, August 5, 1990, p. A6.

3. See John Stratton Hawley, "Naming Hinduism," *Wilson Quarterly* (Summer 1991): 20–34.

4. Whether there actually was a Kautilya, a political advisor to the great ruler Candragupta Maurya, is a subject of some scholarly dispute. The *Artha-sastra* came to light in the twelfth century C.E., and some scholars date the text some seven centuries later than the traditional fourth century B.C.E.

5. The date the panchayat system developed in India is difficult to ascertain, but Basham reports a primitive form of it in ancient India. A. L. Basham, *The Wonder That Was India: A Survey of the Culture of the Indian Sub-continent before the Coming of the Muslims* (New York: Grove Press, 1954), 102–7.

6. Embree, "Brahmanical Ideology and Regional Identities," in *Imagining India*, 9–27. For the way Brahmanical Hinduism encapsulates its competition, see Embree, "The Question of Hindu Tolerance," in *Utopias in Conflict*, 19–37. As early as the mid 1960s, van Leeuwen proclaimed that Hinduism was becoming the national ideology of India. Van Leeuwen, *Christianity in World History*, 365.

7. On the history of the RSS, see Walter K. Andersen and Shridhar

D. Damle, *The Brotherhood in Saffron: The Rashtriya Swayamsevak Sangh and Hindu Revivalism* (Boulder, Colo.: Westview Press, 1987).

8. V. D. Savarkar, "Foreword" to Savitri Devi, *A Warning to the Hindus* (Calcutta: Hindu Mission, 1939).

9. V. D. Savarkar, *Hindutva: Who Is a Hindu?* (Bombay: Veer Savarkar Prakashan, 1969).

10. Quoted in Ainslie T. Embree, "The Function of the Rashtriya Swayamsevak Sangh: To Define the Hindu Nation," in Martin E. Marty and R. Scott Appleby, eds., *Accounting for Fundamentalisms* (Chicago: University of Chicago Press, forthcoming).

11. Nehru, *Discovery of India,* 531.

12. For an analysis of the persistence of what the author calls Hindu fundamentalism in South Asia, see Robert Eric Frykenberg, "Revivalism and Fundamentalism: Some Critical Observations with Special Reference to Politics in South Asia," in James W. Bjorkman, ed., *Fundamentalism, Revivalists and Violence in South Asia* (Riverdale, Md.: Riverdale Company, 1986).

13. Another political issue that exercised Muslims was the Indian Supreme Court's 1986 decision in the Shah Bano case. At issue was the fairness of the Muslim laws regarding compensation for a divorced wife. A Muslim woman in Indore, Shah Bano, argued that she should receive compensation equal to what a divorced Hindu woman would receive, not the meager settlement allowed under Muslim law. The court agreed, and the chief justice added fuel to the fire by stating that the time had come for a unified legal code for all religious communities in India. The outcry from Muslims in response was considerable; in Bombay a procession of 100,000 people denounced the court's verdict. At first Rajiv Gandhi's government defended the court, but after Muslim resistance mounted, it reversed itself, proposing a new piece of legislation known as the Muslim Women's Bill. The bill would nullify the effect of the Supreme Court's decision by exempting Muslims from the provisions of Section 125 of the Criminal Procedure Code, which prescribed the way in which husbands were to support their divorced wives. The new bill attempted to be egalitarian, however, by allowing Muslim women to appeal to the Muslim *waqf,* the charitable fund, for compensation equal to what Hindu women in such circumstances would receive. The bill was attacked by Hindus, secularists, and feminists, but on May 6, 1986, it became law.

14. Opinion poll conducted by *India Today* 16, no. 10 (May 31, 1991): 3.

15. See Peter van der Veer, "Hindu 'Nationalism' and the Discourse of 'Modernity': The Vishva Hindu Parishad," in Martin E. Marty and R. Scott Appleby, eds., *Accounting For Fundamentalisms* (Chicago: University of Chicago Press, forthcoming).

16. The founding date was August 29, which in 1964 corresponded with the date in the lunar calendar when Lord Krishna was said to be born.

17. Swami Chinmayananda was a Shaivite Kshatriya from Kerala who had been active in the Indian independence movement before traveling to Rishikesh, where he sought out the reclusive Swami Topavana for spiritual edification. His Chinmaya Mission had centers in cities throughout India in addition to the main Sandeepany Sadhanalaya ashram near Bombay. He taught a reformed Hinduism emphasizing the value of self-esteem and the dangers of a secularized society. A number of young, Western spiritual seekers were attracted to his ashram in the 1970s, and a branch of the movement established a "Sandeepany West" in California in the 1980s. My thanks to Prof. Ann Berliner of California State University, Fresno, for information on Swami Chinmayananda and his mission.

18. Ayodhya was the third "most important issue" in the 1991 political campaign; "price increase" was first, and "political instability" was second. *India Today* 16, no. 10 (May 31, 1991): 4.

19. These figures were reported by *India Today*. The *Los Angeles Times* placed the number killed in Ayodhya-related incidents at more than a thousand. Mark Fineman, "India Arrests Hindu Party Chief, Sparks Crisis," *Los Angeles Times*, October 24, 1990, p. A12.

20. Quoted in Bernard Weinraub, "A Hindu Nationalist Stirs and Scares," *New York Times*, June 9, 1991, international edition, p. A10.

21. Rajiv Gandhi was killed during the campaign by a bomb blast on May 21, 1991, in the small South Indian town of Sriperumbudur, where he had come to make a speech. Tamils involved in the Sri Lankan separatist movement were implicated in the conspiracy.

22. *India Today* 16, no. 10 (May 31, 1991): 59.

23. Quoted in Sanjoy Hazarika, "Hindu Fundamentalist Threatens India's Government over Temple," *New York Times*, October 18, 1990, international edition, p. A1.

24. Quoted in Mark Fineman, "Hindus Storm Mosque; 32 Die in India Strife," *Los Angeles Times*, October 31, 1990, p. A1.

25. Quoted in Fineman, "India Arrests Hindu Party Chief," A12.

26. Sarvepalli Gopal, "Introduction," in Sarvepalli Gopal, ed., *Anatomy of a Confrontation: The Babri Masjid–Ramjanmabhumi Issue* (New Delhi: Penguin Books, 1991), 13.

27. Quoted in Bernard Weinraub, "A Hindu Nationalist Stirs and Scares," A10.

28. A. B. Vajpayee, BJP leader, quoted in V. Mahurkar, "Gandhian Humanism: BJP Agonizes over Striking New Posture," *India Today*, May 31, 1992, p. 16.

29. Dilip Awasthi and Shahnaz Anklesaria Aiyar, "RSS-BJP-VHP: Hindu Divided Family," *India Today*, November 30, 1991, pp. 14–19.

30. The Unity March, led by BJP leader Murli Manohar Joshi, continued north to the Kashmir border, where he and his marchers were denied access for security reasons. Joshi flew to the Kashmir capital, Srinagar, by airplane to complete the last leg of the march. In 1991, in the midst of the Ayodhya controversy, a similar incident occurred when a group of young Hindu students in Chandigarh, the capital of the Punjab, who were on a hunger strike to show their support for the BJP cause were shot dead by a passing cadre of militant Sikhs.

31. Some Sikhs, however, think they have more in common with the BJP than with the secular Congress party, and for that reason they supported the BJP in the 1989 and 1991 elections.

32. Interview with Jasvinder Singh, member of the Delhi Branch, All-India Sikh Students Federation (Mehta-Chawla group), at Rakabganj Gurdwara, New Delhi, January 13, 1991.

33. Interview with Darshan Singh Ragi, former jatedar, Akal Takhat, at Bhai Vir Singh Sadan, New Delhi, January 13, 1991.

34. Interview with Ragi.

35. Jarnail Singh Bhindranwale, "Address to the Sikh Congregation," transcript of a sermon given in the Golden Temple in November 1983, translated by Ranbir Singh Sandhu, April 1985, and distributed by the Sikh Religious and Educational Trust, Columbus, Ohio, p. 10.

36. For a brief introduction to Guru Nanak and his relation to the other bhakti saints, see John Stratton Hawley and Mark Juergensmeyer, trans., *Songs of the Saints of India* (New York: Oxford University Press, 1988). The leading scholarly work on Guru Nanak's life and writings is W. H. McLeod, *Guru Nanak and the Sikh Religion* (Oxford: Clarendon Press, 1968). Whether Guru Nanak actually took an interest in the societal matters and community issues of his day is a matter of some speculation.

37. See the title essay in W. H. McLeod, *The Evolution of the Sikh Community: Five Essays* (Oxford: Clarendon Press, 1976), 1–19.

38. See Embree, "A Sikh Challenge to the Indian State," in *Utopias in Conflict*, 113–32.

39. For a good account of the Punjab crisis in the 1980s and the events leading up to it, see Mark Tully and Satish Jacob, *Amritsar: Mrs. Gandhi's Last Battle* (London: Cape, 1985); also useful are Amarjit Kaur et al., *The Punjab Story* (New Delhi: Roli Books International, 1984); and Kuldip Nayar and Khushwant Singh, *Tragedy of Punjab: Operation Bluestar and After* (New Delhi: Vision Books, 1984).

40. An extensive analysis of Bhindranwale's speeches may be found in Mark Juergensmeyer, "The Logic of Religious Violence," *Journal of Strate-*

gic Studies 10, no. 4 (December 1987), reprinted in David C. Rapoport, ed., *Inside Terrorist Organizations* (London: Frank Cass, 1988).

41. Fear of the absorption of Sikhism into Hinduism is the refrain of many modern Sikh writers, including the best known, Khushwant Singh. See, for instance, the final chapter of his *History of the Sikhs*, vol. 2 (Princeton, N.J.: Princeton University Press, 1966). In Nayar and Singh, *Tragedy of Punjab*, 19–21, he attributes many of the problems in the Punjab in the mid-1980s to the erosion of Sikh identity.

42. *Qaum* is a Persian word with a Muslim heritage that has tradition-ally been a part of the Sikh vocabulary, where it expresses a sense of religious nationhood. For a discussion of the political implications of the concept in the Punjab, see Mark Juergensmeyer, *Religion as Social Vision: The Movement against Untouchability in 20th Century Punjab* (Berkeley and Los Angeles: University of California Press, 1982), 45.

43. Bhindranwale, "Address to the Sikh Congregation," 9. The de-mand for Khalistan developed largely among Sikhs living abroad. The Indian government's account of Jagjit Singh Chauhan's campaign for a separate Sikh nation while he was in exile in London is detailed in a report prepared by the Indian Home Ministry, "Sikh Agitation for Khalistan," reprinted in Nayar and Singh, *Tragedy of Punjab*, 142–55.

44. On Bhindranwale's use of *miri-piri*, see Joyce Pettigrew, "In Search of a New Kingdom of Lahore," *Pacific Affairs* 60, no. 1 (Spring 1987).

45. Jarnail Singh Bhindranwale, "Two Lectures," given on July 19 and September 20, 1983, translated from the videotaped originals by R. S. Sandhu, and distributed by the Sikh Religious and Educational Trust, Columbus, Ohio, p. 2.

46. Bhindranwale, "Address to the Sikh Congregation," 1.

47. Indira Gandhi, "Don't Shed Blood, Shed Hatred," All India Radio, June 2, 1984, reprinted in V. D. Chopra, R. K. Mishra, and Nirmal Singh, *Agony of Punjab* (New Delhi: Patriot Publishers, 1984), 189.

48. See Ritu Sarin, *The Assassination of Indira Gandhi* (New Delhi: Penguin Books, 1990).

49. There is a good deal of evidence that many of the acts of the "mobs" were orchestrated, or at least facilitated, by anti-Sikh politicians. See *Who Are the Guilty? Report of a Joint Inquiry into the Causes and Impact of the Riots in Delhi from 31 October to 10 November* (Delhi: People's Union for Democratic Rights and People's Union for Civil Liberties, 1984); and Tambiah's interesting study of three riots in South Asia, including the Delhi riot of November 1984: Stanley J. Tambiah, *Levelling Crowds: Ethnic Violence in South Asia* (Berkeley and Los Angeles: University of California Press, forthcoming).

50. The majority of those killed were themselves Sikhs. "Sikhs Worst

Hit by Punjab Terrorism," *Times of India*, March 6, 1992, p. 1. One of the more spectacular incidents in 1991 was the attack of Sikh extremists on the Indian ambassador to Romania in Bucharest. The Romanian government helped to capture the Sikhs, who were killed, and in October, in retaliation, militant Sikhs kidnapped a Romanian diplomat in Delhi.

51. Punjab police are often drawn from the so-called backward castes, such as blacksmiths and carpenters, as well as from the lowest, the scheduled castes, which include chuhras (sweepers). Urban sweepers, known as balmikis, have traditionally been Hindu and have allied with urban merchant-caste Hindus (such as aroras and khatris). Rural chuhras are often Sikh; known as mazhabis (believers), they have traditionally been allies of Jat Sikhs. In modern times, however, economic opportunities offered by government service have drawn large numbers into the army and the police. The assassin of Mrs. Gandhi, Beant Singh, was a mazhabi who had joined the police; he then reverted to his caste's traditional alliance with the Jats and became an instrument of their antipathy toward her. The other major group within the Punjab scheduled castes, the chamars (leatherworkers), who are both Sikh and Hindu, have become economically more successful and less dependent on Jat support than the chuhras; they tend increasingly to ally with khatris. Some, like their mazhabi counterparts, have entered government service. For background on Punjab untouchables, see Juergensmeyer, *Religion as Social Vision*, 11–21.

52. In Kashmir, where Muslims are in the majority, the rise of Hindu nationalism throughout India spurred a Muslim separatist movement. It erupted in 1986–87, led by the Muslim United Front, and in 1988 some elements of the opposition took a turn toward increased stridency, becoming a paramilitary operation: the Kashmir Liberation Front. Allegedly supported by Pakistan, the Front called for secession from India. Members organized demonstrations and responded to police attempts to suppress the operation by throwing bombs and shooting automatic weapons, incurring bloodshed on both sides. In May 1989 the separatists began calling themselves mujahedin (holy warriors) and characterized their conflict with the government as a holy war.

53. Sarin, *Assassination*, 149.

54. Interviews in Amritsar, June 5, 1993.

55. Interview with Uduwawala Chandananda Thero, February 2, 1988. My thanks to Antony Charles for his research assistance on this and other case studies.

56. Interview with Uduwawala Chandananda Thero, February 2, 1988. For the role of Buddhist monks in contemporary Sri Lankan politics, see Stanley J. Tambiah, *Buddhism Betrayed? Religion, Politics and Violence*

in Sri Lanka (Chicago: University of Chicago Press, 1992), and Donald Swearer, "Fundamentalist Movements in Theravada Buddhism," in Martin E. Marty and R. Scott Appleby, eds., *Fundamentalisms Observed* (Chicago: University of Chicago Press, 1991), 628–90.

57. Interview with Uduwawala Chandananda Thero, January 6, 1991.

58. The Pali Chronicles portray a grand Buddhist dynasty from the time of Mahinda up to the fall of the Buddhist capital at Anaradhapura. See Walpola Rahula, *History of Buddhism in Ceylon*, 2d ed. (Colombo: M. D. Gunasena, 1966); and Bardwell L. Smith, "The Ideal Social Order as Portrayed in the Chronicles of Ceylon," in Gananath Obeyesekere, Frank Reynolds, and Bardwell L. Smith, eds., *The Two Wheels of Dhamma: Essays on the Theravada Tradition in India and Ceylon* (Chambersburg, Pa.: American Academy of Religion, 1972), 31–57.

59. The origins of the Sri Lankan flag and the Tamil objections to it are described in Satchi Ponnambalam, *Sri Lanka: National Conflict and the Tamil Liberation Struggle* (London: Zed Books and Tamil Information Centre, 1983), 72–73.

60. Vejayavardhana, *The Revolt in the Temple.* A similar essay, "The Betrayal of Buddhism," is discussed in Tambiah, *Buddhism Betrayed?*

61. The Sinhalization of Sri Lankan politics is well documented in Gananath Obeyesekere, "Religious Symbolism and Political Change in Ceylon" in Gananath Obeyesekere, Frank Reynolds, and Bardwell L. Smith, eds., *The Two Wheels of Dhamma: Essays on the Theravada Tradition in India and Ceylon* (Chambersburg, Pa.: American Academy of Religion, 1972), 58–78; Donald Eugene Smith, "Ceylon: The Politics of Buddhist Resurgence," pt. 4 of Donald Eugene Smith, ed., *South Asian Politics and Religion* (Princeton, N.J.: Princeton University Press, 1966), 453–546; "Religious Revival and Cultural Nationalism," ch. 6 of Wriggins, *Ceylon*, 169–270; and Urmila Phadnis, *Religion and Politics in Sri Lanka* (Columbia, Mo.: South Asia Books, 1976).

62. Ponnambalam, *Sri Lanka*, 2.

63. The government placed the death total at 350, but other estimates went as high as 2,000. Tambiah, *Sri Lanka*, 22. Useful collections of essays discussing the significance of the 1983 riots may be found in James Manor, *Sri Lanka in Change and Crisis* (London: Croom Helm, 1984); and Committee for Rational Development, *Sri Lanka, the Ethnic Conflict: Myths, Realities and Perspectives* (New Delhi: Navrang, 1984); see also the various monographs of the International Centre for Ethnic Studies, Kandy and Colombo, relating to the event, and Tambiah, *Levelling Crowds.*

64. Ponnambalam, *Sri Lanka*, 31.

65. Mark Fineman, "Rebels' Weapon: Cyanide," *Los Angeles Times*, January 20, 1992, p. A1.

66. I am grateful to Ainslie Embree for pointing out this bit of historical irony.

67. For a useful account of the rise and fall of the JVP in the 1980s, see Rohan Gunaratna, *Sri Lanka: A Lost Revolution? The Inside Story of the JVP* (Kandy, Sri Lanka: Institute of Fundamental Studies, 1990).

68. K. M. deSilva, *Managing Ethnic Tensions in Multi-ethnic Societies: Sri Lanka, 1880–1985* (Lanham, Md.: University Press of America, 1986), 204.

69. My information on the JVP comes from a variety of interviews in Colombo, Matara, Tangalle, Humbantota, and Kandy, January 25–February 6, 1988.

70. Interview with Mangala Moonesinghe, director, Political and Institutional Studies Division, Marga Institute, in Colombo, January 27, 1988.

71. Interview with Moonesinghe.

72. Interview with W. G. Ganegama, coordinator, Sarvodaya Rural Technical Services, in Kandy, Sri Lanka, February 4, 1988.

73. Reuter report in *India West* 13, no. 15 (February 19, 1988), 1.

74. I saw the black flags myself in the city of Kandy and the surrounding countryside during the first week of February 1988.

75. This information came from my informal interviews with students at Peradeniya University in February 1988.

76. Interview with the Venerable Palipana Chandananda, mahanayake, Asigiriya Chapter, Sinhalese Buddhist Sangha, in Kandy, Sri Lanka, February 3, 1988.

77. Interview with Uduwawala Chandananda Thero, February 2, 1988.

78. Interview with Uduwawala Chandananda Thero, February 2, 1988.

79. Gunaratna, *Sri Lanka*, 306.

80. Ibid., 307.

81. Ibid., 296.

82. Interview with Merwyn Dominic, member of Sri Lankan Catholic Church, in Colombo, January 3, 1991.

83. Interview with A. T. Ariyaratne, founder and president, Sarvodaya Shramadana Movement, in Moratuwa, Sri Lanka, January 2, 1991. The *Los Angeles Times* asserted that 20,000 were killed; no sources, however, were given for this figure. Mark Fineman, "Sri Lanka's Bizarre Leader Confounds His Foes," *Los Angeles Times*, January 26, 1992, p. A4.

84. Interview with Jamaluddin Farook and other students at the Peradeniya University canteen, January 4, 1991. They told me that soon after one of their friends, a Buddhist monk, publicly spoke out in support of the JVP and against the army's repression, he disappeared. They do not know whether he is in hiding or has been killed.

85. These examples have been cited to me by Sri Lankans and others who visited the country in 1991 and 1992. See also Fineman, "Sri Lanka's Bizarre Leader," A4.

86. Premadasa also created ministries of Muslim and Hindu affairs (for which he did not serve as minister) and attempted to create a ministry of Christian affairs. The Christians turned down the offer, preferring to stay free of government influence.

87. Interview with Palipana Chandananda, January 4, 1991.

88. Interview with Uduwawala Chandananda Thero, January 5, 1991. For a summary of his earlier thoughts about the movement, see Juergensmeyer, "What the Bhikkhu Said."

89. Interview with Uduwawala Chandananda Thero, January 5, 1991.

90. Interview with Uduwawala Chandananda Thero, January 5, 1991.

Chapter 5: Religious Ambivalence toward Socialist Nationalism

1. Sahib Nazarov, prodemocracy member of the Communist-dominated parliament in Tajikistan, quoted in Mark Fineman, "Tide of Islam Stirs Forces in Soviet Asia," *Los Angeles Times*, November 5, 1991, p. A1. Fineman reported that attendance in mosques in the four southern republics of Central Asia had risen from 20 percent in 1989 to 50 percent in 1991, and the majority of the population appeared to favor "the reestablishment of the rule of Islam."

2. The *Great Soviet Encyclopedia* defines nationalism as "a bourgeois and petit bourgeois ideology." Quoted in Walker Connor, *The National Question in Marxist-Leninist Theory and Strategy* (Princeton, N.J.: Princeton University Press, 1984), xiii.

3. Interestingly, both phrases are in the same sentence, in a famous passage in Karl Marx, "Contribution to the Critique of Hegel's Philosophy of Right," reprinted in Reinhold Niebuhr, ed., *Karl Marx and Friedrich Engels on Religion* (New York: Schocken, 1964), 42.

4. See Connor, *National Question.*

5. Joseph Dzugashvili, who adopted the name Stalin (man of steel) in 1913, had studied for the Russian Orthodox priesthood from 1884 to 1889 at a seminary in Tiflis. He became a Marxist while he was in seminary and was expelled for insubordination.

6. For a history of the church's response to this repression, see Jane Ellis, *The Russian Orthodox Church: A Contemporary History* (Bloomington: Indiana University Press, 1986).

7. Alan J. K. Sanders, *Mongolia: Politics, Economics and Society* (London: Frances Pinter, 1987), 34.

8. Richard N. Ostling, "Victory for a Dark Horse," *Time*, June 18, 1990, p. 71.

9. Ellis, *Russian Orthodox Church*. According to William Keller, former Moscow bureau chief for the *New York Times*, the Russian church's previous complicity with Communist leaders keeps it from playing an active political role (private conversation, Honolulu, January 16, 1992).

10. Nikolai Arzhannikov, a deputy in the Russian legislature, quoted in Russell Chandler, "A Russian Force Is Reborn," *Los Angeles Times*, September 28, 1991, p. A1.

11. Interview with S. Bayantsagaan, president, Mogolyhn Süsegtnii Kholboo (Association of Mongolian Believers), and leader, Mongolian Buddhist Party, in Ulan Bator, April 12, 1992. Ordinarily Mongolians use only one name, the one given to them at birth. They have no family names. In order to help differentiate between one person's name and another, the first letter of the father's name often precedes a name in any formal identification, thereby providing a first initial.

12. There appears to be no consistently agreed-on convention for transliterating Mongolian names into romanized English. In general, I have opted for familiar transliterations; hence Ulan Bator rather than Ulaanbaatar, and Genghis Khan rather than Chinggis Khan or Jenghis Khan.

13. Interview with D. Oujun, scientific researcher for government archives and member of the Mongolian People's Revolutionary Party, in Ulan Bator, April 12, 1992.

14. B. Rinchen, ed., *Etnolingvisticheskiy atlas MNR* (*Ethnolinguistic Atlas of the MPR*) (Ulan Bator: Academy of Sciences, 1979), 43–69, cited in Sanders, *Mongolia*, 124. The population of Mongolia today is roughly two million.

15. Interviews with Y. Amgalan, deputy hamba lama (deputy head lama), Gandan Tegchinlen Monastery, in Ulan Bator, April 14, 1992, and Kushok Bakula, rinpoche and Indian ambassador, in Ulan Bator, April 12, 1992.

16. Interview with Y. Amgalan, April 14, 1992.

17. Interview with Kushok Bakula.

18. Interview with Y. Amgalan, April 13, 1992.

19. For a history of the Mongols and the conquests of the great khans, see Walther Heissig, *A Lost Civilisation: The Mongols Rediscovered* (London: Thames and Hudson, 1966), and *The Religions of Mongolia* (London: Routledge & Kegan Paul, 1980); J. J. Saunders, *The History of the Mongol Conquests* (London: Routledge & Kegan Paul, 1971); David Snellgrove and Hugh Richardson, *A Cultural History of Tibet* (London: Weidenfeld and Nicolson, 1968); Bertold Spüler, *History of the Mongols* (London:

Routledge & Kegan Paul, 1968); and Arthur Waley, *The Secret History of the Mongols* (London: Allen & Unwin, 1963).

20. See Morris Rossabi, *Khubilai Khan: His Life and Times* (Berkeley and Los Angeles: University of California Press, 1988).

21. For the history of modern Mongolia, see C. R. Bawden, *The Modern History of Mongolia* (New York: Praeger, 1968); Sanders, *Mongolia;* and Shirin Akiner, ed., *Mongolia Today* (London: Kegan Paul International, 1991). For the official Mongolian People's Revolutionary Party version, see William A. Brown and Urgunge Onon, trans., *History of the Mongolian People's Republic* (Cambridge: East Asian Research Center, Harvard University, 1976).

22. Mongolians in present-day Inner Mongolia are in the minority because that region is inhabited largely by immigrants from China. However, there are areas with Mongolian majorities outside Outer Mongolia, in Russian territory: Buryatia, north of present-day Mongolia, near the Russian city of Irkutsk; and Tuva, to the northwest.

23. Sanders, *Mongolia,* 125.

24. For a description of the Dalai Lama's visit, sponsored by the Asian Buddhist Conference for Peace, see Sanders, *Mongolia,* 126.

25. For a description of post-1989 Mongolia, see Fred Shapiro, "Starting from Scratch," *New Yorker,* January 20, 1992, 39–58; and Lincoln Kaye, "Faltering Steppes," *Far Eastern Economic Review* (April 9, 1992): 16–20.

26. See William R. Heaton, "Mongolia in 1990: Upheaval, Reform, but No Revolution Yet," *Asian Survey* 31 (January 1991): 50–56.

27. N. Zoljargal, quoted in Shapiro, "Starting from Scratch," 42.

28. Interview with A. Mekey, vice-rector, Mongolian State University, in Ulan Bator, April 11, 1992.

29. Quoted in Shapiro, "Starting from Scratch," 43.

30. See Paul C. Woy, "Rebirth of a Nation? Mongolia's Reincarnated Religious Leader," *Contemporary Review* 259 (November 1991): 234–41.

31. Interview with S. Bayantsagaan.

32. For the expansion of Buddhism after the 1990 reforms, see Alan J. K. Sanders, "Guardians of Culture," *Far Eastern Economic Review* 151 (January 3, 1991): 20–23; David Holley, "In Mongolia, a Reincarnation of Buddhism," *Los Angeles Times,* October 8, 1991, p. H6; and John Noble Wilford, "Buddha and Genghis Khan Back in Mongolia," *New York Times,* July 22, 1991, p. A1.

33. Cited in Sanders, *Mongolia,* 127.

34. Interview with G. Luhsantseren, secretary general, Asian Buddhist Conference for Peace, in Ulan Bator, April 13, 1992.

35. Interview with C. Dambajav, khambo lama (head lama), Tashichoeling Monastery, in Ulan Bator, April 11, 1992.

36. Interview with C. Dambajav.

37. Interview with S. Bayantsagaan.

38. The MPRP won 57 percent of the popular vote, with the rest divided among thirteen opposition parties. Out of the seventy-six seats at stake, the MPRP captured seventy, the Democratic Coalition (of three parties) garnered four, the Social Democrats received one, and one seat was won by an independent allied with the MPRP. David Holley, "Ruling Party's Win Is Official in Mongolia," *Los Angeles Times*, July 3, 1992, p. A14.

39. Interview with S. Bayantsagaan.

40. Interview with S. Bayantsagaan.

41. Report on CNN Headline News, April 27, 1992. See also Edward A. Gargan, "After Years of War, Afghan Rebels Easily Take Prize," *New York Times*, April 26, 1992, p. A1.

42. On June 28, 1992, after the major factions appeared to come to an agreement about the way Afghanistan was to be transformed into an Islamic state, Mojaddidi was replaced by the head of the Jamiat-i-Islami, Burhanuddin Rabbani, who was supported by the guerrilla leader Ahmed Shah Masoud. Rabbani, a professor of Islamic theology in Peshawar, Pakistan, was educated at Cairo's Al-Azhar University. He is an ethnic Tajik, less revolutionary in his approach to Islamic politics than his rival, the Pakhtun guerrilla leader Gulbuddin Hekmatyar, who was represented in the new government by Prime Minister Ustad Fareed. It was an uneasy truce, however, and fighting among the factions continued.

43. The English transcriptions of the names of these nations vary widely. I have chosen to use the forms that the current governments prefer, in some cases because the old spelling implies a Russified version of the names. Hence, I use Tajikistan rather than Tadzhikistan, and Kyrgyzstan rather than Kirghizia.

44. When the Republic of Tatar, surrounded entirely by Russia, declared itself a "sovereign state" in March 1992, President Boris Yeltsin was publicly nervous—not only because he feared the unraveling of the Russian Federation but also because he was concerned about forces within his own nation that might encourage the rising tide of Islamic nationalism on the southern boundaries.

45. Vladimir Klimenko, "Opposition Seizes Power in Tajikistan," *Los Angeles Times*, May 8, 1992, p. A45.

46. Abdulrahim Pulatov, leader, Birlik, quoted in Robin Wright, "Report from Turkestan," *New Yorker*, April 6, 1992, p. 60.

47. Martha Brill Olcott, "An Islamic Empire?" *New York Times*, August 29, 1991, p. A19.

48. Mark Fineman, "Tide of Islam Stirs Forces in Soviet Asia," *Los Angeles Times,* November 5, 1991, p. A1.

49. Quoted in Ronald Wixman, "Ethnic Attitudes and Relations in Modern Uzbek Cities," in William Fierman, ed., *Soviet Central Asia: The Failed Transformation* (Boulder, Colo.: Westview Press, 1991), 174.

50. Quoted in Wixman, "Ethnic Attitudes," 172. Regarding circumcision, Wixman reports that the Uzbek students were pleasantly surprised to hear that many American males were circumcised. He further reports that several Russians in the group who heard his description of American practices were shocked and explained that if this were the case, it was only because "the Jews control America." Quoted in Wixman, "Ethnic Attitudes," 174.

51. For the history and culture of Muslims in Central Asia, see Denis Sinor, *The Cambridge History of Inner Asia* (Cambridge: Cambridge University Press, 1990), Alexandre Bennigsen and S. Enders Wimbush, *Muslims of the Soviet Empire: A Guide* (London: C. Hurst, 1985); Shirin Akiner, *The Islamic Peoples of the Soviet Union* (London: Kegan Paul International, 1983); and R. Pierce, *Russian Central Asia, 1867–1917: A Study in Colonial Rule* (Berkeley and Los Angeles: University of California Press, 1960).

52. See Hélène Carrère d'Encausse, *Islam and the Russian Empire: Reform and Revolution in Central Asia,* translated by Quintin Hoare (London: I. B. Tauris, 1988).

53. For the history of Soviet–Central Asian relations, see Alexandre Bennigsen and Marie Broxup, *The Islamic Threat to the Soviet State* (New York: St. Martin's Press, 1983); Edward Allworth, ed., *Central Asia: 120 Years of Russian Rule* (Durham, N.C.: Duke University Press, 1989); Yaacov Ro'i, ed., *The USSR and the Muslim World: Issues in Domestic and Foreign Policy* (London: Allen & Unwin, 1984); and Geoffrey Wheeler, *The Modern History of Soviet Central Asia* (London: Weidenfeld and Nicolson, 1964).

54. Cited in Wright, "Report from Turkestan," 56.

55. Francis X. Cline, "Defiance of Kremlin's Control Is Accelerating in Soviet Asia," *New York Times,* July 1, 1990, p. A1.

56. Wright, "Report from Turkestan," 56. See also "The Next Islamic Revolution," *Economist* 320, no. 7725 (September 21, 1991): 58–60.

57. Ahmed Rashid, "The Islamic Challenge," *Far Eastern Economic Review* 149 (July 12, 1990): 24. His fellow mullahs again attempted to oust the Tashkent mufti, Muhammad Sady Muhammad Yusuf, in January 1992. Martha Brill Olcott, "Central Asia's Post-Empire Politics," *Orbis* 36, no. 2 (Spring 1992): 253–68.

58. Sahib Nazarov, prodemocracy member of the Communist-dominated parliament in Tajikistan, quoted in Fineman, "Tide of Islam," A1.

59. Moldokasymov in *Leninchil Zhash,* August 6, 1987, quoted in Azade-Ayse Rorlich, "Islam and Atheism: Dynamic Tension in Soviet Central Asia," in William Fierman, ed., *Soviet Central Asia: The Failed Transformation* (Boulder, Colo.: Westview Press, 1991), 192.

60. Regarding Uzbek political alignments, see James Critchlow, *Nationalism in Uzbekistan: A Soviet Republic's Road to Sovereignty* (Boulder, Colo.: Westview Press, 1991). For a more general background to Uzbek history and culture, see Edward A. Allworth, *The Modern Uzbeks: From the Fourteenth Century to the Present, a Cultural History* (Stanford, Calif.: Hoover Institution Press, 1990).

61. Tsumbai Lyusanov, quoted in Wright, "Report from Turkestan," 57.

62. For background information on religion and politics in Tajikistan, see Muriel Atkin, *The Subtlest Battle: Islam in Soviet Tajikistan* (Philadelphia: Foreign Policy Research Institute, 1989).

63. Olcott, "Central Asia's Post-Empire Politics," 261.

64. Ibid., 262.

65. Wright, "Report from Turkestan," 74.

66. Vladimir Klimenko, "Wind of Islam Fans Politics in Emergent Tajikistan," *Los Angeles Times,* May 14, 1992, p. A4.

67. Ibid.

68. Quoted in Wright, "Report from Turkestan," 74.

69. For the historical background of present-day Kazakhstan, see Martha Brill Olcott, *The Kazakhs* (Stanford, Calif.: Hoover Institution Press, 1987); and George J. Demko, *The Russian Colonization of Kazakhstan, 1896–1916* (Bloomington: Indiana University Publications, 1969).

70. Wright, "Report from Turkestan," 68.

71. Olcott, "Central Asia's Post-Empire Politics," 260.

72. See Rorlich, "Islam and Atheism," 191.

73. Olcott, "Central Asia's Post-Empire Politics," 264.

74. See Francis X. Cline's essay, "Islamic Militance along Russia's Rim Is Less Than a Sure Bet," *New York Times,* February 9, 1992, p. E2.

75. Interview with Nikolai A. Kolesnik, chairman, Council on Questions of Religion, Ukrainian Soviet Socialist Republic Council of Ministers, at a meeting of the Working Group on Religion and Nationalism, United States Institute of Peace, Washington, D.C., June 20, 1990.

76. See Dan Ionescu, "Romania: Religious Denominations, Change and Resistance to Change at the Top," *Radio Free Europe Report on Eastern Europe* 1, no. 17 (April 17, 1990): 29–33; and Pedro Ramet, "Patterns of Religio-national Symbiosis in Eastern Europe: Poland, Czechoslovakia, Hungary," in *Eastern Europe: Religion and Nationalism,* Occasional Paper 3 (Washington, D.C.: East European Program, European Institute, Wilson Center, December 4, 1985), 48–51.

77. See Henry Kamm, "Rising Verbal Attacks Shake Romania's Jews," *New York Times*, June 19, 1991, international edition, p. A10.

78. In October 1991 Catholic churches in Serbia became a target of attack.

79. See Carol J. Williams, "Ethnic Mix Could Be Explosive in Yugoslav Republic," *Los Angeles Times*, June 10, 1991, p. A4.

80. Interview with Latvian Prime Minister Ivars Godmanis on CNN television news, August 27, 1991.

81. Quoted in Adam Bromke, "A New Juncture in Poland," *Problems of Communism* 25, no. 5 (September–October 1976): 11, cited in Ramet, "Patterns of Religio-national Symbiosis in Eastern Europe."

82. Quoted in Bogdan Szajkowski, *Next to God . . . Poland: Politics and Religion in Contemporary Poland* (New York: St. Martin's Press, 1983), 17.

83. Carl Bernstein, "The Holy Alliance," *Time*, February 24, 1992, pp. 28–35.

84. Quoted in Alain Touraine, François Dubet, Michel Wievorka, and Jan Strzelecki, *Solidarity: Poland, 1980–81*, translated by David Denby (Cambridge: Cambridge University Press, 1983), 46, cited in Ramet, "Patterns of Religio-national Symbiosis in Eastern Europe."

85. See "And unto Poland, What Is God's," *Economist*, May 25, 1991, p. 51.

86. Quoted in a news story from wire sources, "The Ukraine Declares Its Independence," *Honolulu Sunday Star-Bulletin and Advertiser*, August 25, 1991, p. A4.

87. The best description of the present religious turmoil in independent Ukraine is to be found in David Little, *Ukraine: The Legacy of Intolerance* (Washington, D.C.: United States Institute of Peace Press, 1991).

88. Quoted in Jane Ellis, "The Russian Orthodox Church's Attitude to the Situation in Ukraine" (Paper presented at the Working Group on Religion and Nationalism, United States Institute of Peace, Washington, D.C., June 21, 1990), 6.

89. Quoted in ibid.

90. Bohdan R. Bociurkiw, "Institutional Religion and Nationality in the Soviet Union," in S. Enders Wimbush, ed., *Soviet Nationalities in Strategic Perspective* (London: Croom Helm, 1985), 183, cited in Little, *Ukraine*, 53.

91. *Autocephalous* means "independent," literally "self-headed."

92. Interview with Ivan Hrechko, chairman, Commission on Religious Freedom of Rukh, Lviv Chapter, December 13, 1990, by David Little at the United States Institute of Peace. Quoted in Little, *Ukraine*, 74.

93. Denise Hamilton, "Independence Fever," *Los Angeles Times Magazine*, December 1, 1991, p. 54.

94. Father Frank Estocin, "Summary of Remarks" (Presented at the Working Group on Religion and Nationalism, United States Institute of Peace, Washington, D.C., June 21, 1990), 3.

95. Ibid. He added that "*glasnost* and *perestroika* have opened the doors to this possibility."

96. Interview with Kolesnik.

97. See Mark Juergensmeyer, "Tibet," in Stuart Mews, ed., *Religion in Politics: A World Guide* (London: Longman, 1989).

98. These observations about the religious nature of *Juche* thought came from my discussions with Korean officials during a visit to Pyongyang in August 1989.

99. Tambiah, *Buddism Betrayed?* 117–18.

100. Quoted in Chris Hedges, "Vatican II Reforms Gave Rise to Liberation Theology," *Dallas Morning News*, March 2, 1986, p. A29.

101. For a discussion of the importance of religion in the general context of the Nicaraguan revolution (and counterrevolution), see Luis Serra, "Ideology, Religion, and Class Struggle in the Nicaraguan Revolution," in Richard Harris and Carlos M. Vilas, eds., *Nicaragua: A Revolution under Siege* (London: Zed Books, 1985), 151–201; Roger N. Lancaster, *Thanks to God and the Revolution: Popular Religion and Class Consciousness in the New Nicaragua* (New York: Columbia University Press, 1988); and Michael Dodson and Laura Nuzzi O'Shaughnessy, *Nicaragua's Other Revolution: Religious Faith and Political Struggle* (Chapel Hill: University of North Carolina Press, 1990). I am grateful to Darrin McMahon for preparing a background paper on the Nicaraguan situation and its sources.

102. Services held in the streets were much better attended than those in the church building (interview with religious leaders in Managua, June 5, 1988).

103. Teofilo Cabestrero, *Revolutionaries for the Gospel: Testimonies of Fifteen Christians in the Nicaraguan Government*, translated by Phillip Berryman (Maryknoll, N.Y.: Orbis Books, 1986), 37.

104. Ibid., 22.

105. I am grateful to Prof. Charles Hale for pointing out the nationalism of Nicaragua's Roman Catholic right wing as well as its left.

106. See, for instance, Stephen Bruce, "The Moral Majority: The Politics of Fundamentalism in Secular Society," in Lionel Caplan, ed., *Studies in Religious Fundamentalism* (Albany: State University of New York Press, 1987); and Capps, *The New Religious Right*.

107. See, for instance, Weston LaBarre, *The Ghost Dance: The Origins of Religion* (New York: Dell, 1970).

108. See David Chidester, *Shots in the Street: Violence and Religion in South Africa* (Boston: Beacon Press, 1991).

109. John Hickey, *Religion and the Northern Ireland Problem* (Totawa, N.J.: Barnes & Noble, 1984), 57–88; and W. Dennis D. Cooke, "The Religious Dimension in the Northern Ireland Problem," *Lexington Theological Quarterly* 16, no. 3 (July 1981): 85–93.

110. See Gary Lease, "The Origins of National Socialism: Some Fruits of Religion and Nationalism," in Peter Merkl and Ninian Smart, eds., *Religion and Politics in the Modern World* (New York: New York University Press, 1983).

111. In his book *Nostradamus: Fearful Prophecies*, Okawa said that Japan will be the only nation to survive a great apocalyptic battle that will destroy the United States and the former Soviet Union. American civilization, which he claimed "produced nothing more than weapons, cars, Coca-Cola and hamburgers," will be "laughed at." His writings include quotations from Jesus, Moses, Confucius, Isaac Newton, and Albert Einstein. Mari Yamaguchi, "Self Proclaimed Messiah Rises out of Postwar Prosperity," *Japan Times* (Tokyo), October 29, 1991.

112. Samuel P. Huntington, "How Countries Democratize," *Political Science Quarterly* 106, no. 4 (Winter 1991–92): 605–20. Huntington's first guideline is especially consistent with the approach taken by religious revolutionaries: "Focus attention on the illegitimacy or dubious legitimacy of the authoritarian regime" (607–8).

Chapter 6:
Why Religious Confrontations Are Violent

1. From an excerpt of one of Bhindranwale's speeches, translated in Pettigrew, "In Search of a New Kingdom of Lahore."

2. Khomeini, *Collection*, 7.

3. Interview with Lerner.

4. René Girard, *Violence and the Sacred*, translated by Patrick Gregory (Baltimore: Johns Hopkins University Press, 1977), and *The Scapegoat*, translated by Yvonne Freccero (Baltimore: Johns Hopkins University Press, 1986); Walter Burkert, *Homo Necans: The Anthropology of Ancient Greek Sacrificial Ritual and Myth*, translated by Peter Bing (Berkeley and Los Angeles: University of California Press, 1972); Walter Burkert, René Girard, and Jonathan Z. Smith, *Violent Origins: Ritual Killing and Cultural Formation*, edited by Robert G. Hamerton-Kelly (Stanford, Calif: Stanford University Press, 1987); Eli Sagan, *The Lust to Annihilate: A Psychoanalytic Study of Violence in Ancient Greek Culture* (New York: Psychohistory Press, 1972), and *Cannibalism: Human Aggression and Cultural Form* (New York: Psychohistory Press, 1974).

5. Girard, *Violence and the Sacred*, 36.

6. Ibid.

7. I discuss Girard's theories, agree with some of them, and offer alternatives to other aspects of them in Mark Juergensmeyer, "Sacrifice and Cosmic War," in Mark Juergensmeyer, ed., *Violence and the Sacred in the Modern World* (London: Frank Cass, 1992), 101–17.

8. Attempts to apply Girard's theories to modern cases of religious violence may be found in Mark Juergensmeyer, ed., *Violence and the Sacred in the Modern World* (London: Frank Cass, 1992).

9. For a discussion of the definition of violence and terror in political contexts, see Thomas Perry Thornton, "Terrorism as a Weapon of Political Agitation," in Harry Eckstein, ed., *Internal War: Problems and Approaches* (New York: Free Press, 1964); and David C. Rapoport, "The Politics of Atrocity," in Y. Alexander and S. Finger, eds., *Terrorism: Interdisciplinary Perspectives* (New York: John Jay, 1977).

10. Martin Kramer, "Sacrifice and Fratricide in Shi'ite Lebanon," in Mark Juergensmeyer, ed., *Violence and the Sacred in the Modern World* (London: Frank Cass, 1992).

11. Hamas Communiqué #64, September 26, 1990, quoted in Legrain, "Defining Moment," 75–76.

12. Juergensmeyer, "Logic of Religious Violence."

13. Rev. Wayne E. Anderson, "Battle Cry," television program, KWHE-TV, Channel 14, Honolulu, January 30, 1991.

14. For an interesting analysis of "Onward Christian Soldiers" and other hymns of U.S. frontier revival movements, see Sandra Sizer, *Gospel Hymns and Social Religion: The Rhetoric of Nineteenth-Century Revivalism* (Philadelphia: Temple University Press, 1978).

15. Harriet Crabtree, "Quest for True Models of the Christian Life: An Evaluative Study of the Use of Traditional Metaphor in Contemporary Popular Theologies of the Christian Life" (Th.D. diss., Harvard University, 1989). Her findings with regard to warfare are summarized in Harriet Crabtree, "Onward Christian Soldiers? The Fortunes of a Traditional Christian Symbol in the Modern Age," *Bulletin of the Center for the Study of World Religion* (Harvard University) 16, no. 2 (1989–90): 6–27.

16. Quoted in Crabtree, "Onward Christian Soldiers?" 10. The italics are in the original.

17. *Bhagavad Gita,* chapter 1, verse 45. The cousins are not quite morally equal however. One set, the Pandavas, are more wicked than the other.

18. Ibid., chapter 2, verses 19–34.

19. Ibid. As Ernst Becker has observed in *The Denial of Death* (New York: Free Press, 1973) and *Escape from Evil* (New York: Free Press, 1975), religious imagination serves to enlarge one's sense of the potential

for life and to deny death. Although in general I agree with Becker, it seems to me that it is possible to employ the language of sacrifice, martyrdom, and warfare to reassert the primacy of structure over chaos in general rather than death in particular, as Becker suggests.

20. Crabtree, "Onward Christian Soldiers?" 7.

21. Kramer, "Sacrifice and Fratricide in Shi'ite Lebanon," 38–40. Among the Huron and Seneca Indians may be found another example of the sacrifice of humans who are in an ambiguous or incorrect category: a captured enemy is made a member of the household and feted and adored before being ritually tortured to death. See Anthony F. C. Wallace, *The Death and Rebirth of the Seneca* (New York: Random House, 1969), 102–7.

22. Herman Melville's *Billy Budd* trades on this same theme. In a book of essays on sainthood and morality, the authors consistently come to a similar conclusion—that social misfits make good candidates for sainthood. They must be perceived as "sublimely wacky" in order for their martyrdom and self-sacrifice to be seen as saintly. John Stratton Hawley, "Introduction: Saints and Virtues," in John Stratton Hawley, ed., *Saints and Virtues* (Berkeley and Los Angeles: University of California Press, 1987), xvi–xxiii.

23. Bhindranwale, "Two Lectures," 2.

24. Bhindranwale, "Address to the Sikh Congregation," 1.

25. Bhindranwale, "Two Lectures," 22.

26. Khomeini, *Collection*, 6.

27. Bani-Sadr, *Fundamental Principles and Precepts of Islamic Government*, 28–35.

28. Khomeini, *Collection*, 30.

29. Khomeini, *Islam and Revolution*, 27–28.

30. Khomeini, *Collection*, 24.

31. Ibid., 3.

32. Ibid., 25.

33. Ernesto Cardenal, in Teofilo Cabastrero, *Ministers of God, Ministers of the People: Testimonies of Faith from Nicaragua*, translated by Robert R. Barr (Maryknoll, N.Y.: Orbis Books, 1983), 22–23.

34. My interviews with the bhikkhu, Rev. Uduwawala Chandananda Thero, were conducted in Sri Lanka on February 4–5, 1988, in English. For a fuller account, see Juergensmeyer, "What the Bhikkhu Said."

35. Rabbi Meir Kahane, speech on the announcement of the creation of an independent state of Judea, Jerusalem, January 18, 1989 (from my notes taken on that occasion).

36. Ibid.

37. Interview with Lerner.

38. "Guidelines for the Panth" and other excerpts from the speeches of

Bhindranwale are included as an appendix in Surjeet Jalandhary, *Bhindran-*
wale Sant (Jalandhar, India: Punjab Pocket Books, n.d. [c. 1985]), 164.

39. Bhindranwale, excerpt from a speech, in Pettigrew, "In Search of a
New Kingdom of Lahore."

40. Bhindranwale, "Address to the Sikh Congregation," 9; see also
Jalandhary, *Bhindranwale Sant*, 165.

41. See Mohinder Singh, "Gandhi, Sikhs and Non-violence," *Khera* 9,
no. 3 (July-September 1990): 72–87. For the ethic of nonviolence in
Sikhism, see W. Owen Cole and Piara Singh Sambhi, *The Sikhs: Their*
Religious Beliefs and Practices (London: Routledge & Kegan Paul, 1978),
138. For Sikh ethical attitudes in general, see Avtar Singh, *Ethics of the*
Sikhs (Patiala, India: Punjabi University Press, 1970); and S. S. Kohli,
Sikh Ethics (New Delhi: Munshiram Manoharlal, 1975).

42. Bhindranwale, "Two Lectures," 21.

43. See Mark Juergensmeyer, "Nonviolence," in Mircea Eliade, ed.,
The Encyclopedia of Religion, vol. 10 (New York: Macmillan, 1987), 463–
67. An excellent anthology of statements of Christian theologians on the
ethical justification for war is Albert Marrin, ed., *War and the Christian*
Conscience: From Augustine to Martin Luther King, Jr. (Chicago: Regnery,
1971). On the development of the just-war doctrine in Christianity, with its
secular parallels, see James Turner Johnson, *Ideology, Reason, and the*
Limitation of War: Religious and Secular Concepts, 1200–1740 (Princeton,
N.J.: Princeton University Press, 1975).

44. Robert McAfee Brown, *Religion and Violence*, 2d ed. (Philadelphia: Westminster Press, 1987), 56–61.

45. Interview with Kahane.

46. Speech given by Kahane at the event proclaiming an independent
state of Judea, Jerusalem, January 18, 1989. For a summary of the discussion in the Gush Emunim about the appropriateness of using violence,
see Lustick, *For the Land and the Lord*, 93–100.

47. Kahane speech.

48. Ibid.

49. Interview with Lerner.

50. Interview with Kahane in Mergui and Simonnot, *Israel's Aya-*
tollahs, 52.

51. Ibid., 50.

52. Interview with Yassin.

53. Interview with Yassin.

54. Interview with 'Odeh in *Islam and Palestine*, Leaflet 5 (Limassol,
Cyprus, June 1988).

55. Ibid.

56. Interview with Shitta, January 11, 1989.

57. Interviews in Sri Lanka, January 1988.

58. Interviews in Sri Lanka, January 1988.

59. Interviews in Sri Lanka, January 1988.

60. Bandaranaike was gunned down by a bhikkhu, Talduwe Somarama Thero, when Somarama came to the prime minister's house with a group of petitioners on September 25, 1959. The court determined that the bhikkhu was part of a larger conspiracy masterminded by the most politically powerful monk of the day, Mapitigama Buddharakkhita Thero, whom Smith has called the Rasputin of Sri Lankan politics. Donald Eugene Smith, "The Political Monks and Monastic Reform," in Donald Eugene Smith, ed., *South Asian Politics and Religion* (Princeton, N.J.: Princeton University Press, 1966), 495.

61. For the social makeup of the Iranian revolution, see Robin Wright, *Sacred Rage: The Wrath of Militant Islam* (New York: Linden Press, Simon & Schuster, 1985); Sick, *All Fall Down;* and Simpson, *Inside Iran.*

62. Kim Murphy, "Islamic Party Wins Power in Algeria," *Los Angeles Times,* December 28, 1991, p. A15.

63. Gombrich, Richard, and Gananath Obeyesekere, *Buddhism Transformed: Religious Change in Sri Lanka* (Princeton, N.J.: Princeton University Press, 1988). See also Tambiah, *Buddhism Betrayed?*

64. This analysis is based on twenty obituaries printed in the *World Sikh News* during 1988. I appreciate the assistance of Gurinder Singh in compiling this information.

65. For a comparative study of this issue, see the essays in Hawley, *Fundamentalism and Gender.*

66. Quoted in Kim Murphy, "Algerian Election to Test Strength of Radical Islam," *Los Angeles Times,* December 26, 1991, p. 19.

67. Quited in ibid.

68. The intense loyalties of male comrades in these militant groups suggest in some cases a homoerotic element. In India, some of the young men in militant Sikh cadres pair off and are bonded as blood brothers in a quasi-religious ceremony.

69. Frantz Fanon, *The Wretched of the Earth* (New York: Grove Press, 1963).

Chapter 7: Democracy, Human Rights, and the Modern Religious State

1. Sarvepalli Gopal, "Introduction," in Gopal, *Anatomy of a Confrontation,* 13.

2. Quoted in Kim Murphy, "Algerian Election to Test Strength of Radical Islam," *Los Angeles Times,* December 26, 1991, p. A19.

3. Dina Nath Mishra, *RSS: Myth and Reality* (New Delhi: Vikas, 1980), 73; see also Embree, "Function of the Rashtriya Swayamsevak Sangh," 9–17.

4. Interview with Yassin.

5. Quoted in Mergui and Simonnot, *Israel's Ayatollahs*, 40–41.

6. Interview with Yassin.

7. Interview with Uduwawala Chandananda Thero, February 2, 1988.

8. Interview with el-Arian.

9. Interview with Levinger.

10. Interview with Shitta, January 10, 1989.

11. Interview with Yassin.

12. Kahane, quoted in Mergui and Simonnot, *Israel's Ayatollahs*, 35.

13. "The goal of democracy is to let people do what they want," Kahane claimed. "Judaism wants to make them better." Quoted in ibid., 36.

14. Interview with Uduwawala Chandananda Thero, February 2, 1988.

15. Plato, *The Republic*, translated by B. Jowett (New York: Modern Library, n.d.), 312.

16. The separation of legislative and executive branches was a further attempt to balance these two functions of government, one representing particular districts and the other representing the whole. See Locke, "Of the Legislative, Executive, and Federative Power of the Commonwealth," ch. 12 of *The Second Treatise on Government*, 410.

17. See *The Federalist Papers* (New York: Mentor Books, 1961), 378.

18. Interview with el-Geyoushi.

19. Speech by Yoel Lerner at the celebration to establish an independent state of Judea, Jerusalem, January 18, 1989. I appreciate the simultaneous translation of his speech at that occasion provided by Ehud Sprinzak and his students.

20. Interview with Lerner.

21. Hamid Algar, trans., *Constitution of the Islamic Republic of Iran* (Berkeley, Calif.: Mizan Press, 1980), 68.

22. The leader is leader for life, presumably, and when he dies, the constitution specifies that "experts elected by the people" will choose a new leader; if none is to be found, they will appoint from three to five members of a leadership council, which will perform the leader's functions. Algar, *Constitution*, 66.

23. See H. E. Chehabi, "Religion and Politics in Iran: How Theocratic Is the Islamic Republic?" *Daedalus* (Summer 1991): 69–92. For the clergy's ambivalence toward politics in the period immediately prior to the revolution, see Shahrough Akhavi, *Religion and Politics in Contemporary Iran: Clergy-State Relations in the Pahlavi Period* (Albany: State University of New York Press, 1980).

24. Sick, *All Fall Down*, 193–94.

25. Ibid., 185.

26. Arjomand, "Victory for the Pragmatists," 57. See also Simpson, *Inside Iran*, 92–93.

27. Although Sikhism does not have a tradition of clergy, it does have groups of teachers in what amounts to monastic orders; Bhindranwale was in one of these, the Damdami Taksal.

28. Interview with Yassin.

29. Interview with Uduwawala Chandananda Thero, February 2, 1988.

30. Interview with el-Arian.

31. Interview with Uduwawala Chandananda Thero, February 2, 1988.

32. Interview with Shitta, January 10, 1989.

33. Interview with Kahane. Michael ben Horin, a leader of the event for proclaiming a state of Judea, explained that all the delegates had been chosen from Judea and Sumaria, two elected from each settlement. Leaders of the founding congress were elected by a secret ballot. The list of people nominated for the executive committee was read out (and other names could be added); each candidate gave a little nominating speech. Interview with Michael ben Horin, manager, Kach office, in Jerusalem, January 15, 1989.

34. See Louis Dumont, *From Mandeville to Marx: The Genesis and Triumph of Economic Ideology* (Chicago: University of Chicago Press, 1977).

35. Quoted in Mark Fineman, "Riding the Crest of India's Hindu Revival," *Los Angeles Times,* June 11, 1991, p. H1.

36. Interview with Kahane.

37. Bani-Sadr, *Fundamental Principles and Precepts of Islamic Government*, 40.

38. The International Centre for Ethnic Studies in Colombo produced a series of television programs describing the "unity through diversity" in Sri Lankan society. The Hindu god Vishnu, for instance, was shown to be frequently worshiped at Buddhist temples, and the distinctly Sri Lankan god Kataragama was seen to be venerated equally by Buddhists and Hindus.

39. A solution frequently offered for India's problems with the Sikhs (and, perhaps more important, with the much larger Muslim minority) is the creation of an ethnic branch of government: either councils made up of representatives from each religious community to advise the government on social legislation or an upper house of parliament to provide representation on the basis of religious and ethnic affiliation.

40. Interviews with Shitta, January 10, 1989; el-Arian; el-Geyoushi; and Yassin. Their comments about a two-level shari'a were made without knowing that similar comments had been made by the others.

41. Interview with el-Geyoushi.

42. Prabhu Chawla, "Ambitious Alliances," *India Today,* April 30, 1991, p. 44.

43. Interview with Kenneth Fernando. Anthony Fernando, Kelaniya University, Colombo, has also written extensively on the importance of Buddhism for Christians.

44. Carl W. Ernst, "The Symbolism and Psychology of World Empire in the Delhi Sultanate" (Paper given at a conference, Religion and National-ism, at the University of California, Santa Barbara, April 20, 1989), 15. Ernst is quoting the chronicle of the Muslim historian Ziyamal-Din Barani.

45. Algar, *Constitution,* 32, 36.

46. See Bakhash, *Reign of the Ayatollahs,* 24; and Simpson, *Inside Iran,* 213–19.

47. Interview with el-Arian. He claimed that, like Muslims, Copts have their own concentric circles of identity, one of which is Egypt.

48. Interviews with Shitta, January 10, 1989; and el-Geyoushi.

49. Interview with Father Aramea Marcari, Coptic monk, in Abba Marcarios Monastery, Egypt, May 28, 1990.

50. Interview with el-Hamamsy.

51. Interview with Kahane.

52. Interview with Kahane. See also Meir Kahane, *They Must Go* (Jerusalem: Institute of the Jewish Idea, 1981).

53. Interview with ben Horin.

54. Interviews with Shitta, January 10, 1989; el-Arian; el-Geyoushi; and Yassin.

55. Interview with el-Geyoushi.

56. For a discussion of human rights in comparative perspective, see David Little, John Kelsay, Abdulaziz A. Sachedina, *Human Rights and the Conflict of Cultures: Western and Islamic Perspectives on Religious Lib-erty* (Columbia: University of South Carolina Press, 1988); Max L. Stackhouse, *Creeds, Society, and Human Rights: A Study in Three Cul-tures* (Grand Rapids, Mich.: W. B. Eerdmans, 1984); Arlene Swidler, ed., *Human Rights in Religious Traditions* (New York: Pilgrim Press, 1982); Leroy S. Rouner, ed., *Human Rights and the World's Religions* (Notre Dame, Ind.: University of Notre Dame Press, 1988); Kenneth W. Thomp-son, ed., *Moral Imperative of Human Rights* (Washington, D.C.: Univer-sity Press of America, 1980); and Irene Bloome, Paul Martin, and Wayne Proudfoot, eds., *Religion and Human Rights* (New York: Columbia Univer-sity Press, forthcoming). For an exploration of the interesting thesis that human rights is itself a religious tradition, see Robert Traer, *Faith in Human Rights: Support in Religious Traditions for a Global Struggle* (Washington, D.C.: Georgetown University Press, 1991).

57. David Little, "The Development in the West of the Right to Freedom of Religion and Conscience: A Basis for Comparison with Islam," in David Little, John Kelsay, and Abdulaziz A. Sachedina, *Human Rights and the Conflict of Cultures: Western and Islamic Perspectives on Religious Liberty* (Columbia: University of South Carolina Press, 1988), 30.

58. Speech given by Rabbi Meir Kahane, Jerusalem, January 18, 1989 (the English translation was supplied to me on that occasion by Ehud Sprinzak and his students). See also the transcript of an interview with Kahane in Mergui and Simonnot, *Israel's Ayatollahs*, 33–34.

59. Robert Bellah et al., *Habits of the Heart: Individualism and Commitment in American Life* (Berkeley and Los Angeles: University of California Press, 1985).

60. Alasdair MacIntyre, *After Virtue: A Study in Moral Theory* (Notre Dame, Ind.: University of Notre Dame Press, 1981).

61. Interview with el-Arian.

62. Algar, *Constitution*, 27.

63. Ibid., 38.

64. Ibid., 43.

65. Ibid., 91.

66. Interview with Yassin.

67. A number of Muslims I interviewed insisted that Islam is especially tolerant of differences of opinion and open discourse because, as one of them put it, "aside from the Qur'an, everything in Islam is open to argument." Interview with Ashur.

68. See Embree, "Function of the Rashtriya Swayamsevak Sangh," 5.

69. Zafar Agha, "BJP Government: What Will It Be Like?" *India Today*, May 15, 1991, pp. 20–21.

70. Interview with Levinger.

71. Madhu Jain, "BJP Supporters: Invasion of the Scuppies," *India Today*, May 15, 1991, pp. 18–19.

72. Quoted in Murphy, "Algerian Election to Test Strength of Radical Islam," 19.

73. Lawrence, *Defenders of God*, 27.

74. Giddens, *Nation-State*, 215–16.

75. Gerald Larson, "Fast Falls the Eventide: India's Anguish over Religion" (Presentation at a conference, Religion and Nationalism, at the University of California, Santa Barbara, April 21, 1989).

76. Wilfred Cantwell Smith, *Islam in Modern History* (Princeton, N.J.: Princeton University Press, 1957), 47.

77. Sick, *All Fall Down*, 185.

Conclusion:
Can We Live with Religious Nationalism?

1. Sick, *All Fall Down*, 186.

2. Imam Abu Kheireiddine, quoted in Kim Murphy, "Islamic Party Wins Power in Algeria," *Los Angeles Times*, December 28, 1991, p. A1.

3. A "senior Administration official" quoted in Robin Wright, "U.S. Struggles to Deal with Global Islamic Resurgence," *Los Angeles Times*, January 26, 1992, p. A1.

4. Interview with Palipana Chandananda, February 3, 1988.

5. Murphy, "Islamic Party Wins Power in Algeria," A15.

6. Robin Wright, "Islam, Democracy, and the West," *Foreign Affairs* 71, no. 3 (Summer 1992): 108–30.

7. The appeals to religion come from both ends of the political spectrum. The conservative political theorist Eric Voegelin, for instance, has called for a greater influence of Christianity in American political thinking in order to counter what he regards as a Gnostic tendency toward utopianism that corrupts the "civil theology" of the modern West. Eric Voegelin, *The New Science of Politics: An Introduction*, 2d ed. (Chicago: University of Chicago Press, 1987), 162. Interestingly, Islamic activists have also encouraged the United States to take biblical religion more seriously. Alann Steen reports that while he was held hostage in Lebanon, his Islamic captors, loyal followers of the Ayatollah Khomeini, gave the hostages Bibles and encouraged them to read them. Interview with Alann Steen, in Honolulu, March 11, 1992.

8. Mohandas Gandhi, *Hind Swaraj, or Indian Home Rule* (Ahmedabad, India: Navajivan Press, 1938), 33–34.

9. Schlesinger, who served in the administrations of Franklin D. Roosevelt and John F. Kennedy, said that Niebuhr "cast an intellectual spell" on him and his generation of political thinkers. Arthur Schlesinger, Jr., "Reinhold Niebuhr's Long Shadow," *New York Times*, June 22, 1992, p. A13. See also Arthur Schlesinger, Jr., "Reinhold Niebuhr's Role in American Political Thought," in Charles W. Kegley, ed., *Reinhold Niebuhr: His Religious, Social and Political Thought*, rev. ed. (New York: Pilgrim Press, 1984), 189–222. Niebuhr was highly critical of Gandhi's "sentimental" view of human nature and its implications for politics.

10. Reinhold Niebuhr, *Moral Man and Immoral Society* (New York: Scribner's, 1932), 255.

11. Embree, *Utopias in Conflict*, 45.

12. Niebuhr, *Moral Man and Immoral Society*, 277.

13. Ibid.

Bibliography

General Works

Alpher, Joseph, ed. *Nationalism and Modernity: A Mediterranean Perspective.* New York: Praeger, 1986.

Anderson, Benedict. *Imagined Communities: Reflections on the Origin and Spread of Nationalism.* London: Verso, 1983.

Antoun, Richard T., and Mary Elaine Hegland, eds. *Religious Resurgence: Contemporary Cases in Islam, Christianity, and Judaism.* Syracuse, N.Y.: Syracuse University Press, 1987.

Apter, David, ed. *Ideology and Discontent.* New York: Free Press, 1964.

Arendt, Hannah. *On Revolution.* New York: Viking Press, 1963.

Baron, Salo Wittmayer. *Modern Nationalism and Religion.* New York: Harper & Bros., 1947.

Baumann, Red E., and Kenneth M. Jensen, eds. *Religion and Politics.* Charlottesville: University Press of Virginia, 1989.

Becker, Ernest. *The Denial of Death.* New York: Free Press, 1973.

———. *Escape from Evil.* New York: Free Press, 1975.

Bellah, Robert, Richard Madsen, William Sullivan, Ann Swidler, and Steven Tipton, *Habits of the Heart: Individualism and Commitment in American Life.* Berkeley and Los Angeles: University of California Press, 1985.

Benavides, Gustavo, and M. W. Daly, eds. *Religion and Political Power.* Albany: State University of New York Press, 1989.

Berger, Peter. *The Heretical Imperative.* New York: Doubleday, 1980.

———. *The Sacred Canopy: Elements of a Sociological Theory of Religion.* Garden City, N.Y.: Doubleday, 1967.

Bloome, Irene, Paul Martin, and Wayne Proudfoot, eds. *Religion and Human Rights.* New York: Columbia University Press, forthcoming.

Bohannan, Paul, ed. *Law and Warfare: Studies in the Anthropology of Conflict.* Garden City, N.Y.: Natural History Press, 1967.

Breuilly, John. *Nationalism and the State.* Manchester: Manchester University Press, 1982.

Brinton, Crane. *The Anatomy of Revolution.* Rev. ed. New York: Random House, Vintage Books, 1957.

Brown, Robert McAfee. *Religion and Violence.* 2d ed. Philadelphia: Westminster Press, 1987.

Burkert, Walter. *Homo Necans: The Anthropology of Ancient Greek Sacrificial Ritual and Myth.* Translated by Peter Bing. Berkeley and Los Angeles: University of California Press, 1983.

Burkert, Walter, René Girard, and Jonathan Z. Smith. *Violent Origins: Ritual Killing and Cultural Formation.* Edited by Robert G. Hamerton-Kelly. Stanford, Calif.: Stanford University Press, 1987.

Candland, Christopher, comp. *The Spirit of Violence: An Annotated Bibliography on Religious Violence.* New York: Harry Frank Guggenheim Foundation, forthcoming.

Caplan, Lionel, ed. *Studies in Religious Fundamentalism.* Albany: State University of New York Press, 1987.

Cassirer, Ernst. *The Philosophy of the Enlightenment.* Boston: Beacon Press, 1955.

Connor, Walker. *The National Question in Marxist-Leninist Theory and Strategy.* Princeton, N.J.: Princeton University Press, 1984.

Cox, Richard H. *Ideology, Politics, and Political Theory.* Belmont, Calif.: Wadsworth, 1969.

de Tocqueville, Alexis. *The Old Régime and the French Revolution.* Translated by Stuart Gilbert. New York: Doubleday, Anchor Books, 1955.

Detienne, Marcel, and Jean-Pierre Vernant. *The Cuisine of Sacrifice among the Greeks.* Translated by Paula Wissing. Chicago and London: University of Chicago Press, 1989.

Deutsch, Eliot, ed. *Culture and Modernity: East-West Philosophical Perspectives.* Honolulu: University of Hawaii Press, 1991.

Deutsch, Karl. *Nationalism and Social Communication.* Cambridge: MIT Press, 1966.

Doob, L. *Patriotism and Nationalism.* New Haven, Conn.: Yale University Press, 1964.

Douglas, Mary. "The Effects of Modernization on Religious Change." *Daedalus* 111, no. 1 (Winter 1982): 1–19.

Dumont, Louis. *From Mandeville to Marx: The Genesis and Triumph of Economic Ideology.* Chicago: University of Chicago Press, 1977.

Dumouchel, Paul, ed. *Violence and Truth: On the Work of René Girard.* Stanford, Calif.: Stanford University Press, 1988.

Dupré, Louis. *Transcendent Selfhood: The Loss and Rediscovery of the Inner Life.* New York: Seabury Press, 1976.

Dupuy, Jean-Pierre. *Ordres et désordres: Enquêtes sur un nouveau paradigme.* Paris: Editions du Seuil, 1982.

Durkheim, Emile. *The Elementary Forms of the Religious Life.* 1915. Translated by Joseph Ward Swain. London: Allen & Unwin, 1976.

Emerson, Rupert. *From Empire to Nation: The Rise to Self-Assertion of Asian and African Peoples.* Boston: Beacon Press, 1960.

Fanon, Frantz. *The Wretched of the Earth.* New York: Grove Press, 1963.

Fukuyama, Francis. "The End of History." *The National Interest* 16 (Summer 1989): 3–18.

————. *The End of History and the Last Man.* New York: Free Press, 1992.

Geertz, Clifford. Ideology as a Cultural System." In David Apter, ed., *Ideology and Discontent.* New York: Free Press, 1964.

————, ed. *Old Societies and New States: The Quest for Modernity in Asia and Africa.* New York: Free Press, 1963.

————. "Religion as a Cultural System." Reprinted in William A. Lessa and Evon Z. Vogt, eds., *Reader in Comparative Religion: An Anthropological Approach,* 3d ed. New York: Harper & Row, 1972.

Gellner, Ernest. *Nations and Nationalism.* Oxford: Basil Blackwell, 1983.

Giddens, Anthony. *Central Problems in Social Theory: Action, Structure and Contradiction in Social Analysis.* Berkeley and Los Angeles: University of California Press, 1979.

————. *The Nation-State and Violence.* Vol. 2 of *A Contemporary Critique of Historical Materialism.* Berkeley and Los Angeles: University of California Press, 1985.

Girard, René. *The Scapegoat.* Translated by Yvonne Freccero. Baltimore: Johns Hopkins University Press, 1986. Originally published as *Le bouc émissaire.* Paris: Editions Grasset et Fasquelle, 1982.

————. *Violence and the Sacred.* Translated by Patrick Gregory. Baltimore: Johns Hopkins University Press, 1977. Originally published as *La Violence et le sacré.* Paris: Editions Bernard Grasset, 1972.

Goldstone, Jack. *Revolution and Rebellion in the Early Modern World.* Berkeley and Los Angeles: University of California Press, 1991.

Greenawalt, Kent. *Religious Convictions and Political Choice.* New York: Oxford University Press, 1988.

Gurr, Ted Robert. *Why Men Rebel.* Princeton, N.J.: Princeton University Press, 1971.

Habermas, Jürgen. *Legitimation Crisis.* Translated by Thomas McCarthy. Boston: Beacon Press, 1975.

Hadden, Jeffrey K., and Anson Shupe, eds. *Prophetic Religions and Poli-*

tics: Religion and the Political Order, vol. 1. New York: Paragon House, 1984.

Hawley, John Stratton, ed. *Fundamentalism and Gender.* New York: Oxford University Press, forthcoming.

————, ed. *Saints and Virtues.* Berkeley and Los Angeles: University of California Press, 1987.

Hayes, Carleton J. H. *Essays on Nationalism.* New York: Russell and Russell, 1966.

————. *The Historical Evolution of Modern Nationalism.* New York: Richard R. Smith, 1931.

————. *Nationalism: A Religion.* New York: Macmillan, 1960.

Hobsbawm, Eric J. *The Age of Empire, 1875–1914.* New York: Pantheon Books, 1987.

————. *Revolutionaries.* New York: Pantheon Books, 1973.

Huntington, Samuel P. "How Countries Democratize." *Political Science Quarterly* 106, no. 4 (Winter 1991–92): 579–616.

————. *The Third Wave: Democratization in the Late Twentieth Century.* Norman: University of Oklahoma Press, 1991.

James, E. O. *Origins of Sacrifice: A Study in Comparative Religion.* 1933. Port Washington, N.Y.: Kennikat Press, 1971.

Jelen, Ted G., ed. *Religion and Political Behavior in the United States.* New York: Praeger, 1989.

Johnson, Chalmers. *Revolution and the Social System.* Stanford, Calif.: Hoover Institution on War, Revolution, and Peace, 1964.

————. *Revolutionary Change.* Boston: Little, Brown, 1966.

Johnson, James Turner. *Ideology, Reason, and the Limitation of War: Religious and Secular Concepts, 1200–1740.* Princeton, N.J.: Princeton University Press, 1975.

Juergensmeyer, Mark. "Nonviolence." In Mircea Eliade, ed., *The Encyclopedia of Religion*, vol. 10. New York: Macmillan, 1987.

————. "Sacrifice and Cosmic War." In Mark Juergensmeyer, ed., *Violence and the Sacred in the Modern World.* London: Frank Cass, 1992.

————. "Violence and Religion." In Jonathan Z. Smith, ed., *The Harper Dictionary of Religion.* New York: HarperCollins, forthcoming.

————, ed. *Violence and the Sacred in the Modern World.* London: Frank Cass, 1992.

Kedourie, Elie, ed. *Nationalism in Asia and Africa.* New York: New American Library, 1970.

Keyes, Charles F., ed. *Ethnic Change.* Seattle: University of Washington Press, 1981.

Kohn, Hans. *The Age of Nationalism.* New York: Harper, 1962.

————. *Nationalism: Its Meaning and History.* Princeton, N.J.: D. Van Nostrand, 1955.

Kramer, Martin. "Sacrifice and Fratricide in Shi'ite Lebanon." In Mark Juergensmeyer, ed., *Violence and the Sacred in the Modern World.* London: Frank Cass, 1992.

Krejci, Jaroslav. "What Is a Nation?" In Peter Merkl and Ninian Smart, eds., *Religion and Politics in the Modern World.* New York: New York University Press, 1983.

Lawrence, Bruce B. *Defenders of God: The Fundamentalist Revolt against the Modern Age.* San Francisco: Harper & Row, 1989.

Lease, Gary. *Religion as Politics and Politics as Religion: Tales from Europe's Twentieth Century Woods.* Forthcoming.

Lewy, Guenter. *Religion and Revolution.* New York: Oxford University Press, 1974.

Lincoln, Bruce, ed. *Religion, Rebellion, Revolution: An Interdisciplinary and Cross-cultural Collection of Essays.* New York: St. Martin's Press, 1985.

Little, David, John Kelsay, and Abdulaziz A. Sachedina. *Human Rights and the Conflict of Cultures: Western and Islamic Perspectives on Religious Liberty.* Columbia: University of South Carolina Press, 1988.

Livingston, Paisley, ed. *Disorder and Order: Proceedings of the Stanford International Symposium (Sept. 14–16, 1981).* Stanford Literature Series 1. Saratoga, Calif.: Anma Libri, 1984.

London, Kurt. *New Nations in a Divided World: The International Relations of the Afro-Asian States.* New York: Praeger, 1983.

MacIntyre, Alasdair. *After Virtue: A Study in Moral Theory.* Notre Dame, Ind.: University of Notre Dame Press, 1981.

Mannheim, Karl. *Ideology and Utopia.* New York: Harcourt, Brace and World, 1936.

Martin, David. "Fundamentalism: An Observational and Definitional *Tour d'Horizon.*" *Political Quarterly* 61, no. 2 (April–June 1990):129–31.

Marty, Martin E., and R. Scott Appleby, eds. *Accounting for Fundamentalisms: The Dynamic Character of Movements.* Chicago: University of Chicago Press, forthcoming.

Marty, Martin E., and R. Scott Appleby, eds. *Fundamentalisms Observed.* Chicago: University of Chicago Press, 1991.

Merkl, Peter H., and Ninian Smart, eds. *Religion and Politics in the Modern World.* New York: New York University Press, 1983.

Mews, Stuart, ed. *Religion in Politics: A World Guide.* London: Longman, 1989.

Molnar, Thomas. "The Medieval Beginnings of Political Secularization." In George W. Carey and James V. Schall, eds., *Essays on Christianity and Political Philosophy.* Lanham, Md.: University Press of America, 1985.

Moore, Barrington, Jr. *The Social Origins of Dictatorship and Democracy: Lord and Peasant in the Making of the Modern World.* Boston: Beacon Press, 1966.

Niebuhr, Reinhold, ed. *Karl Marx and Friedrich Engels on Religion.* New York: Schocken, 1964.

————. *Man's Nature and His Communities.* New York: Scribner's, 1965.

————. *Moral Man and Immoral Society.* New York: Scribner's, 1932.

————. *The Nature and Destiny of Man,* vol. 2. New York: Scribner's, 1941.

Packard, Sidney R. *12th Century Europe: An Interpretive Essay.* Amherst: University of Massachusetts Press, 1973.

Pollard, Sidney. *Peaceful Conquest: The Industrialization of Europe, 1760–1970.* New York: Oxford University Press, 1981.

Rapoport, David C., ed. *Inside Terrorist Organizations.* New York: Columbia University Press, 1988.

————. "The Politics of Atrocity." In Y. Alexander and S. Finger, eds., *Terrorism: Interdisciplinary Perspectives.* New York: John Jay, 1977.

Rapoport, David C., and Yonah Alexander, eds. *The Morality of Terrorism: Religious and Secular Justifications.* New York: Pergamon Press, 1982.

Rouner, Leroy S., ed. *Human Rights and the World's Religions.* Notre Dame, Ind.: University of Notre Dame Press, 1988.

Rubenstein, Richard L., ed. *Spirit Matters: The Worldwide Impact of Religion on Contemporary Politics.* New York: Paragon House, 1987.

Sagan, Eli. *Cannibalism: Human Aggression and Cultural Form.* New York: Psychohistory Press, 1974.

————. *The Lust to Annihilate: A Psychoanalytic Study of Violence in Ancient Greek Culture.* New York: Psychohistory Press, 1972.

Sahliyeh, Emile, ed. *Religious Resurgence and Politics in the Contemporary World.* Albany: State University of New York Press, 1990.

Schafer, Boyd C. *Faces of Nationalism: New Realities and Old Myths.* New York: Harcourt Brace Jovanovich, 1972.

Schlesinger, Arthur, Jr. "Reinhold Niebuhr's Role in American Political Thought." In Charles W. Kegley, ed., *Reinhold Niebuhr: His Religious, Social and Political Thought,* rev. ed. New York: Pilgrim Press, 1984.

Schorske, Carl E. *Fin-de-Siècle Vienna: Politics and Culture.* New York: Knopf, 1980.

Seton-Watson, Hugh. *Nations and States: An Enquiry into the Origins of Nations and the Politics of Nationalism.* Boulder, Colo.: Westview Press, 1977.

Smart, Ninian. "Religion, Myth, and Nationalism." In Peter H. Merkl and Ninian Smart, eds., *Religion and Politics in the Modern World.* New York: New York University Press, 1983.

———. *Worldviews: Crosscultural Explorations of Human Beliefs.* New York: Scribner's, 1983.

Smith, Anthony D. *Nationalism in the Twentieth Century.* Oxford: Martin Robertson, 1979.

———, ed. *Nationalist Movements.* New York: St. Martin's Press, 1977.

———. *Theories of Nationalism.* London: Duckworth, 1971.

Smith, Donald Eugene, ed. *Religion and Political Modernization.* New Haven, Conn.: Yale University Press, 1974.

———, ed. *Religion, Politics, and Social Change in the Third World: A Sourcebook.* New York: Free Press, 1971.

———, ed. *South Asian Politics and Religion.* Princeton, N.J.: Princeton University Press, 1966.

Smith, Wilfred Cantwell. *The Meaning and End of Religion: A New Approach to the Religious Traditions of Mankind.* New York: Macmillan, 1962.

Snyder, Louis L. *The Dynamics of Nationalism: Readings in Its Meaning and Development.* Princeton, N.J.: D. Van Nostrand, 1964.

Stackhouse, Max L. *Creeds, Society, and Human Rights: A Study in Three Cultures.* Grand Rapids, Mich.: W. B. Eerdmans, 1984.

Strayer, Joseph. *Medieval Statecraft and the Perspectives of History.* Princeton, N.J.: Princeton University Press, 1971.

Swatos, William H., Jr., ed. *Religious Politics in Global and Comparative Perspective.* New York: Greenwood Press, 1989.

Swidler, Arlene, ed. *Human Rights in Religious Traditions.* New York: Pilgrim Press, 1982.

Thompson, Kenneth W., ed. *Moral Imperative of Human Rights.* Washington, D.C.: University Press of America, 1980.

Thornton, Thomas Perry. "Terrorism as a Weapon of Political Agitation." In Harry Eckstein, ed., *Internal War: Problems and Approaches.* New York: Free Press, 1964.

Tilly, Charles. *Coercion, Capital, and European States.* Cambridge, Mass.: Basil Blackwell, 1990.

Traer, Robert. *Faith in Human Rights: Support in Religious Traditions for a Global Struggle.* Washington, D.C.: Georgetown University Press, 1991.

van Leeuwen, Arend Theodor. *Christianity in World History: The Meeting of the Faiths of East and West.* Translated by H. H. Hoskins. New York: Scribner's, 1964.

Voegelin, Eric. *The New Science of Politics: An Introduction,* 2d ed. Chicago: University of Chicago Press, 1987.

————. *Science, Politics, and Gnosticism.* Washington, D.C.: Regnery Gateway, 1968.

Wallace, Anthony F. C. *The Death and Rebirth of the Seneca.* New York: Random House, 1969.

Wallerstein, Immanuel. *Geopolitics and Geoculture: Essays on the Changing World-System.* New York: Cambridge University Press, 1991.

————. *The Modern World-System: Capitalist Agriculture and the Origins of the European World-Economy in the Sixteenth Century.* New York: Academic Press, 1974.

————. *The Modern World-System II: Mercantilism and the Consolidation of the European World-Economy, 1600–1750.* New York: Academic Press, 1980.

Walzer, Michael. *The Revolution of the Saints: A Study in the Origins of Radical Politics.* New York: Atheneum, 1974.

Waxman, Chaim I., ed. *The End of Ideology Debate.* New York: Simon & Schuster, 1964.

Weber, Max. "Politics as a Vocation." In Hans H. Gerth and C. Wright Mills, eds., *From Max Weber: Essays in Sociology.* New York: Oxford University Press, 1946.

Whitehead, Alfred North. *Religion in the Making.* Reprinted in F. S. C. Northup and Mason W. Gross, eds., *Alfred North Whitehead: An Anthology.* New York: Macmillan, 1961.

Williams, James G. *The Bible, Violence, and the Sacred: Liberation from the Myth of Sanctioned Violence.* San Francisco: Harper San Francisco, 1991.

Wolf, Eric R. *Europe and the People without History.* Berkeley and Los Angeles: University of California Press, 1982.

Wright, Robin, and Doyle McManus. *Flashpoints: Promise and Peril in a New World.* New York: Knopf, 1992.

Islamic Nationalism

Abdallah, Umar F. *The Islamic Struggle in Syria.* Berkeley, Calif.: Mizan Press, 1983.

Abrahamian, Ervand. *Radical Islam: The Iranian Mojahedin.* London: I. B. Tauris, 1989.

Adams, Charles. "The Ideology of Mawlana Mawdudi." In Donald Eugene Smith, ed., *South Asian Politics and Religion.* Princeton, N.J.: Princeton University Press, 1966.

Ahmad, Aziz. "The Ulama in Politics." In Nikki R. Keddie, ed., *Scholars, Saints, and Sufis.* Berkeley and Los Angeles: University of California Press, 1972.

Ahmad, Jalal Al-e. *The School Principal.* Translated by John K. Newton. Minneapolis: Bibliotheca Islamica, 1974.

Ahmad, Mumtaz. "Islamic Fundamentalism in South Asia: The Jamaat-i-Islami and the Tablighi Jamaat." In Martin E. Marty and R. Scott Appleby, eds., *Fundamentalisms Observed.* Chicago: University of Chicago Press, 1991.

Akhavi, Shahrough. "The Impact of the Iranian Revolution on Egypt." In John L. Esposito, ed., *The Iranian Revolution: Its Global Impact.* Miami: Florida International University Press, 1990.

———. *Religion and Politics in Contemporary Iran: Clergy-State Relations in the Pahlavi Period.* Albany: State University of New York Press, 1980.

Akiner, Shirin. *The Islamic Peoples of the Soviet Union.* London: Kegan Paul International, 1983.

Algar, Hamid, trans. *Constitution of the Islamic Republic of Iran.* Berkeley, Calif.: Mizan Press, 1980.

Allworth, Edward, ed. *Central Asia: 120 Years of Russian Rule.* Durham, N.C.: Duke University Press, 1989.

———. *The Modern Uzbeks: From the Fourteenth Century to the Present. A Cultural History.* Stanford, Calif.: Hoover Institution Press, 1990.

al-Razzaz, Munif. *The Evolution of the Meaning of Nationalism.* Translated by Ibrahim Abu-Lughod. Garden City, N.Y.: Doubleday, 1963.

Amjad, Mohammed. *Iran: From Royal Dictatorship to Theocracy.* Westport, Conn.: Greenwood Press, 1989.

Arjomand, Said Amir, ed. *Authority and Political Culture in Shi'ism.* Albany: State University of New York Press, 1988.

———. *The Shadow of God and the Hidden Imam: Religion, Political Order, and Societal Change in Shi'ite Iran from the Beginning to 1890.* Chicago: University of Chicago Press, 1984.

———. *The Turban for the Crown: The Islamic Revolution in Iran.* New York: Oxford University Press, 1988.

———. "A Victory for the Pragmatists: The Islamic Fundamentalist Reaction in Iran." In James P. Piscatori, ed., *Islamic Fundamentalisms and the Gulf Crisis.* Chicago: Fundamentalism Project, American Academy of Arts and Sciences, 1991.

Atkin, Muriel. *The Subtlest Battle: Islam in Soviet Tajikistan.* Philadelphia: Foreign Policy Research Institute, 1989.

Auda, Gehad. "The Normalization of the Islamic Movement in Egypt." In Martin E. Marty and R. Scott Appleby, eds., *Accounting for Fundamentalisms: The Dynamic Character of Movements.* Chicago: University of Chicago Press, forthcoming.

———. "An Uncertain Response: The Islamic Movement in Egypt." In

James P. Piscatori, ed., *Islamic Fundamentalisms and the Gulf Crisis.* Chicago: Fundamentalism Project, American Academy of Arts and Sciences, 1991.

Baker, Raymond William. *Sadat and After: Struggles for Egypt's Political Soul.* Cambridge: Harvard University Press, 1990.

Bakhash, Shaul. *The Reign of the Ayatollahs: Iran and the Islamic Revolution.* New York: Basic Books, 1984.

Bani-Sadr, Abolhassan. *The Fundamental Principles and Precepts of Islamic Government.* Translated by Mohammed R. Ghanoonparvar. Lexington, Ky.: Mazda Publishers, 1981.

Bennigsen, Alexandre, and Marie Broxup. *The Islamic Threat to the Soviet State.* New York: St. Martin's Press, 1983.

Bennigsen, Alexandre, and S. Enders Wimbush. *Muslims of the Soviet Empire: A Guide.* London: C. Hurst, 1985.

Binder, Leonard. *Religion and Politics in Pakistan.* Berkeley and Los Angeles: University of California Press, 1961.

Burke, Edmund, III, and Ira M. Lapidus, eds. *Islam, Politics, and Social Movements.* Berkeley and Los Angeles: University of California Press, 1988.

Carrère d'Encausse, Hélène. *Islam and the Russian Empire: Reform and Revolution in Central Asia.* Translated by Quintin Hoare, London: I.B. Tauris, 1988. Originally published as *Réforme et révolution chez les Musulmans de l'Empire russe.* Paris: Presses de la Fondation Nationale des Sciences Politiques, 1966.

Chehabi, H. E. "Religion and Politics in Iran: How Theocratic Is the Islamic Republic?" *Daedalus* (Summer 1991):69–92.

Cole, Juan R. I., and Nikki R. Keddie. *Shi'ism and Social Protest.* New Haven, Conn.: Yale University Press, 1986.

Critchlow, James. *Nationalism in Uzbekistan: A Soviet Republic's Road to Sovereignty.* Boulder, Colo.: Westview Press, 1991.

Curtis, Michael, ed. *Religion and Politics in the Middle East.* Boulder, Colo.: Westview Press, 1981.

Deeb, Marius. "Egypt." In Stuart Mews, ed., *Religion in Politics: A World Guide.* London: Longman, 1989.

Demko, George J. *The Russian Colonization of Kazakhstan, 1896–1916.* Bloomington: Indiana University Publications, 1969.

Dessouki, Ali E. Hillal, ed. *Islamic Resurgence in the Arab World.* New York: Praeger, 1982.

Enayat, Hamid. *Modern Islamic Political Thought: The Response of the Shi'i and Sunni Muslims to the Twentieth Century.* London: Macmillan, 1982.

Entelis, John P. *Algeria: The Revolution Institutionalized.* Boulder, Colo.: Westview Press, 1986.

Esposito, John L., ed. *The Iranian Revolution: Its Global Impact*. Miami: Florida International University Press, 1990.

―――. *Islam and Politics*. Syracuse: Syracuse University Press, 1987.

―――, ed. *Voices of Resurgent Islam*. New York: Oxford University Press, 1983.

Farazmand, Ali. *The State, Bureaucracy, and Revolution in Modern Iran: Agrarian Reforms and Regime Politics*. New York: Praeger, 1989.

Fierman, William, ed. *Soviet Central Asia: The Failed Transformation*. Boulder, Colo.: Westview Press, 1991.

Ghayasuddin, M., ed. *The Impact of Nationalism on the Muslim World*. London: Open Press, Al-Hoda, 1986.

Gilsenan, Michael. *Recognizing Islam: Religion and Society in the Modern Arab World*. New York: Pantheon, 1982.

Gladney, Dru. *Muslim Chinese: Ethnic Nationalism in the People's Republic*. Cambridge, Mass.: Council on East Asian Studies, Harvard University, 1991.

Haddad, Yvonne V. "Sayyid Qutb: Ideologue of Islamic Revival." In John L. Esposito, ed., *Voices of Resurgent Islam*. New York: Oxford University Press, 1983.

Heikal, Mohammed. *Autumn of Fury: The Assassination of Sadat*. London: Andre Deutsch, 1983.

Hinnebusch, Raymond A. "The Islamic Movement in Syria: Sectarian Conflict and Urban Rebellion in an Authoritarian-Populist Regime." In Ali E. Hillal Dessouki, ed. *Islamic Resurgence in the Arab World*. New York: Praeger, 1982.

Hopkins, Nicholas S., and Saad Eddin Ibrahim, eds. *Arab Society: Social Science Perspectives*. Cairo: American University in Cairo Press, 1985.

Humphreys, R. Stephen. "The Contemporary Resurgence in the Context of Modern Islam." In Ali E. Hillal Dessouki, ed., *Islamic Resurgence in the Arab World*. New York: Praeger, 1982.

Hunter, Shireen T., ed. *The Politics of Islamic Revivalism: Diversity and Unity*. Bloomington: Indiana University Press, 1988.

Ibrahim, Saad Eddin. "Islamic Militancy as a Social Movement: The Case of Two Groups in Egypt." In Ali E. Hillal Dessouki, ed., *Islamic Resurgence in the Arab World*. New York: Praeger, 1982.

Jansen, Johannes J. G. *The Neglected Duty: The Creed of Sadat's Assassins and Islamic Resurgence in the Middle East*. New York: Macmillan, 1986.

Keddie, Nikki R., ed. *Religion and Politics in Iran: Shi'ism from Quietism to Revolution*. New Haven, Conn.: Yale University Press, 1983.

―――. *Scholars, Saints, and Sufis*. Berkeley and Los Angeles: University of California Press, 1972.

————. "Shi'ism and Revolution." In Bruce Lincoln, ed., *Religion, Rebellion, Revolution: An Interdisciplinary and Cross-Cultural Collection of Essays.* New York: St. Martin's Press, 1985.

Keddie, Nikki R., and Eric Hooglund, eds. *The Iranian Revolution and the Islamic Republic.* Syracuse, N.Y.: Syracuse University Press, 1986.

Kepel, Gilles. *Muslim Extremism in Egypt: The Prophet and Pharaoh.* Berkeley and Los Angeles: University of California Press, 1986.

Khomeini, Ayatollah Sayyed Ruhollah Mousavi. *A Clarification of Questions: An Unabridged Translation of Resaleh Towzih al-Masael.* Translated by J. Borujerdi. Boulder, Colo., and London: Westview Press, 1984.

————. *Collection of Speeches, Position Statements.* Translated from "Najaf Min watha 'iq al-Imam al-Khomeyni did al-Quwa al Imbiriyaliyah wa al-Sahyuniyah wa al-Raj'iyah" ("From the Papers of Imam Khomeyni against Imperialist, Zionist and Reactionist Powers"), 1977. Translations on Near East and North Africa 1902. Arlington, Va.: Joint Publications Research Service, 1979.

————. *Sayings of the Ayatollah Khomeini: Political, Philosophical, Social and Religious.* Extracts from *Valayate-Faghih* (*The Kingdom of the Learned*), *Kashfol-Asrar* (*The Key to Mysteries*), and *Towzihol-Masael* (*The Explanation of Problems*). Selected and translated into French by Jean-Marie Xaviere and published as *Principes de l'Ayatollah Khomeiny: philosophiques, sociaux et réligieux,* Paris: Editions Libres-Hallier, 1979. Translated from French into English by Harold J. Salemson and edited by Tony Hendra. New York: Bantam Books, 1980.

Khomeini, Imam [Ayatollah]. *Islam and Revolution: Writings and Declarations.* Translated and annotated by Hamid Algar. Berkeley, Calif.: Mizan Press, 1981; London: Routledge & Kegan Paul, 1985.

Kramer, Martin, ed. *Shi'ism, Resistance and Revolution.* Boulder, Colo.: Westview Press, 1987.

Lapidus, Ira M. *A History of Islamic Societies.* Cambridge: Cambridge University Press, 1988.

Legrain, Jean-François. "A Defining Moment: Palestinian Islamic Fundamentalism." In James P. Piscatori, ed., *Islamic Fundamentalisms and the Gulf Crisis.* Chicago: Fundamentalism Project, American Academy of Arts and Sciences, 1991.

————. "The Islamic Movement and the Intifada." In Jamal R. Nassar and Roger Heacock, eds., *Intifada: Palestine at the Crossroads.* New York: Praeger, 1990.

————. "Islamistes et lutte nationale palestinienne dans les territoires occupés par Israel." *Revue française de science politique* 36, no. 2 (April 1986): 227–47.

Lewis, Bernard. *The Assassins: A Radical Sect in Islam.* New York: Oxford University Press, 1967.

——, ed. *Islam: From the Prophet Muhammad to the Capture of Constantinople.* 2 vols. New York: Oxford University Press, 1987.

——. *The Political Language of Islam.* Chicago: University of Chicago Press, 1988.

——. "The Return of Islam." In Michael Curtis, ed., *Religion and Politics in the Middle East.* Boulder, Colo.: Westview Press, 1981.

Lewy, Guenter. "Nasserism and Islam: A Revolution in Search of Ideology." In Guenter Lewy, *Religion and Revolution.* New York: Oxford University Press, 1974.

Martin, Richard C. "Religious Violence in Islam: Towards an Understanding of the Discourse on *Jihad* in Modern Egypt." In Paul Wilkinson and A. M. Stewart, eds., *Contemporary Research on Terrorism.* Aberdeen. University Press, 1987.

Mitchell, Richard P. *The Society of the Muslim Brothers.* London: Oxford University Press, 1969.

Mortimer, Edward. *The Politics of Islam.* New York: Random House, Vintage Books, 1982.

Mottahedeh, Roy P. *The Mantle of the Prophet.* New York: Pantheon, 1986.

Munson, Henry, Jr. *Islam and Revolution in the Middle East.* New Haven, Conn.: Yale University Press, 1988.

Muslih, Muhammad. *The Origins of Palestinian Nationalism.* New York: Columbia University Press, 1988.

Nassar, Jamal R., and Roger Heacock. *Intifada: Palestine at the Crossroads.* New York: Praeger, 1990.

Nettler, Ronald L. *Past Trials and Present Tribulations: A Muslim Fundamentalist's View of the Jews.* New York: Pergamon Press, 1987.

"The Next Islamic Revolution." *Economist* 320, no. 7725 (September 21, 1991):58–60.

Olcott, Martha Brill. "Central Asia's Catapult to Independence." *Foreign Affairs* 71: 3 (Summer 1992):131–45.

——. "Central Asia's Post-Empire Politics." *Orbis* 36, no. 2 (Spring 1992):253–68.

——. *The Kazakhs.* Stanford, Calif.: Hoover Institution Press, 1987.

Peters, Rudolph. *Islam and Colonialism: The Doctrine of Jihad in Modern History.* The Hague: Mouton, 1979.

Pierce, R. *Russian Central Asia, 1867–1917: A Study in Colonial Rule.* Berkeley and Los Angeles: University of California Press, 1960.

Piscatori, James P. *Islam in the Political Process.* Cambridge: Cambridge University Press, 1983.

————, ed. *Islamic Fundamentalisms and the Gulf Crisis*. Chicago: Fundamentalism Project, American Academy of Arts and Sciences, 1991.

Qutb, Sayyid. *This Religion of Islam (Hadha 'd-Din)*. Translated by Islamdust. Palo Alto, Calif.: Al-Manar Press, 1967.

Rashid, Ahmed. "The Islamic Challenge." *Far Eastern Economic Review* 149 (July 12, 1990):24.

Rekhess, Elie. "The Iranian Impact on the Islamic Jihad Movement in the Gaza Strip." In David Menashri, ed., *The Iranian Revolution and the Muslim World*. Boulder, Colo.: Westview Press, 1990.

Roberts, Hugh. "Radical Islamism and the Dilemma of Algerian Nationalism: The Embattled Arians of Algiers." *Third World Quarterly* 10, no. 2 (April 1988):556–89.

Ro'i, Yaacov, ed. *The USSR and the Muslim World: Issues in Domestic and Foreign Policy*. London: George Allen & Unwin, 1984.

Rorlich, Azade-Ayse. "Islam and Atheism: Dynamic Tension in Soviet Central Asia." In William Fierman, ed., *Soviet Central Asia: The Failed Transformation*. Boulder, Colo.: Westview Press, 1991.

Roy, Olivier. *Islam and Resistance in Afghanistan*. Cambridge: Cambridge University Press, 1990. Originally published as *L'Afghanistan: Islam et modernité politique*. Paris: Editions du Seuil, 1985.

Sachedina, Abdulaziz Abdulhussein. "Activist Shi'ism in Iran, Iraq, and Lebanon." In Martin E. Marty and R. Scott Appleby, eds., *Fundamentalisms Observed*. Chicago: University of Chicago Press, 1991.

————. *The Just Ruler (al-sultan al-'adil) in Shi'ite Islam: The Comprehensive Authority of the Jurist in Imamite Jurisprudence*. New York: Oxford University Press, 1988.

Satha-Anand, Chaiwat. *Islam and Violence: A Case Study of Violent Events in the Four Southern Provinces, Thailand, 1976–1981*. Monographs in Religion and Public Policy. Tampa: Department of Religious Studies, University of South Florida, 1986.

Sick, Gary. *All Fall Down: America's Tragic Encounter with Iran*. Rev. ed. New York: Penguin, 1986.

Siddiqui, Kalim. "Nation-States as Obstacles to the Total Transformation of the *Ummah*." In M. Ghayasuddin, ed., *The Impact of Nationalism on the Muslim World*. London: Open Press, Al-Hoda, 1986.

Simpson, John. *Inside Iran: Life under Khomeini's Regime*. New York: St. Martin's Press, 1988.

Sinor, Denis. *The Cambridge History of Inner Asia*. Cambridge: Cambridge University Press, 1990.

Sivan, Emmanuel. "The Islamic Resurgence: Civil Society Strikes Back." *Journal of Contemporary History* (London) 25 (1990):353–64.

————. *Radical Islam: Medieval Theology and Modern Politics.* New Haven, Conn.: Yale University Press, 1985.

————. "Sunni Radicalism in the Middle East and the Iranian Revolution." *International Journal for Middle East Studies* 21 (1989):1–30.

Sivan, Emmanuel, and Menachem Friedman, eds. *Religious Radicalism and Politics in the Middle East.* Albany: State University of New York Press, 1990.

Smith, Wilfred Cantwell. *Islam in Modern History.* Princeton, N.J.: Princeton University Press, 1957.

Steinberg, Matti. "The PLO and Palestinian Islamic Fundamentalism." *Jewish Quarterly* 52 (Fall 1989):37–54.

Syed, Anwar. *Pakistan: Islam, Politics, and National Solidarity.* New York: Praeger, 1982.

Wasserstein, Bernard. "Patterns of Communal Conflict in Palestine." In Ada Rapoport and Steven J. Zipperstein, eds., *Jewish History: Essays in Honour of Chimen Abramsky.* London: Peter Halban, 1988.

Watt, W. Montgomery. *Islamic Fundamentalism and Modernity.* London: Routledge, 1988.

Wendell, Charles, trans. *Five Tracts of Hasan al-Banna (1906–1949).* Berkeley and Los Angeles: University of California Press, 1978.

Wheeler, Geoffrey. *The Modern History of Soviet Central Asia.* London: Weidenfeld and Nicolson, 1964.

Wixman, Ronald. "Ethnic Attitudes and Relations in Modern Uzbek Cities." In William Fierman, ed., *Soviet Central Asia: The Failed Transformation.* Boulder, Colo.: Westview Press, 1991.

Wright, Robin. *In the Name of God: The Khomeini Decade.* New York: Simon & Schuster, 1989.

————. "Islam, Democracy, and the West." *Foreign Affairs* 71: 3 (Summer 1992):131–45.

————. "Report from Turkestan." *New Yorker,* April 6, 1992, 53–75.

————. *Sacred Rage: The Wrath of Militant Islam.* New York: Linden Press, Simon & Schuster, 1985.

Jewish Nationalism

Agus, Jacob B. *Banner of Jerusalem: The Life, Times, and Thought of Rabbi Abraham Isaac Kuk.* New York: Bloch, 1946.

Aran, Gideon. "From Religious Zionism to Zionist Religion: The Roots of Gush Emunim." In Peter Medding, ed., *Studies in Contemporary Jewry,* vol. 2. New York: Oxford University Press, 1986.

————. "Jewish Zionist Fundamentalism: The Bloc of the Faithful in Israel (Gush Emunim)." In Martin E. Marty and R. Scott Appleby, eds.,

Fundamentalisms Observed. Chicago: University of Chicago Press, 1991.

Biale, David J. "Mysticism and Politics in Modern Israel: The Messianic Ideology of Abraham Isaac Ha-Cohen Kook." In Peter H. Merkl and Ninian Smart, eds., *Religion and Politics in the Modern World.* New York: New York University Press, 1983.

Buchanan, George W. *Revelation and Redemption: Jewish Documents of Deliverance from the Fall of Jerusalem to the Death of Nahmanides.* Dillsboro, N.C.: Western North Carolina Press, 1978.

Cromer, Gerald. *The Debate about Kahanism in Israeli Society, 1984–1988.* Occasional Papers 3. New York: Harry Frank Guggenheim Foundation, 1988.

Frankel, Jonathan, ed. *Jews and Messianism in the Modern Era: Metaphor and Meaning.* Vol. 7 of *Studies in Contemporary Jewry.* New York: Oxford University Press, and Jerusalem: Institute of Contemporary Jewry, Hebrew University of Jerusalem, 1991.

Friedman, Robert. *The False Prophet: Rabbi Meir Kahane—From FBI Informant to Knesset Member.* London: Faber and Faber, 1990.

Grossman, David. *The Yellow Wind.* Translated from the Hebrew by Haim Watzman. New York: Farrar, Straus & Giroux, 1988.

Kahane, Meir. *Listen World, Listen Jew.* Jerusalem: Institute of the Jewish Idea, 1978.

———. *They Must Go.* Jerusalem: Institute of the Jewish Idea, 1981.

Kotler, Yair. *Heil Kahane.* New York: Adama Books, 1986.

Lustick, Ian S. *For the Land and the Lord: Jewish Fundamentalism in Israel.* New York: Council on Foreign Relations, 1989.

Mergui, Raphael, and Philippe Simonnot. *Israel's Ayatollahs: Meir Kahane and the Far Right in Israel.* London: Saqi Books, 1987. Originally published as *Meir Kahane: Le rabbin qui fait peur aux juifs.* Lausanne: Editions Pierre-Marcel Favre, 1985.

Metzger, Alter B. Z. *Rabbi Kook's Philosophy of Repentence: A Translation of "Orot Ha-Teshuvah."* Studies in Torah Judaism 11. New York: Yeshiva University Press, 1968.

Paz, Reuven. *Ha-'imna ha-islamit umichma'utah 'iyyon rechoni utargum (The Covenant of the Islamicists and Its Significance—Analysis and Translation).* Tel Aviv: Dayan Center, Tel Aviv University, 1988.

Reich, Walter. *A Stranger in My House: Jews and Arabs in the West Bank.* New York: Holt, Rinehart & Winston, 1984.

Sprinzak, Ehud. *The Ascendance of Israel's Radical Right.* New York: Oxford University Press, 1991.

———. *Gush Emunim: The Politics of Zionist Fundamentalism in Israel.* New York: American Jewish Committee, 1986.

Zucker, Norman L. "Secularization Conflicts in Israel." In Donald Eugene Smith, ed., *Religion and Political Modernization*. New Haven, Conn.: Yale University Press, 1974.

Buddhist Nationalism

Abeysekera, Charles, and Newton Gunasinghe, eds. *Facets of Ethnicity in Sri Lanka*. Colombo: Social Scientists Association, 1987.

Akiner, Shirin, ed. *Mongolia Today*. London: Kegan Paul International, 1991.

Aung-Thwin, Michael. *Pagan: The Origins of Modern Burma*. Honolulu: University of Hawaii Press, 1985.

Bawden, C. R. *The Modern History of Mongolia*. New York: Praeger, 1968.

Bechert, Heinz. "Buddhism and Mass Politics in Burma and Ceylon." In Donald Eugene Smith, ed., *Religion and Political Modernization*. New Haven, Conn.: Yale University Press, 1974.

Bobilin, Robert. *Revolution from Below: Buddhist and Christian Movements for Justice in Asia: Four Case Studies from Thailand and Sri Lanka*. Lanham, Md.: University Press of America, 1988.

Brown, William A., and Urgunge Onon, trans. *History of the Mongolian People's Republic*. Cambridge: East Asian Research Center, Harvard University, 1976.

Buddhadasa, Bhikkhu. *Dhammic Socialism*. Translated and edited by Donald K. Swearer. Bangkok: Thai Inter-religious Commission for Development, 1986.

Committee for Rational Development. *Sri Lanka, the Ethnic Conflict: Myths, Realities, and Perspectives*. New Delhi: Navrang, 1984.

Davis, Winston. "Fundamentalism in Japan: Religious and Political." In Martin E. Marty and R. Scott Appleby, eds., *Fundamentalisms Observed*. Chicago: University of Chicago Press, 1991.

deSilva, K. M. *Managing Ethnic Tensions in Multi-ethnic Societies: Sri Lanka, 1880–1985*. Lanham, Md.: University Press of America, 1986.

Gombrich, Richard, and Gananath Obeyesekere. *Buddhism Transformed: Religious Change in Sri Lanka*. Princeton, N.J.: Princeton University Press, 1988.

Goulet, Denis. *Survival with Integrity: Sarvodaya at the Crossroads*. Colombo: Marga Institute, 1981.

Gunaratna, Rohan. *Sri Lanka: A Lost Revolution? The Inside Story of the JVP*. Kandy, Sri Lanka: Institute of Fundamental Studies, 1990.

Heaton, William R. "Mongolia in 1990: Upheaval, Reform, but No Revolution Yet." *Asian Survey* 31 (January 1991):50–56.

Heissig, Walther. *A Lost Civilization: The Mongols Rediscovered.* London: Thames and Hudson, 1966.

———. *The Religions of Mongolia.* London: Routledge & Kegan Paul, 1980.

Juergensmeyer, Mark. "Sri Lanka." In Stuart Mews, ed., *Religion in Politics: A World Guide.* London: Longman, 1989.

———. "Tibet." In Stuart Mews, ed., *Religion in Politics: A World Guide.* London: Longman, 1989.

———. "What the Bhikkhu Said: Reflections on the Rise of Militant Religious Nationalism." *Religion* 20, no. 1 (1990):53–75.

Kaye, Lincoln. "Faltering Steppes." *Far Eastern Economic Review* (April 9, 1992):16–20.

Keyes, Charles F. *Thailand: Buddhist Kingdom as Modern Nation-State.* Boulder, Colo.: Westview Press, 1987.

Lewy, Guenter. "Militant Buddhist Nationalism: The Case of Burma." In Guenter Lewy, *Religion and Revolution.* New York: Oxford University Press, 1974.

———. "The Sinhalese Buddhist Revolution of Ceylon." In Guenter Lewy, *Religion and Revolution.* New York: Oxford University Press, 1974.

Manogaran, Chelvadurai. *Ethnic Conflict and Reconciliation in Sri Lanka.* Honolulu: University of Hawaii Press, 1987.

Manor, James. *Sri Lanka in Change and Crisis.* London: Croom Helm, 1984.

McGowan, William. *The Tragedy of Sri Lanka.* New York: Farrar, Straus & Giroux, 1992.

Moonesinghe, Mangala. *The Sri Lanka Ethnic Conflict: A Documentation of Literature 1983–1987.* Colombo: Marga Institute, 1987.

Obeyesekere, Gananath. "Religious Symbolism and Political Change in Ceylon." In Gananath Obeyesekere, Frank Reynolds, and Bardwell L. Smith, eds., *The Two Wheels of Dhamma: Essays on the Theravada Tradition in India and Ceylon.* Chambersburg, Pa.: American Academy of Religion, 1972.

Obeyesekere, Gananath, Frank Reynolds, and Bardwell L. Smith, eds. *The Two Wheels of Dhamma: Essays on the Theravada Tradition in India and Ceylon.* Chambersburg, Pa.: American Academy of Religion, 1972.

Phadnis, Urmila. *Religion and Politics in Sri Lanka.* Columbia, Mo.: South Asia Books, 1976.

Ponnambalam, Satchi. *Sri Lanka: National Conflict and the Tamil Liberation Struggle.* London: Zed Books and Tamil Information Centre, 1983.

Rahula, Walpola. *History of Buddhism in Ceylon,* 2d ed. Colombo: M. D. Gunasena, 1966.

Rossabi, Morris. *China and Inner Asia: From 1368 to the Present Day.* New York: Pica Press, 1975.

————. *Khubilai Khan: His Life and Times.* Berkeley and Los Angeles: University of California Press, 1988.

Sanders, Alan J. K. "Guardians of Culture." *Far Eastern Economic Review* 151 (January 3, 1991):20–23.

————. *Mongolia: Politics, Economics and Society.* London: Frances Pinter, 1987.

Sarkisyanz, E. *Buddhist Backgrounds of the Burmese Revolution.* The Hague: Martinus Nijhoff, 1965.

Saunders, J. J. *The History of the Mongol Conquests.* London: Routledge & Kegan Paul, 1971.

Smith, Bardwell L. "The Ideal Social Order as Portrayed in the Chronicles of Ceylon." In Gananath Obeyesekere, Frank Reynolds, and Bardwell L. Smith, eds., *The Two Wheels of Dhamma: Essays on the Theravada Tradition in India and Ceylon.* Chambersburg, Pa.: American Academy of Religion, 1972.

————, ed. *Religion and Legitimation of Power in Thailand, Laos, and Burma.* Chambersburg, Pa.: Anima Books, 1978.

Smith, Donald Eugene. "The Political Monks and Monastic Reform." In Donald Eugene Smith, ed., *South Asian Politics and Religion.* Princeton, N.J.: Princeton University Press, 1966.

————, ed. *Religion and Politics in Burma.* Princeton, N.J.: Princeton University Press, 1965.

Smith, Donald Eugene, Jeyaratnam Wilson, and D. S. Siriwardane. "Ceylon: The Politics of Buddhist Resurgence." Pt. 4 of Donald Eugene Smith, ed., *South Asian Politics and Religion.* Princeton, N.J.: Princeton University Press, 1966.

Snellgrove, David, and Hugh Richardson. *A Cultural History of Tibet.* London: Weidenfeld and Nicolson, 1968.

Spencer, Jonathan. *Sri Lanka: History and the Roots of Conflict.* London: Routledge, 1990.

Spüler, Bertold. *History of the Mongols.* London: Routledge & Kegan Paul, 1968.

Suksamran, Somboon. *Buddhism and Politics in Thailand: A Study of Socio-political Change and Political Activism of the Thai Sangha.* Singapore: Institute of Southeast Asian Studies, 1982.

Swearer, Donald K. *Buddhism and Society in Southeast Asia.* Chambersburg, Pa.: Anima Books, 1981.

————. "Fundamentalist Movements in Theravada Buddhism." In Martin

E. Marty and R. Scott Appleby, eds., *Fundamentalisms Observed* (Chicago: University of Chicago Press, 1991).

Tambiah, Stanley J. *Buddhism Betrayed? Religion, Politics and Violence in Sri Lanka*. Chicago: University of Chicago Press, 1992.

————. *Levelling Crowds: Ethnic Violence in South Asia*. Berkeley and Los Angeles: University of California Press, forthcoming.

————. *Sri Lanka: Ethnic Fratricide and the Dismantling of Democracy*. Chicago: University of Chicago Press, 1986.

————. *World Conqueror and World Renouncer: A Study of Buddhism and Polity in Thailand against a Historical Background*. Cambridge: Cambridge University Press, 1976.

Vejayavardhana, D. C. *The Revolt in the Temple: Composed to Commemorate 2,500 Years of the Land, the Race, and the Faith*. Colombo: Sinha Publications, 1953. Reprinted in Donald Eugene Smith, *Religion, Politics and Social Change in the Third World: A Sourcebook*. New York: Free Press, 1971.

von der Mehden, Fred R. *Religion and Nationalism in Southeast Asia: Burma, Indonesia, the Philippines*. Madison: University of Wisconsin Press, 1963.

————. "Secularization of Buddhist Polities: Burma and Thailand." In Donald Eugene Smith, ed., *Religion and Political Modernization*. New Haven, Conn.: Yale University Press, 1974.

Waley, Arthur. *The Secret History of the Mongols*. London: Allen & Unwin, 1963.

Woy, Paul C. "Rebirth of a Nation? Mongolia's Reincarnated Religious Leader." *Contemporary Review* 259 (November 1991):234–41.

Wriggins, W. Howard. *Ceylon: Dilemmas of a New Nation*. Princeton, N.J.: Princeton University Press, 1960.

Sikh and Hindu Nationalism

Andersen, Walter K., and Shridhar D. Damle. *The Brotherhood in Saffron: The Rashtriya Swayamsevak Sangh and Hindu Revivalism*. Boulder: Colo.: Westview Press, 1987.

Basham, A. L. *The Wonder That Was India: A Survey of the Culture of the Indian Sub-continent before the Coming of the Muslims*. New York: Grove Press, 1954.

Baxter, Craig. *The Jana Sangh: A Biography of an Indian Political Party*. Philadelphia: University of Pennsylvania Press, 1969.

Bhindranwale, Jarnail Singh. "Address to the Sikh Congregation." Transcript of a sermon given in the Golden Temple in November 1983, translated by Ranbir Singh Sandhu, April 1985, and distributed by the Sikh Religious and Educational Trust, Columbus, Ohio.

―――. "Two Lectures." Given on July 19 and September 20, 1983, translated from the videotaped originals by R. S. Sandhu, and distributed by the Sikh Religious and Educational Trust, Columbus, Ohio.

Bjorkman, James W., ed. *Fundamentalism, Revivalists and Violence in South Asia.* Riverdale, Md.: Riverdale Company, 1986.

Chaddah, Mehar Singh. *Are Sikhs a Nation?* Delhi: Delhi Sikh Gurdawara Management Committee, 1982.

Chatterjee, Margaret. *Gandhi's Religious Thought.* Notre Dame, Ind.: Notre Dame University Press, 1983.

Chopra, V. D., R. K. Mishra, Nirmal Singh. *Agony of Punjab.* New Delhi: Patriot Publishers, 1984.

Citizens for Democracy. *Oppression in Punjab.* Columbus, Ohio: Sikh Religious and Educational Trust, 1985.

Cole, W. Owen, and Piara Singh Sambhi. *The Sikhs: Their Religious Beliefs and Practices.* London: Routledge & Kegan Paul, 1978.

Das, Veena, ed. *The Word and the World: Fantasy, Symbol and Record.* New Delhi: Sage Publications, 1986.

Devi, Savitri. *A Warning to the Hindus.* Calcutta: Hindu Mission, 1939.

Duara, Prasenjit. "The New Politics of Hinduism." *Wilson Quarterly* (Summer 1991):35–42.

Editors of *Executive Review. Derivative Assassination: Who Killed Indira Gandhi?* New York: New Benjamin Franklin House, 1985.

Embree, Ainslie T. "The Function of the Rashtriya Swayamsevak Sangh: To Define the Hindu Nation." In Martin E. Marty and R. Scott Appleby, eds., *Accounting for Fundamentalisms.* Chicago: University of Chicago Press, forthcoming.

―――. *Imagining India: Essays on Indian History.* Delhi and New York: Oxford University Press, 1989.

―――. *Utopias in Conflict: Religion and Nationalism in Modern India.* Berkeley and Los Angeles: University of California Press, 1990.

Freitag, Sandria B. *Collective Action and Community: Public Arenas and the Emergence of Communalism in North India.* Berkeley and Los Angeles: University of California Press, 1989.

French, Hal W., and Arvind Sharma. *Religious Ferment in Modern India.* New York: St. Martin's Press, 1981.

Frykenberg, Robert Eric. "Revivalism and Fundamentalism: Some Critical Observations with Special Reference to Politics in South Asia." In James W. Bjorkman, ed., *Fundamentalism, Revivalists and Violence in South Asia.* Riverdale, Md.: Riverdale Company, 1986.

Gandhi, Indira. "Don't Shed Blood, Shed Hatred." All India Radio, June

2, 1984. Reprinted in V. D. Chopra, R. K. Mishra, and Nirmal Singh, *Agony of Punjab.* New Delhi: Patriot Publishers, 1984.

Gandhi, Mohandas. *Hind Swaraj, or Indian Home Rule.* Ahmedabad: Navajivan Press, 1938.

George, Alexandra. *Social Ferment in India.* New York: Athlone, 1986.

Gold, Daniel. "Organized Hinduisms: From Vedic Tradition to Hindu Nation." In Martin E. Marty and R. Scott Appleby, eds., *Fundamentalisms Observed.* Chicago: University of Chicago Press, 1991.

————. "Rational Action and Uncontrolled Violence: Explaining Hindu Communalism." *Religion* 21 (1991): 357–70.

Gopal, Sarvepalli, ed. *Anatomy of a Confrontation: The Babri Masjid-Ramjanmabhumi Issue.* New Delhi: Penguin Books, 1991.

Graham, B. D. *Hindu Nationalism and Indian Politics: The Origins and Development of the Bharatiya Jana Sangh.* Cambridge: Cambridge University Press, 1990.

Gulati, Kailash Chander. *The Akalis Past and Present.* New Delhi: Ashajanak Publications, 1974.

Gupta, Lina. "Indian Secularism and the Problem of the Sikhs." In Gustavo Benavides and M. W. Daly, eds., *Religion and Political Power.* New York: State University of New York Press, 1989.

Hawley, John Stratton. "Naming Hinduism." *Wilson Quarterly* (Summer 1991):20–34.

Hawley, John Stratton, and Mark Juergensmeyer, trans. *Songs of the Saints of India.* New York: Oxford University Press, 1988.

Jalandhary, Surjeet. *Bhindranwale Sant.* Jalandhar, India: Punjab Pocket Books, n.d. (c. 1985).

Jeffrey, Robin. *What's Happening to India? Punjab, Ethnic Conflict, Mrs. Gandhi's Death and the Test for Federalism.* New York: Holmes and Meier, 1986.

Juergensmeyer, Mark. "India." In Stuart Mews, ed., *Religion in Politics: A World Guide.* London: Longman, 1989.

————. "The Logic of Religious Violence." In David C. Rapoport, ed., *Inside Terrorist Organizations.* London: Frank Cass, 1988.

————. *Radhasoami Reality: The Logic of a Modern Faith.* Princeton, N.J.: Princeton University Press, 1991.

————. *Religion as Social Vision: The Movement against Untouchability in 20th Century Punjab.* Berkeley and Los Angeles: University of California Press, 1982. Revised edition: *Religious Rebels in the Punjab: The Social Vision of Untouchables.* Delhi: Ajanta Publications, 1988.

Juergensmeyer, Mark, and N. Gerald Barrier, eds. *Sikh Studies: Comparative Perspectives on Changing Tradition.* Berkeley Religious Studies Series 1. Berkeley, Calif.: Graduate Theological Union, 1979.

Kapur, Rajiv A. *Sikh Separatism: The Politics of Faith.* London: Allen & Unwin, 1986.

Kaur, Amarjit, Shourie Arun, J. S. Aurora, Khushwant Singh, M. V. Kamath, Shekhar Gupta, Subhash Kirpekar, Sunil Sethi, and Tavleen Singh. *The Punjab Story.* New Delhi: Roli Books International, 1984.

Kohli, S. S. *Sikh Ethics.* New Delhi: Munshiram Manoharlal, 1975.

McLeod, W. H. *The Evolution of the Sikh Community: Five Essays.* Oxford: Clarendon Press, 1976.

———. *Guru Nanak and the Sikh Religion.* Oxford: Clarendon Press, 1968.

———. *Who Is a Sikh? The Problem of Sikh Identity.* Oxford: Clarendon Press, 1989.

Madan, T. N. "The Double-Edged Sword: Fundamentalism and the Sikh Religious Tradition." In Martin E. Marty and R. Scott Appleby, eds., *Fundamentalisms Observed.* Chicago: University of Chicago Press, 1991.

Mahmood, Cynthia Keppley. "Sikh Rebellion and the Hindu Concept of Order." *Asian Survey* 29, no. 3 (1989):326–40.

Majahid, Abdul Mali. *Conversion to Islam: Untouchables' Strategy for Protest in India.* Chambersburg, Pa.: Anima Press, 1989.

Malik, Yogendra, and Dhirendra Vajpeyi. "The Rise of Hindu Militancy: India's Secular Democracy at Risk." *Asian Survey* 29, no. 3 (1989): 308–25.

Mishra, Dina Nath. *RSS: Myth and Reality.* New Delhi: Vikas, 1980.

Mulgrew, Ian. *Unholy Terror: The Sikhs and International Terrorism.* Toronto: Key Porter Books, 1988.

Nandy, Ashis. "An Anti-secularist Manifesto." In John Hick and Lamont C. Hempel, eds., *Gandhi's Significance for Today: The Elusive Legacy.* London: Macmillan, 1989.

Nayar, Baldev Raj. *Minority Politics in the Punjab.* Princeton, N.J.: Princeton University Press, 1966.

———. "Sikh Separatism in the Punjab." In Donald Eugene Smith, ed., *South Asian Politics and Religion.* Princeton, N.J.: Princeton University Press, 1966.

Nayar, Kuldip, and Khushwant Singh. *Tragedy of Punjab: Operation Bluestar and After.* New Delhi: Vision Books, 1984.

Nehru, Jawaharlal. *A Bunch of Old Letters.* Bombay: Asia Publishing House, 1958.

———. *The Discovery of India.* New York: John Day, 1946.

O'Brien, Conor Cruise. "Holy War against India." *Atlantic Monthly* 262 (August 1988).

O'Connell, Joseph T., Milton Israel, and Willard G. Oxtoby, eds. *Sikh*

History and Religion in the Twentieth Century. Toronto: Centre for South Asian Studies, University of Toronto, 1988.

Oddie, G. A., ed. *Religion in South Asia: Religious Conversion and Revival Movements in South Asia in Medieval and Modern Times.* Columbia, Mo.: South Asia Books, 1977.

Pettigrew, Joyce. "In Search of a New Kingdom of Lahore." *Pacific Affairs* 60, no. 1 (Spring 1987).

Premdas, Ralph R., S.W.R. de A. Samarasinghe, and Alan B. Anderson, eds. *Secessionist Movements in Comparative Perspective.* London: Pinter Publishers, 1990.

Sarin, Ritu. *The Assassination of Indira Gandhi.* New Delhi: Penguin Books, 1990.

Savarkar, V. D. *Hindutva: Who Is a Hindu?* Bombay: Veer Savarkar Prakashan, 1969.

Seshadri, H. V., ed. *RSS: A Vision in Action.* Bangalore, India: Jagarana Prakashana, 1988.

Singh, Amrik, ed. *Punjab in Indian Politics: Issues and Trends.* New Delhi: Ajanta Books, 1985.

Singh, Avtar. *Ethics of the Sikhs.* Patiala, India: Punjabi University Press, 1970.

Singh, Jagjit. *The Sikh Revolution.* New Delhi: Bahri Publications, 1981.

Singh, Khushwant. *History of the Sikhs,* vol. 2. Princeton, N.J.: Princeton University Press, 1966.

Singh, Mohinder. "Gandhi, Sikhs and Non-violence." *Khera* 9, no. 3 (July-September 1990):72–87.

Smith, Donald Eugene. *India as a Secular State.* Princeton, N.J.: Princeton University Press, 1963.

Tambiah, Stanley J. *Levelling Crowds: Ethnic Violence in South Asia.* Berkeley and Los Angeles: University of California Press, forthcoming.

Thapar, Romila. "Imagined Religious Communities? Ancient History and the Modern Search for a Hindu Identity." *Modern Asian Studies* 23, no. 2 (1989): 209–31.

Tully, Mark, and Satish Jacob. *Amritsar: Mrs. Gandhi's Last Battle.* London: Cape, 1985.

van der Veer, Peter. "God Must Be Liberated! A Hindu Liberation Movement in Ayodhya." *Modern Asian Studies* 21, no. 2 (1985): 283–301.

———. "Hindu 'Nationalism' and the Discourse of 'Modernity': The Vishva Hindu Parishad." In Martin E. Marty and R. Scott Appleby, eds., *Accounting for Fundamentalisms.* Chicago: University of Chicago Press, forthcoming.

Wallace, Paul, ed. *Region and Nation in India.* New Delhi: Oxford and IBH, 1985.

Wallace, Paul, and Surendra Chopra, eds. *Political Dynamics and Crisis in Punjab.* Amritsar: Guru Nanak Dev University Press, 1988.

Who Are the Guilty? Report of a Joint Inquiry into the Causes and Impact of the Riots in Delhi from 31 October to 10 November. Delhi: People's Union for Democratic Rights and People's Union for Civil Liberties, 1984.

Christian Nationalism

Ammerman, Nancy T. "North American Protestant Fundamentalism." In Martin E. Marty and R. Scott Appleby, eds., *Fundamentalisms Observed.* Chicago: University of Chicago Press, 1991.

Balmer, Randall. *Mine Eyes Have Seen the Glory: A Journey into the Evangelical Subculture in America.* New York: Oxford University Press, 1989.

Batstone, David. *From Conquest to Struggle: Jesus of Nazareth in Latin America.* Albany: State University of New York Press, 1991.

Bellah, Robert N. "Civil Religion in America," *Daedalus* 96, no. 1 (Winter 1967):1–21.

———. "Transcendence in Contemporary Piety." In Donald R. Cutler, ed., *The Religious Situation: 1969.* Boston: Beacon Press, 1969.

Berryman, Phillip. *Liberation Theology: The Essential Facts about the Revolutionary Movements in Latin America and Beyond.* Maryknoll, N.Y.: Orbis Books, 1984.

———. *The Religious Roots of Rebellion: Christians in Central American Revolutions.* Maryknoll, N.Y.: Orbis Books, 1984.

Bociurkiw, Bohdan R. "Institutional Religion and Nationality in the Soviet Union." In S. Enders Wimbush, ed., *Soviet Nationalities in Strategic Perspective.* London: Croom Helm, 1985.

Borge, Tomas, Carlos Fonseca, Daniel Ortega, Humberto Ortega, and Jaime Wheelock. *Sandinistas Speak.* New York: Pathfinder Press, 1986.

Bradstock, Andrew. *Saints and Sandinistas: The Catholic Church in Nicaragua and Its Response to the Revolution.* London: Epworth Press, 1987.

Bruce, Stephen. "The Moral Majority: The Politics of Fundamentalism in Secular Society." In Lionel Caplan, ed., *Studies in Religious Fundamentalism.* Albany: State University of New York Press, 1987.

Cabastrero, Teofilo. *Ministers of God, Ministers of the People: Testimonies of Faith from Nicaragua.* Translated by Robert R. Barr. Maryknoll, N.Y.: Orbis Books, 1986.

———. *Revolutionaries for the Gospel: Testimonies of Fifteen Christians in the Nicaraguan Government.* Translated by Phillip Berryman. Maryknoll, N.Y.: Orbis Books, 1986.

Capps, Walter H. *The New Religious Right: Piety, Patriotism, and Politics.* Columbia: University of South Carolina Press, 1990.

Carey, George W., and James V. Schall, eds. *Essays on Christianity and Political Philosophy.* Lanham, Md.: University Press of America, 1985.

Carey, Michael J. "Catholicism and Irish National Identity." In Peter H. Merkl and Ninian Smart, eds., *Religion and Politics in the Modern World.* New York: New York University Press, 1983.

Casaldaliga, Bishop Pedro. *Prophets in Combat: The Nicaraguan Journal of Bishop Pedro Casaldaliga.* Oak Park, Ill: Meyer-Stone Books, 1987.

Chidester, David. *Shots in the Streets: Violence and Religion in South Africa.* Boston: Beacon Press, 1991.

Chodak, Szymon. "People and the Church versus the State: The Case of the Roman Catholic Church in Poland." In Richard L. Rubenstein, ed. *Spirit Matters: The Worldwide Impact of Religion on Contemporary Politics.* New York: Paragon House, 1987.

Cooke, W. Dennis D. "The Religious Dimension in the Northern Ireland Problem." *Lexington Theological Quarterly* 16, no. 3 (July 1981):85–93.

Crabtree, Harriet. "Onward Christian Soldiers? The Fortunes of a Traditional Christian Symbol in the Modern Age." *Bulletin of the Center for the Study of World Religion* (Harvard University) 16, no. 2 (1989/90): 6–27.

Demko, George J. *The Russian Orthodox Church: A Contemporary History.* London and Sydney: Croom Helm Ltd., 1986.

Dodson, Michael, and Laura Nuzzi O'Shaughnessy. *Nicaragua's Other Revolution: Religious Faith and Political Struggle.* Chapel Hill: University of North Carolina Press, 1990.

Ellis, Jane. *The Russian Orthodox Church: A Contemporary History.* Bloomington: Indiana University Press, 1986.

Gibellini, Rosino, ed. *Frontiers of Theology in Latin America.* Translated by John Drury. Maryknoll, N.Y.: Orbis Books, 1983.

Girardi, Giulio. "Democracy and Ideological Struggle in Nicaragua Today." *Cross Currents* 39, no. 1 (Spring 1989).

Griffin, Leslie, ed. *Religion and Politics in the American Milieu.* Notre Dame, Ind.: *Review of Politics* and Office of Policy Studies, University of Notre Dame, 1989.

Gutierrez, Gustavo. *A Theology of Liberation: History, Politics, and Salvation.* Rev. ed. Maryknoll, N.Y.: Orbis Books, 1988.

Hammond, Phillip E. "Religion and Nationalism in the United States." In Gustavo Benavides and M. W. Daly, eds., *Religion and Political Power.* Albany: State University of New York Press, 1989.

Harris, Richard, and Carlos M. Vilas, eds. *Nicaragua: A Revolution under Siege.* London: Zed Books, 1985.

Haslam, David. *Faith in Struggle: The Protestant Churches and Their Response to the Revolution.* London: Epworth Press, 1987.

Hickey, John. *Religion and the Northern Ireland Problem.* Totawa, N.J.: Barnes & Noble, 1984.

Hoover, Arlie J. *The Gospel of Nationalism: German Patriotic Preaching from Napoleon to Versailles.* Stuttgart: Franz Steiner Verlag, 1986.

Hudson, Winthrop S., ed. *Nationalism and Religion in America: Concepts of American Identity and Mission.* New York: Harper & Row, 1970.

Ionescu, Dan. "Romania: Religious Denominations, Change and Resistance to Change at the Top." *Radio Free Europe Report on Eastern Europe* 1, no. 17 (April 17, 1990):29–33.

Kennedy, Michael D., and Maurice D. Simon. "Church and Nation in Socialist Poland." In Peter H. Merkl and Ninian Smart, eds., *Religion and Politics in the Modern World.* New York: New York University Press, 1983.

LaBarre, Weston. *The Ghost Dance: The Origins of Religion.* New York: Dell, 1970.

Lancaster, Roger N. *Thanks to God and the Revolution: Popular Religion and Class Consciousness in the New Nicaragua.* New York: Columbia University Press, 1988.

Lease, Gary. "The Origins of National Socialism: Some Fruits of Religion and Nationalism." In Peter Merkl and Ninian Smart, eds., *Religion and Politics in the Modern World.* New York: New York University Press, 1983.

Lewellen, Ted C. "Holy and Unholy Alliances: The Politics of Catholicism in Revolutionary Nicaragua." *Journal of Church and State* 31, no. 1 (Winter 1989).

Little, David. *Ukraine: The Legacy of Intolerance.* Washington, D.C.: United States Institute of Peace Press, 1991.

Marrin, Albert, ed. *War and the Christian Conscience: From Augustine to Martin Luther King, Jr.* Chicago: Regnery, 1971.

Marsden, George M. *Fundamentalism and American Culture: The Shaping of Twentieth-Century Evangelicalism, 1870–1925.* New York: Oxford University Press, 1980.

McManners, John. *The French Revolution and the Church.* Westport, Conn.: Greenwood Press, 1969.

Motyl, Alexander J. *Sovietology, Rationality, Nationality: Coming to Grips with Nationalism in the USSR.* New York: Columbia University Press, 1990.

———, ed. *Thinking Theoretically about Soviet Nationalities: History and Comparison in the Study of the USSR.* New York: Columbia University Press, 1992.

O'Brien, Conor Cruise. "God and Man in Nicaragua." *Atlantic* 258, no. 2 (1986):50–72.

Ramet, Pedro, ed. *Eastern Christianity and Politics in the Twentieth Century.* Durham, N.C.: Duke University Press, 1988.

————. "Patterns of Religio-national Symbiosis in Eastern Europe: Poland, Czechoslovakia, Hungary." In *Eastern Europe: Religion and Nationalism.* Occasional Paper 3. Washington, D.C.: East European Program, European Institute, Wilson Center, December 4, 1985.

————, ed. *Religion and Nationalism in Soviet and East European Politics.* Durham, N.C.: Duke University Press, 1989.

Randall, Margaret. *Christians in the Nicaraguan Revolution.* Translated by Mariana Valverde. Vancouver: New Star Books, 1983.

Sanders, Thomas G. "The New Latin American Catholicism." In Donald Eugene Smith, ed., *Religion and Political Modernization.* New Haven, Conn.: Yale University Press, 1974.

Serra, Luis. "Ideology, Religion, and Class Struggle in the Nicaraguan Revolution." In Richard Harris and Carlos M. Vilas, eds., *Nicaragua: A Revolution under Siege.* London: Zed Books, 1985.

Sigmund, Paul. *Liberation Theology at the Crossroads: Democracy or Revolution?* New York: Oxford University Press, 1990.

Sizer, Sandra. *Gospel Hymns and Social Religion: The Rhetoric of Nineteenth-Century Revivalism.* Philadelphia: Temple University Press, 1978.

Szajkowski, Bogdan. *Next to God . . . Poland: Politics and Religion in Contemporary Poland.* New York: St. Martin's Press, 1983.

Walker, Thomas. *Nicaragua: The Land of Sandino.* Boulder, Colo.: Westview Press, 1981.

Wlasowsky, Ivan. *Outline History of the Ukrainian [Autocephalous] Orthodox Church.* New York: Ukrainian Orthodox Church, 1974.

List of Interviews

Amgalan, Y. Deputy Hamba Lama (Deputy Head Lama), Gandan Tegchinlen Monastery. In Ulan Bator, April 14, 1992.

Amunagama, Dr. Sarath. Associate Secretary-General, Worldview International Foundation. In Colombo, January 2, 1991.

Arafat, Dr. Fathi. President, Palestine Red Crescent Society. In Cairo, May 30, 1990.

Ariyaratne, A. T. Founder and President, Sarvodaya Shramadana Movement. In Moratuwa, Sri Lanka, January 2, 1991.

Asafi, Dr. Muhammad, and other Palestinian refugee camp leaders. In Jabaliya camp, Gaza, January 14, 1989.

Asfour, Gaber. Professor of Arabic Literature, Cairo University. In Cairo, May 26, 1990.

Ashur, Prof. A. K. Dean of the Faculty of Education, Al-Azhar University. In Cairo, May 27, 1990.

Auda, Gehad. Research Scholar, Al Ahram Institute. In Cairo, May 31, 1990.

Bakula, Kushok. Rinpoche and Indian Ambassador. In Ulan Bator, April 12, 1992.

bar Nathan, Arie. Settler in Mitzpeh Jericho. In Gush Emunim tent in front of Knesset, Jerusalem, January 16, 1989.

Batsukh, D. Official, Asian Buddhist Conference for Peace. In Ulan Bator, April 10, 11, and 13, 1992.

Bayantsagaan, S. President, Mongolyn Süsegtnii Kholboo (Association of Mongolian Believers). In Ulan Bator, April 12, 1992.

Bayarsuren, Ts., Chairman, Mongolian Religious Party. In Ulan Bator, April 12, 1992.

Bayasakh, K. Director, School of Foreign Service, and Head, Department of Oriental Studies, Mongolia State University. In Seoul, April 10, 1992.

ben Horin, Michael. Manager, Kach Office. In Jerusalem, January 15, 1989.

Bishoy, Father Sedrack Anbas. Coptic Monk. In Anbas Bishoy Coptic Monastery, Egypt, May 28, 1990.

Chandananda, Venerable Palipana. Mahanayake, Asgiri Chapter, Sinhalese Buddhist Sangha. In Kandy, Sri Lanka, February 3, 1988, and January 4, 1991.

Chandananda Thero, Rotapokune. Principal, Vidyasara Vidyayathana Pirvena. In Kalutara, Sri Lanka, January 3, 1991.

Chandananda Thero, Rev. Uduwawala. Member, Karaka Sabha, Asgiri Chapter, Sinhalese Buddhist Sangha. In Kandy, Sri Lanka, February 2, 1988, and January 5, 1991.

Chandra, Ram. Office Worker, Bharatiya Janata Party. In Delhi, January 10, 1991.

Charny, Israel W. Executive Director, Institute of the International Conference on the Holocaust and Genocide. In Jerusalem, January 15, 1989.

Choijants, D. Lama, Gandan Monastery, and Member, Great Hural (Upper House of Parliament). In Ulan Bator, April 12, 1992.

Coomaraswamy, Radhika. Research Scholar, International Centre for Ethnic Studies. In Colombo, January 28, 1988.

Dambajav, C. Hamba Lama (Head Lama), Tashichoeling Monastery. In Ulan Bator, April 11 and 13, 1992.

Dandinsuren, B. Hamba Lama (Head Lama), Gandan Tegchinlen Monastery. In Ulan Bator, April 14, 1992.

deSilva, K. M. Chairman, International Centre for Ethnic Studies. In Kandy, Sri Lanka, January 4, 1991.

deSilva, Padmasiri. Professor of Philosophy, Peradeniya University. In Kandy, Sri Lanka, February 4, 1988.

Desouki, Ali. Member, Muslim Brotherhood. In Cairo, January 11, 1989.

Dewasumananayaka Thero, D. Buddhist Teacher, Dharmavijaya Pirivena. In Kalutara, Sri Lanka, January 3, 1991.

Dhaman, Kuldip Kumar. Student, Guru Nanak Dev University. In Amritsar, January 11 and 12, 1991.

Dharmasiri, Gunapala. Professor of Philosophy, Peradeniya University. In Kandy, Sri Lanka, February 5, 1988.

Dheerasekera, J. D. Professor, University of Colombo. In Colombo, February 2, 1988.

Dominic, Merwyn. Member, Sri Lankan Catholic Church. In Colombo, January 3, 1991.

Dorji, D. Rector, Mongolian State University. In Seoul, April 10, 1992.

el-Arian, Essam. Medical Doctor; Member, National Assembly; and Member, Muslim Brotherhood. In Cairo, January 11, 1989.

el-Geyoushi, Dr. Muhammad Ibraheem. Dean of the Faculty of Dawah, Al-Azhar University. In Cairo, May 30, 1990.

el-Hamamsy, Prof. Leila. Director, Social Research Center, American University. In Cairo, January 10, 1989.

Farook, Jamaluddin. Student, Peradeniya University. In Kandy, Sri Lanka, January 4, 1991.

Fernando, Rev. Kenneth. Ecumenical Institute for Study and Dialogue. In Colombo, January 27, 1988.

Ganegama, W. G. Coordinator, Sarvodaya Rural Technical Services. In Kandy, Sri Lanka, February 4, 1988.

Gunatilake, Godfrey. Research Scholar, Marga Institute. In Colombo, January 28, 1988.

Gutierrez, Rev. Gustavo. Roman Catholic Priest. In Managua, Nicaragua, June 12, 1988.

Hanafi, Hasan. Student Leader, Muslim Brotherhood, Cairo University. In Cairo, May 30, 1990.

Hernandez, Norman J. Catholic Student Leader. In Managua, Nicaragua, June 14, 1988.

Ibrahim, Saad. Professor of Sociology, American University. In Cairo, January 10, 1989.

Jawahir, A. L. Student, Peradeniya University. In Kandy, Sri Lanka, February 6, 1988.

Kahane, Rabbi Meir. Former Member, Knesset, and Leader, Kach Party. In Jerusalem, January 18, 1989.

Kaur, Surjit. President, Delhi Branch, Women's Akali Dal (Mann group). In Rakabganj Gurdwara, New Delhi, January 13, 1991.

Khalifa, Muhammad. Professor of Comparative Religion, Department of Oriental Languages, Cairo University. In Cairo, January 9, 1989.

Khisamutdinov, Amir. President, Far Eastern Studies Society, Vladivostok. In Honolulu, February 18, 1992.

Kolesnik, Nikolai A. Chairman, Council on Questions of Religion, Ukrainian Soviet Socialist Republic Council of Ministers. In a meeting of the Working Group on Religion and Nationalism, United States Institute of Peace, Washington, D.C., June 20, 1990.

Lamba, Navneet. Librarian, Bhai Vir Singh Sadan. In New Delhi, January 9, 1991.

Lerner, Yoel. Director, Sanhedrin Institute. In Jerusalem, January 20, 1989.

Levinger, Rabbi Moshe. Leader, Gush Emunim. In Gush Emunim tent in front of Knesset, Jerusalem, January 16, 1989.

Lubsantseren, G. Secretary General, Asian Buddhist Conference for Peace. In Ulan Bator, April 13, 1992.

Marcari, Father Aramea. Coptic Monk. In Abba Marcarios Monastery, Egypt, May 28, 1990.

Marzel, Baruch. Settler in Kalpat Arba, Hebron. In Jerusalem, January 17, 1989.

Mekey, A. Vice-Rector, Mongolian State University. In Ulan Bator, April 11 and 14, 1992.

Moonesinghe, Mangala. Director, Political and Institutional Studies Division, Marga Institute. In Colombo, January 27, 1988.

Mykmar, J. Assistant, Torgon Zam Co. In Ulan Bator, April 13, 1992.

Nandy, Ashis. Research Scholar, Center for Developing Societies. In Delhi, January 20, 1988.

Narang, Surjit Singh. Professor of Political Science, Guru Nanak Dev University. In Amritsar, January 11, 1991.

Nasar, Mrs., and other Palestinian leaders. In Marna Hotel, Gaza, January 14, 1989.

Oujun, D. Scientific Researcher for Government Archives and Member, Mongolian People's Revolutionary Party. In Ulan Bator, April 12, 1992.

Padmasiri, Rev. T. Sinhalese Monk. In Humbantota, Sri Lanka, February 3, 1988.

Palihawardene, Mahinda. Professor of English, University of Sri Jayawardena. In Colombo, January 27, 1988.

Parajon, Gustavo. Leader, CEPAD. In Managua, Nicaragua, June 14, 1988.

Puri, Harish. Professor of Political Science, Guru Nanak Dev University. In Delhi, January 10, 1991; in Amritsar, January 11, 1991.

Ragi, Darshan Singh. Former Jatedar, Akal Takhat. In Bhai Vir Singh Sadan, New Delhi, January 13, 1991.

Rajagopal, Hari. Office Worker, BJP. In Delhi, January 9, 1991.

Rajapaksa, Mahinda. Lawyer and Member, SLFP. In Tangalle, Sri Lanka, February 3, 1988.

Salameh, Sheik. Spiritual Teacher, al-Nur Mosque. In Cairo, May 28, 1990.

Salem, Mohamed Elmisilhi. Professor of Educational Psychology, Al-Azhar University. In Cairo, May 27, 1990.

Salomon, Gershom. Head, Faithful of Temple Mount. In Jerusalem, May 25, 1990.

Samarasinghe, S.W.R. deA. Director, International Centre for Ethnic Studies. In Kandy, Sri Lanka, January 4, 1991.

Saydhom, Arian. Member, Coptic Orthodox Church. In Cairo, May 28, 1990.

Schleiffer, Prof. Abdullah. Director, Communications Center, American University. In Cairo, January 7, 1989.

Shiha, Abdul Hamid. Professor of dar el-Alum, Cairo University. In Cairo, May 27, 1990.

Shitta, Ibrahim Dasuqi. Professor of Persian Literature, Cairo University. In Cairo, January 10 and 11, 1989.

Shohdy, Nancy A. Director of Public and Ecumenical Relations, Coptic Orthodox Church. In Cairo, May 28, 1990.

Singh, Dr. Amrik. Member, All-India Sikh Students Federation (Mehta-Chawla group). In Rakabganj Gurdwara, New Delhi, January 13, 1991.

Singh, Bhagwan. Mulgranthi (Chief Worship Leader), Golden Temple. In Amritsar, January 11, 1991.

Singh, Gurmit. President, Delhi Branch, All-India Sikh Students Federation (Mehta-Chawla group). In Rakabganj Gurdwara, New Delhi, January 13, 1991.

Singh, Gurnam. Professor of Political Science, Guru Nanak Dev University. In Amritsar, January 11, 1991.

Singh, Harbinder. General Secretary, Delhi Branch, All-India Sikh Students Federation (Mehta-Chawla group). In Rakabganj Gurdwara, New Delhi, January 13, 1991.

Singh, Harcharand. Former Jatedar, Golden Temple. In Rakabganj Gurdwara, New Delhi, January 13, 1991.

Singh, Jasvinder. Member, Delhi Branch, All-India Sikh Students Federation (Mehta-Chawla group). In Rakabganj Gurdwara, New Delhi, January 13, 1991.

Singh, Mohinder. Director, National Institute for Punjab Studies. In Bhai Vir Singh Sadan, New Delhi, January 9, 1991.

Singh, Yashwant Pal. Manager, Delhi Office, All-India Sikh Students Federation (Mehta-Chawla group). In Rakabganj Gurdwara, New Delhi, January 13, 1991.

Sodnom, Sh. Dean of the Faculty, Mongolia State University. In Ulan Bator, April 11, 1992.

Steen, Alann. Former hostage held by Islamic militants in Lebanon. In Honolulu, March 11, 1992.

Sumanawansa Thero, N. Principal, Dharmavijaya Pirivena. In Kalutara, Sri Lanka, January 3, 1991.

Thiruchelvam, Neelan. Director, International Centre for Ethnic Studies. In Colombo, January 27, 1988.

Wangchindorj, B. Editor-in-Chief, *Buddhists for Peace*. In Ulan Bator, April 13, 1992.

Wangchuk, S. Assistant to Rinpoche Kushok Bakula. In Ulan Bator, April 12, 1992.

Wijeratne, Tissa. Manager, Sinhaputra Finance Co. In Kandy, Sri Lanka, February 6, 1988.

Wijesekera, Mahinda. Lawyer and Member, SLFP. In Matara, Sri Lanka, February 2, 1988.

Yassin, Sheik Ahmed. Leader, Hamas. In Gaza, January 14, 1989.

Zamlot, Saleh. Student Leader, Fateh, Palestine Liberation Organization. In Al-Azhar University, Cairo, May 27, 1990.

Zilberman, Dr. Ifrah. Research Scholar, Hebrew University. In Jerusalem, January 18, 1989, and May 25, 1990.

Index

Compositor:	Huron Valley Graphics
Text:	11 / 13 Caledonia
Display:	Caledonia
Printer and Binder:	Maple-Vail Book Mfg. Group